AF802965

"This book takes a helpful evidence-based approach to reviewing and classifying the many psychological biases relevant to those working in organizations and with change practices—it offers important insights for research and practice around how these biases affect us and the social motives behind them."

—**Thomas Calvard,** *University of Edinburgh Business School, UK*

"A reliable compass and guideline for the theory and practice of organizational change."

—**John Rijsman,** *Tilburg University*

Organizational Behaviour and Change Management

Humans are social animals, and change is a social process. To understand this social process and explain the thoughts, feelings and behaviours of individuals, knowledge of how the presence of others influences people is crucial. In this regard, bias is a concept with a lot of potential. Because cognitive and social biases influence human thinking, feelings, and behaviour, these provide insights and knowledge that are helpful, if not essential, for the field of organizational behaviour and change management.

The preceding statements may seem obvious and self-evident, but practice as well as science show that they are neither. *Organizational Behaviour and Change Management: The Impact of Cognitive and Social Bias* aims at unleashing the potential of cognitive and social biases to develop a more effective change management theory and practice. To do so, we analysed and assessed thousands of scientific articles. The most prominent biases are structured by using a practical and comprehensible framework based on five core social motives (belonging, understanding, controlling, trusting, and self-enhancing).

With its evidence-based, systematic, and integrative approach, this book provides scientists and practitioners in the field of organizational behaviour and change management with the best-available evidence linking biases to organizational behaviour and change and further enriching the field of change management.

Cornell Vernooij, MSc, is a business consultant at TEN HAVE Change Management, the Netherlands. Organizational behaviour and change are the main focus in his work as a board room and organizational consultant. Biases form a dominant perspective in his efforts to better understand and change organizational behaviour. He currently leads the long-term team research project concerning biases and is working towards his PhD on biases at TEN HAVE Change Management in accordance with the Vrije Universiteit Amsterdam.

Judith Stuijt, MSc, is a business consultant at TEN HAVE Change Management, the Netherlands, with a background in social and organizational psychology.

Maarten Hendriks, MSc, LLM, is a business consultant at TEN HAVE Change Management, the Netherlands, with a background in organizational psychology and corporate law. He is currently working towards his PhD regarding the effects of social psychology in relation to corporate governance.

Wouter ten Have, PhD, is a full professor of organization and change at the Vrije Universiteit Amsterdam, the Netherlands, member of two supervisory boards, and partner and consultant at TEN HAVE Change Management, the Netherlands.

Steven ten Have, PhD, is a full professor of strategy and change at the Vrije Universiteit Amsterdam, the Netherlands, the former chairman of the Foundation for Evidence Based Management, and partner and consultant at TEN HAVE Change Management, the Netherlands.

Routledge Studies in Organizational Change & Development
Series Editor: Bernard Burnes

6. **Leadership and Digital Change**
   The Digitalization Paradox
   Einar Iveroth and Jacob Hallencreutz

7. **Critical Perspectives on Diversity in Organizations**
   Thomas Calvard

8. **Leadership, Organizational Change and Sensemaking**
   Ronald Skea

9. **Organizational Change and Relational Resources**
   Edited by Karol Marek Klimczak and Yochanan Shachmurove

10. **Organizational Behaviour and Change Management**
    The Impact of Cognitive and Social Bias
    Edited by Cornell Vernooij, Judith Stuijt, Maarten Hendriks, Wouter ten Have and Steven ten Have

11. **Organizational Cognition**
    The Theory of Social Organizing
    Edited by: Davide Secchi, Rasmus Gahrn-Andersen and Stephen John Cowley

12. **Organizational Change, Leadership and Ethics**
    Leading Organizations towards Sustainability, 2E
    Edited by Rune By, Bernard Burnes and Mark Hughes

For more information about this series, please visit: https://www.routledge.com/Routledge-Studies-in-Organizational-Change--Development/book-series/SE0690

Organizational Behaviour and Change Management

The Impact of Cognitive and Social Bias

Edited by Cornell Vernooij, Judith Stuijt, Maarten Hendriks, Wouter ten Have and Steven ten Have

Routledge
Taylor & Francis Group
NEW YORK AND LONDON

First published 2023
by Routledge
605 Third Avenue, New York, NY 10158

and by Routledge
4 Park Square, Milton Park, Abingdon, Oxon, OX14 4RN

Routledge is an imprint of the Taylor & Francis Group, an informa business

© 2023 Cornell Vernooij, Judith Stuijt, Maarten Hendriks, Wouter ten Have and Steven ten Have

The right of Cornell Vernooij, Judith Stuijt, Maarten Hendriks, Wouter ten Have and Steven ten Have to be identified as authors of this work has been asserted in accordance with sections 77 and 78 of the Copyright, Designs and Patents Act 1988.

All rights reserved. No part of this book may be reprinted or reproduced or utilised in any form or by any electronic, mechanical, or other means, now known or hereafter invented, including photocopying and recording, or in any information storage or retrieval system, without permission in writing from the publishers.

Trademark notice: Product or corporate names may be trademarks or registered trademarks, and are used only for identification and explanation without intent to infringe.

ISBN: 978-1-032-26423-3 (hbk)
ISBN: 978-1-032-26424-0 (pbk)
ISBN: 978-1-003-28823-7 (ebk)

DOI: 10.4324/9781003288237

Typeset in Bembo
by Apex CoVantage, LLC

Contents

Overview of authors and research team ix
List of tables and figures xi
Foreword xii
Preface xvii

1 **Bias in organizations and change** 1
STEVEN TEN HAVE, CORNELL VERNOOIJ, AND MAARTEN HENDRIKS

2 **Model and methodology** 11
WOUTER TEN HAVE, CORNELL VERNOOIJ, AND JUDITH STUIJT

3 **Understanding, biases, organizational behaviour, and change** 30
JUDITH STUIJT, CORNELL VERNOOIJ, AND FLORE LOUWERS

4 **Controlling, biases, organizational behaviour, and change** 80
MAARTEN HENDRIKS, CORNELL VERNOOIJ, AND RUBEN TEN HAVE

5 **Trusting, biases, organizational behaviour and change** 110
JUDITH STUIJT, CORNELL VERNOOIJ, AND FLORE LOUWERS

6 **Self-enhancing, biases, organizational behaviour and change** 143
MAARTEN HENDRIKS, CORNELL VERNOOIJ, AND FLORE LOUWERS

7 Belonging, biases, organizational behaviour, and change 181
JUDITH STUIJT, CORNELL VERNOOIJ, AND JULIUS WINTER

8 The impact of bias on organizational behaviour and change 210
CORNELL VERNOOIJ, JUDITH STUIJT, STEVEN TEN HAVE, AND WOUTER TEN HAVE

Appendix: A Overview of primary and secondary biases 228
Appendix: B Examples of Matrix for Each Core Social Motive 235
Index 259

Authors and research team

Authors

Cornell Vernooij, MSc, is a business consultant at TEN HAVE Change Management, the Netherlands. Organizational behaviour and change are the main focus of his work as a board room and organizational consultant. Biases form a dominant perspective in his efforts to better understand and change organizational behaviour. He currently leads the long-term team research project concerning biases and is working towards his PhD on biases at TEN HAVE Change Management in accordance with the Vrije Universiteit Amsterdam.

Judith Stuijt, MSc, is a business consultant at TEN HAVE Change Management, the Netherlands, with a background in social and organizational psychology.

Maarten Hendriks, MSc, LLM, is a business consultant at TEN HAVE Change Management, the Netherlands, with a background in organizational psychology and corporate law. He is currently working towards his PhD regarding the effects of social psychology in relation to corporate governance.

Wouter ten Have, PhD, is a full professor of organization and change at the Vrije Universiteit Amsterdam, the Netherlands, member of two supervisory boards, and partner and consultant at TEN HAVE Change Management, the Netherlands.

Steven ten Have, PhD, is a full professor of strategy and change at the Vrije Universiteit Amsterdam, the Netherlands, former chairperson of the Foundation for Evidence Based Management, and partner and consultant at TEN HAVE Change Management, the Netherlands.

Foreword author

John Rijsman, PhD, is a full professor of social psychology at Tilburg University, the Netherlands. He obtained his PhD in experimental social psychology from the University of Louvain in 1970, and, after a short stay at the University of Southern Illinois, was asked in 1972 to become chair of social psychology at the new faculty of psychology in Tilburg, where he has stayed ever since.

Research team

Flore Louwers, student of culture, organization, and management at the Vrije Universiteit Amsterdam, the Netherlands, and research assistant at TEN HAVE Change Management.

Julius Winter, student of business administration: leadership and change management (LCM) at Vrije Universiteit Amsterdam, the Netherlands, and research assistant at TEN HAVE Change Management.

Ruben ten Have, MSc, student of law and politics of international security at the Vrije Universiteit Amsterdam, the Netherlands, with a background in philosophy, politics, and economics, and research assistant at TEN HAVE Change Management.

Tables and figures

Tables

2.1 Relationships among Core Social Motives 14
2.2 List of All Included Biases Categorized Using the Five Core Social Motives 17
2.3 Five Levels to Determine the Methodological Appropriateness of the Research Design of the Studies Included 25
8.1 Elaboration on Evidence Levels and Probability Levels 215
8.2 Overview of Biases and Their Probability Levels 216
8.3 Change Management Topics 218
8.4 Change Management Topics, Social Motives, and Social Psychological Biases Illustrated 222

Figures

2.1 The Five Motives Ordered Using the Lemniscate 14
2.2 Change-Competence Model 15
2.3 Primary Biases Categorized by the Five Core Social Motives 20
2.4 Sources Contributing to the Best Available Evidence 21
2.5 Overview of the Research Steps 24
3.1 Primary Biases Related to the Core Social Motive of Understanding 31
4.1 Primary Biases Related to the Core Social Motive of Controlling 81
5.1 Primary Biases Related to the Core Social Motive of Trusting 111
6.1 Primary Biases Related to the Core Social Motive of Self-Enhancing 144
7.1 Primary Biases Related to the Core Social Motive of Belonging 182
8.1 The Change-Competence Model Enriched with the Core Social Motives and One Related Change Management Topic Per Factor 222

Foreword

The privilege of writing a foreword to this well-written, sound, and highly inspiring book is deceptively simple, because one feels inclined to simply say "I agree," and I leave it to the readers to understand for themselves what I agree with. Adding more words to it (just like adding more notes to a Partita [ordered set of instrumental music] or more lines to a Miro), might not improve the final product but rather diminish it. I need to say one thing in advance, though, with which I do not agree: The authors refer to me as one of the giants on whose shoulders they stood on to write this book. Although I had several profound conversations with them on numerous occasions and on various issues in social psychology including bias, I always felt the need to learn *at least* as much from them as they have hopefully learnt from me. I, therefore, consider this statement more an expression of a *generosity bias* than a rational judgement. But since I learnt that bias is also linked to survival, I will not disregard it, but take it home as a precious gift.

The topic of this book—biases and their possible implications for change management—is central to social psychology. Social psychology, indeed, is the study of human interaction as far as it is the production and processing of meaning. If social psychology were merely the study of the interaction, then the study of stones and plants would also be social psychological because they also interact; however, they do so only in a mechanical or biological way and not in a psychological way. Social sciences, unlike the sciences of matter, are characterized by a paradoxical distinction, namely between description and prescription. Astronomers never say what stars *should* do but only what they *will* do, based on what they have seen them do in the past. When they say something about the future of stars, it is prediction, not prescription. In the world of meaning, on the other hand, we can describe the habits of thought in a cultural and historical context and then suggest doing it differently in the future. This involves the use of standards that are moral, or legal, but also *rational*. In fact, that is what happens in the study of biases—first looking at the *typical* or *frequent* deviations from these standards and then informing those deviating about their *tendencies* to help them become better when needed. I have often felt that social psychology as a whole is about such discrepancies, because many experiments are used as mirrors of reflection to see on the stage of research what we usually do in ordinary life, and then analyse the remnants of these reflections for use in education or politics, or, as is the case here, in the field of change management.

My first encounter with the concept of 'bias' as describing the difference between description and prescription—or between how things appear to be in the continuous world of meaning and how we think they should be—was when I attended the fourth interdisciplinary research conference "Utility, Probability, and Human Decision Making," held at the Mathematical Institute of the University of Rome in 1973. In the second session, right after the opening session by Bruno De Finetti on the value of studying subjective evaluations of probability, two relative newcomers in field (at least in the eyes of social psychologists), Amoz Tversky and Daniel Kahneman, presented and discussed three so called 'biases'—(1) representativeness, (2) availability, and (3) adjustment—right from the beginning in their talk "Judgment under Uncertainty: Heuristics and Biases." I still remember the laudatory comments at the end of their talk, but nobody could have imagined that this was the start of a new area of research that would dominate psychology for decades and would finally convince experts in related domains, such as economics, that their standards of rationality were normative and not representative of what people really do, unless highly trained and very reflective (sometimes not even then) because many of the studies on bias were actually done on experts, including mathematicians. Apparently, we need more than expertise to avoid biases; we also need mirrors that speak and teach. The peak of this new type of research was Kahneman and Tversky's 1979 publication 'prospect theory,' or the study of how a particular form of bias called 'loss aversion,' influences decision-making under conditions of risk. It was primarily for this publication that Kahneman (Tversky had passed away by then) was awarded the Nobel Prize in economics in 2002, marking the public recognition of a new field of economics called 'behavioural economics.' Before that, an explicit recognition of that type of research had already existed within psychology but much less within the department of economics or at management schools. At my own university in Tilburg, a chair on 'economic psychology' was created in 1971 and a new association and related journal, *The Journal of Economic Psychology*, was launched shortly after, but these were restricted to the faculty of psychology and did not extend to the department of economics. The attitude towards this field in these related faculties or departments has changed enormously since, and this book is only one of the signs of that, and fortunately a very good one. It is sound, rooted in reliable observations, and is well organized, so that we can not only identify the biases but also grasp their relations in terms of function and underlying motivation.

For me, the idea of loss aversion—or weighting losses more heavily than symmetrical gains—was not new at all. In fact, I had already developed that same idea, but in a somewhat different way, in my own work on social comparison that formed the core of my doctoral dissertation in 1970 and part of which was published in the *European Journal of Social Psychology* in 1974. (It has also been published in different ways in various books and journals, but never under 'bias,' only as a matter of fact.) To cut a long story short, I simply analysed the process of comparative preference in a formal way and found that the motivational structure of such a preference is *by definition* asymmetrical with negative outcomes (or losses) looming larger than positive ones, thus not as a bias but as a formal necessity. The logic of that conclusion can easily be grasped by realizing that to *compare,* one needs to assimilate the entities of the comparison in the same category of meaning; hence, a pressure towards similarity. Similarly, to prefer one must also discriminate the preferred entity from the nonpreferred one in a positive direction; hence, a positive discrimination *and* pressure towards similarity at the same time. The equilibrium of these two pressures together is obviously just better. However, since comparability or the possibility to associate elements in the same category of meaning diminishes with distance, the linear sum of these pressures has to be weighted with distance. This results in a curvelinear function of motivation, with negative outcomes, or losses, looming larger than positive ones—in other words, the same conclusion Kahneman and Tversky drew a decade later—but with high motivational value at the point of equality and a complete loss of motivation at the extremes, or very large loss and very large gain. The notion of gain and loss that Kahneman and Tversky used was not between the self and the other, as in my case, but between the current wealth of self and prior wealth of self. Needless to say, the general principle of comparative preference is exactly the same in both cases.

The functional representation of motivational asymmetry between gains and losses that Kahneman and Tversky used was intuitive and not based on any formalism at all. It is not so much on the basis of that representation that they gained recognition in the field of economic decision-making but on the basis of their concrete studies of decision-making under conditions of risk, which often left rational observers flabbergasted. For example, in a famous experiment (of which I present here only an abstracted version), when they let people starting from a possession of 0 to choose between a certain gain of +1 and gambling with 1/3 chance to gain +3 and 2/3 chance to gain nothing, they found that most people preferred the former, or certainty above risk. If, however, they let people starting from a possession of 3 to choose between a certain loss of −2 and gambling with 2/3 chance of losing −3 and 1/3 chance of losing nothing, most people preferred the latter, or risk above certainty. This cannot obviously be explained in classic terms of rational decision-making, or of maximizing absolute outcomes, because the final absolute outcome is exactly the same in both cases—1 (starting from 0, a gain of 1 leads to 1, just as starting from 3, a loss of 2 leads to 1, and the expected utilities of the gambles, or the sum of their possible outcomes weighted with their respective probability of occurrence, is also 1). Kahneman and Tversky explained this in terms of their model of motivational asymmetry, with losses looming larger than gains, but it is easy to demonstrate (as I actually did in a manuscript that I shared with the authors of this book) that it is not their assumed asymmetry that might explain this, but the nonlinearity, or the assumption that the attraction to gains and the aversion to losses, bends off at the extremes. In fact, when we remove the nonlinearity from their representation and keep only the asymmetry in a linear form on both sides, the explanation in terms of motivational asymmetry not only fails to work, but also makes the reversal of attitude towards risk depending on framing impossible.

Anybody familiar with the experiment in question looking at it in a rational *unbiased* way can verify this immediately. However, in comparing my own model of motivational asymmetry (which was developed in the context of social comparison) with that of Kahneman and Tversky's (which was developed in the context of economic decision-making), I also hit upon what is probably the most important bias in the social sciences field as a whole, and extremely relevant to change management: the logic of the observer versus that of the motivated actor. My approach to motivational asymmetry was from the standpoint of what happens to the self-referent actor or the 'ego subject' as I call it. However, in prospect theory and in economic theory in general, the actor is defined as a third person, a he or she, to whom certain characteristics are attributed that are inferred from what the theorist sees when looking at the world as a noninvolved external observer. From such a noninvolved perspective, it is obvious that all actors should be motivated in the same way by maximal absolute gain and minimal absolute loss, because they all represent the same theoretical homo economicus. In real life, however, nobody is a representation of the he or she we talk about. Instead, everyone becomes the one and only ego-subject with the one and only self in which all other people are the other ones. Therefore, when using the knowledge and understanding of biases in change management, I think we need to add this simple insight to the list of biases because nobody can live and work in a position of the he or she in a theory but only in a position of a living ego with a living self.

It becomes easier to understand the moment we translate the word *change* to Dutch: *ver-Anderen*, or literally 'othering.' When change is interpreted that way, then, as research and practice has shown very clearly, we immediately get *resistance to change*, or resistance to othering. Normal loving parents know this very well because they treat their children not as other people but as people like themselves and sketch a positive image of that self even before any assessment centre has any proof of this. Those who get that message are then usually very eager to prove the validity of what they hear, which is not othering, but just the opposite, namely, of changing behaviour in a way that confirms what they were told they already have—the value of their self. Therefore, normal parents can be very strict and *realistic*, or look at their children's potential in directions that *can* be fulfilled in practice. This theme of 'motivation' as the underlying basis of bias in human judgement and decision-making could be added to the list of motivations mentioned in the book already, unless we see it as part of what the authors, along with Fiske, call 'the motivation to belong.' This brings me back to what I learnt in the initial days of my education as a psychologist from my highly esteemed professor in general psychology, Jozef Nuttin Sr., then president of the division of motivation in the World Union of Psychology—that human learning and development are offered as projects wherein the things that we need to learn (e.g., new skills and performances) contribute to what does not change—the beloved self. No wonder then biases exist in the evaluation of probabilities, because if we were to start from pure realism in judging newcomers, we would throw them all away immediately because nothing good is there yet. It is only by looking through responsible eyes, or eyes that *help* make things happen that biases become reality. I believe that this book, used in a reflective way, can be extremely helpful in making change managers, or anybody in a position of responsibility dealing with people—and are we not all somewhat in such a position—better agents of change.

John Rijsman

Preface

In 2017, three leading thinkers of evidence-based management (EBM) claimed: "In management education and practice, too much attention is paid to unfounded beliefs, 'new' insights, and success stories from famous business leaders. Instead, managers always need to ask whether the underlying evidence bears scrutiny."[1] Continuing in their spirit, we have started a journey to fuel the field of organizational behaviour and change management with evidence-based insights. The first stage focused on separating the wheat from the chaff by assessing 18 popular change management assumptions. The second stage aimed at unlocking the potential of social psychology for the field of change management by describing and assessing 40 relevant theories, including the social learning theory, social reinforcement, and social cohesion.

Now we have come to the third stage of our evidence-based journey—"Organizational Behaviour and Change Management. The Impact of Cognitive and Social Bias." It builds on the first two stages, particularly on the second, and its social psychological theories. It is inspired not only by the ideas and insights of people like Kahneman, Tversky, and Rijsman, but also by those of Kurt Lewin, one of the founding fathers of modern change management and the master builder of the essential bridge between science and practice. In 1947 Lewin stated: "The study of the conditions for change begins appropriately with an analysis of the conditions for 'no change', that is, for the state of equilibrium."[2] The concept of bias has the potential to contribute to this analysis and the understanding of resistance to change and seemingly inconceivable organizational behaviour. Together with our very first book on change competence in the series, this is our fourth book in the Routledge Studies in Organizational Change and Development. We are proud to present this book and with it a more than promising next generation, personified by Cornell Vernooij, Judith Stuijt, and Maarten Hendriks as co-authors. This book is also the result of the contributions of Flore Louwers, Julius Winter, and Ruben ten Have, our very talented and committed research team. We like to thank the strong, humble, knowledgeable, open, wise, and generous John Rijsman for his constant inspiration and support. We are honored by his willingness to write the foreword of this book.

Inspired by John Rijsman and Kurt Lewin and other leading thinkers such as Susan T. Fiske and James Q. Wilson, our overarching goal is to make the world a better place by studying practical social and organizational issues and fueling the development of scientific practitioners.

Steven ten Have and Wouter ten Have

Notes

1 Barends, E., Briner, R., & Rousseau, D. M. (2016). Foreword. In S. Ten Have, W. D. ten Have, A. Huijsmans, & M. Otto (Eds.), *Reconsidering change management: Applying evidence-based insights in change management practice*. Routledge.

2 Lewin, K. (1947). Quasi-stationary social equilibria and the problem of permanent change. *Organization Change: A Comprehensive Reader*, 73–77.

1 Bias in organizations and change

Steven ten Have, Cornell Vernooij, and Maarten Hendriks

Introduction

Decades ago, particularly between 1971 and 1979, Nobel Prize winner Daniel Kahneman and Amos Tversky, two of the most influential thinkers on human decision-making, put the traditional rational decision-making model up for discussion. They focused on the systematic deviations and put forward recognizable patterns in the judgement (errors) of humans. We have learned to call these systematic deviations 'biases' or 'heuristics.' In his bestseller *Thinking, Fast and Slow* (2011), Kahneman declares: "I hope to enrich the vocabulary that people use when they talk about the judgements and choices of others, the company's new policies or a colleague's investment decisions." And, as we can conclude decades later, he and Tversky surely did. They enriched our vocabulary with concepts such as groupthink, confirmation bias, framing, and priming. These labels are being used more often and are indispensable when thinking about human behaviour these days.

An explorative search on Google on the term 'bias' shows a wide range of more popular articles and dozens of books concerning the topic. Individual biases also have been thoroughly discussed in science; thousands of scientific journal articles have been published. Biases are 'all over' and numerous; Wikipedia shows a total of around 175 biases listed and grouped into a set of categories (e.g., decision-making biases, social biases, and memory biases). These biases are not always mutually exclusive, while some overlap with other biases with other names. However, it illustrates without doubt, the popularity of and the attention to the concept 'bias.' It also indicates that the knowledge and insights regarding biases is in a way fragmented and not always well structured and evidence based. Bias is a popular and strong concept with a lot of potential and deserves to be further developed in a structured and evidence-based way. In doing this, science and practice will be served, bridging to a certain extent the gap between popular books and scientific insights.

To illustrate its popularity and relevance, we point at a McKinsey survey of 800 corporate board directors regarding bias. The researchers found

DOI: 10.4324/9781003288237-1

that reducing biases was the number one aspiration of high-impact boards (Sibony, 2019). It appears that business leaders are increasingly beginning to realize that they should understand more and do something with their understanding about this phenomenon or concept in their organizations and for their own strategic decisions. But how to understand this complex topic with its fragmented knowledge? What does practice tell us? What can science teach us? What will help organizations, their people, and leaders to move further? In this book, we aim to answer questions such as these regarding biases. To do this, we have analysed and assessed thousands of scientific peer-reviewed journal articles. Based on this, we will provide scientists and practitioners with the best available evidence, linking biases to organizational behaviour and change. This is the purpose of our book, 'Organizational Behaviour and Change Management: The Impact of Cognitive and Social Bias.'

Given the purpose and the related book title, a point to be noted is the relationship between the concept of bias and social psychology. Although not an exclusive one, it is obviously an important and fruitful one. In this book, we explore and structure this relationship, making use of the practical insights and evidence-based findings from our earlier book 'The Social Psychology of Change Management.'

In this introductory chapter, we elaborate on the concepts of bias, organizational behaviour, change management, and their conceptual and practical relationships. In addition, we pay attention to the evolutionary origin of biases and the positioning of social motives as driving forces behind biases. We also explain the approach and structure of the book.

Biases, organizational behaviour, and change

According to American psychologist and personality theorist George Kelly, who is considered the father of cognitive clinical psychology, people act as naive scientists when trying to make sense of the world around them: people want to understand themselves and their surroundings, make predictions about what will happen next, and create theories to explain events or their behaviours and those of others. However, our predictions and theories are not formalized as a professional scientist's would be. Instead, we believe people see the world through their own lenses, based on their uniquely organized systems of construction, which they use to anticipate events of behaviours. Human thinking is thus not purely rational; instead it is hampered by numerous mental shortcuts. Because humans do not conform to the economists' theoretical model of rational decision-making, they are prone to making shortcuts, and therefore, mistakes—and not just any mistake, but systematic, nonrandom, and predictable mistakes. We call these systematic deviations from economic reality 'biases.' An organization is exclusively made up of and governed by humans embodied with biased thinking, which makes organizations eminently prone to biased behaviour.

Weick (1979) describes an organization as "a body of thought, thought by thinking thinkers." From this perspective, an organization is not a stable, objectively determined unit, but instead a dynamic, subjectively and inter-subjectively determined phenomenon. From their own perspectives, members of organizations, groups, and subgroups in collaborative settings develop their own subjective or intersubjective social reality. In the case of decision-making, biases in the negative sense are cognitive mistakes. They arise from conscious or subconscious irrational thought processes. Businesses and institutions, however, are understood to perform objectively, resolutely, and effectively, based on their purpose—their economic or social remit—and to change where required (Bower, 2000). In addition to arbitrary and favourable circumstances, an organization needs a clear direction and the capacity to actually do so. 'Decision making' is a key concept in organizational behaviour when it relates to direction, and 'collaboration' is a key concept in relation to capacity. Biases can have a strong influence on both decision-making and collaboration. For instance, Kahneman describes the 'halo effect' as an example: a particular positive quality, such as good looks, suggests that the person also has other positive qualities such as intelligence or social skills. This halo effect also applies to organizations (Rosenzweig, 2007). High-performing organizations, such as Google, are thus attributed with a brilliant strategy or excellent leadership, even though this has not necessarily been proven. Kahneman (2011) states that the availability of diagnostic labels for this type of very human tendency makes them easier to anticipate, recognize, and understand.

The bias blind spot

Before we start diving deep, it is crucial to point out the meta-bias that fosters all biases, the so-called 'bias blind spot.' The bias blind spot causes people to believe they are less biased in their judgements than others. The term, named after the visual blind spot, was introduced by social psychologist Emily Pronin and her colleagues Daniel Lin and Lee David Ross in 2002. Kahneman once said: "We can be blind to the obvious and we are also blind to our blindness. When someone is blind to ones' own biases one cannot change or influence their own biased behaviour." Creating awareness of biased behaviour in a person is the first step towards reducing the possible negative effects of biases. This book helps in creating knowledge and awareness regarding biases. The knowledge gained from this book can subsequently be used to create meaningful and effective interventions within organizations to reduce the possible negative effects of biases. We provide diagnostic labels for the tendencies and biases as referred to by Kahneman in so far as they relate to organizations and changes. We use examples to link those biases to the important organizational processes such as decision-making and collaboration. It is our aim to help managers, advisors, employees, and everyone related to organizations to recognize and perhaps prevent the negative sides of biases, respond to biased behaviour, or use biases to their advantage. Shown biased behaviour must be understood and handled with respect. Attention to biases and other distortions in our thinking will lead to a better understanding of behaviour and change in organizations. Biases and tendencies are markers and together form the heat maps helpful during our search for functional and dysfunctional individual and social human behaviour in organizations. Recognizing and acknowledging biases will help choose targeted interventions and methods. This makes the application of those interventions and methods more likely to succeed, less risky, and above all, more human.

Negative bias about bias

With 'preoccupation' and 'prejudice,' the most common translations of bias illustrate the 'negative bias about bias.' The often used and more neutral translation of bias 'tendency' can be seen as an exception. Biases are generally seen as cognitive errors or are described as irrational, erroneous lines of thought in humans. All-in-all, not very positive or constructive. However, biases, as biological or society-based bundles of knowledge and experience, do or can have positive effects. There is a positive side to biases as a product and factor of biological and social processes; therefore, we must not only look at biases negatively. It seems wiser and more helpful to approach and *manage* biases in a nuanced, appreciative, and balanced way. If biases are negative, then this is mainly related to excess influence towards one end of the spectrum. For instance, conformity to a group is in basis a good thing. Learning from each other and adapting to each other and increasing efficiency and speed can be important basic elements for the survival, functioning, and performance of groups. Nevertheless, when individuals lose their own opinion and identity, it becomes problematic. In addition, a bias can also be undesirable due to the obsolescence or absence of a function of once-useful routines and mechanisms, the evolutionary remnants rest deep in our brain (Vroon, 1989). Biases are, after all, mental shortcuts formed through millions of years of evolution. If biases were not useful for human survival, the responsible genes would have not been conveyed to the next generations. What made or makes biases useful for humans and why is there a generally negative attitude towards biases nowadays?

The evolutionary origin of biases

The starting point of finding an answer to the origin of biases lies in the biology of the human brain. The human brain makes up only 2 percent of the body's mass and uses approximately 20 percent of the body's energy (Rolfe & Brown, 1997). The brain thus uses a disproportionate share of a human's available energy intake. It is remarkable that during evolution, the human brain has tripled its size relative to the body and that the neural density of the brain has increased significantly (Harris et al., 2012). The growth of the brain was accompanied by greater cognitive powers, which gave humans their evolutionary edge to survive and thrive over thousands of years. The human cognitive capabilities compensated for a lack of strength, speed, and claws. However, with great cognitive power comes great energy consumption. The brain's neural computation is a metabolically expensive process. Therefore, the human brain adapted itself to use the available energy as efficiently as possible. The evolved brain uses only a measly 20 watts in rest, which is much less than a glowing lightbulb. To put this into perspective, with current technology a supercomputer thousand times as powerful as the best supercomputer in existence, with an energy input stemming from a fully operating nuclear power plant, is estimated to have abilities equal to the human brain (Furber, 2012). Biases are one of the important evolutionary energy-saving measures and are therefore crucial to our survival and day-to-day functioning.

Biases help quickly assess and respond in (social) situations without using too much of the brain's valuable processing power. They are part of the fast, effortless, and irrational system 1 thinking introduced by Daniel Kahneman (Kahneman, 2011). Kahneman introduced two systems of thinking, systems 1 and 2. System 1 thinking is intuitive and unconscious and can be considered the autopilot mode of thinking. We use system 1 when driving a car on an empty road, solve 2 + 2=? or read a billboard sign. System 2 however is slow, rational, effortful, calculating, and conscious. We use system 2 when directing our focus on a deliberate task such as solving a puzzle, trying to remember what we did last weekend, or when riding a bike for the first time. To save energy, humans mostly use system 1 thinking. Automatic thinking is an efficient process that enables saving up our full focus and energy for important matters that require attention. The brain's energy consumption would simply be inconceivably high if a person has to consciously register all the details in its surroundings and make choice with meticulous calculation.

Evolution has thus made the human brain very energy efficient, but this limited energy use places restrictions on the brain's information processing capacity (Harris et al., 2012). Cognitive biases work quick and dirty, which leave room for mistakes. Humans have a built-in margin of error that is, from an evolutionarily point of view, acceptable when compared to the upside of biases. When humans were hunter gatherers, survival was their main priority. This came down to not dying, which meant preventing fatal situations and learning from these to avoid such circumstances altogether became more important than seeking positive situations. Humans have, therefore, a built-in negativity bias (the tendency to give more weight to negative compared with positive information), which makes the memory of the time they almost got eaten by a bear more vivid and significant than the time they ate a delicious apple.

Nowadays people do not encounter deadly predators, which makes survival considerably easier and not the main priority anymore. Most contemporary humans have shifted their focus from survival to living a fulfilling and happy life. As the once-valuable negativity bias can hinder humans in the quest for their newfound life goal, the current society has rejected it. The same applies to the well-known bias 'groupthink.' For early humans, being banished from their tribe to live the life of a lone wanderer was akin to a near-death sentence. It was therefore evolutionarily beneficial to maintain harmony and conformity in the group and be overly agreeable. These days, however, critical thinking and creativity are valued when it comes to decision-making processes in organizations. Consequently, board room members, managers, and employees are expected to convey a multitude of perspectives and challenge the status quo. The modern-day focus on diversity in organizations is a good example of the desire to bring different perspectives to the table.

Evolution takes millions of years, modern society, however, develops at an exceedingly high pace, which could make the human brain outdated. Biases can be seen as the evolutionary collateral damage of something that was once a very useful built-in script. However, certain biases in general are still basic useful human tendencies that we should not immediately discard. As said earlier, most biases have unfavourable effects when they drive people too far towards irrational behaviour. But it is valuable to keep in mind humans are irrational beings, and their irrationality is also one of their greatest powers. We argued that groupthink is unfavourable in modern organizations. This is only the case when excessive groupthink hinders decision-making. Groupthink in itself is a useful construct that makes people in general strive for harmony and conformity. Organizations and teams without any harmony and conformity would end up with undesirable decisions and working conditions. The same applies to the negativity bias. The tendency to put more weight on negative rather than positive information motivates people to learn from negative situations and help them to avoid these situations in the future.

Using biases to our advantage

We could compare biases to medicines; the right doses can help us thrive, but we must be careful not to overdose, or underdose. Therefore, as said before, it is essential to approach biases in an appreciative and balanced manner without completely condemning them. In addition, biases also help to make organizational behaviour more predictable. While human behaviour is unpredictable, understanding the tendencies of all humans helps understand and subsequently reshape certain unwanted behaviours in ourselves and within organizations. When biases are properly understood, they can contribute to efficiency, speed, pragmatism, and risk management as well as explain, predict, and manage the consistency and perseverance of organizations and organizational change. It is difficult, or even impossible, to persuade people in organizations to go along with a plan or concept, even if there are clear benefits or gains for those people. Understanding their cognitive biases increases the chances of successfully influencing them. A useful example is the 'outcome bias.' The intended or actual result of a change process can be of high value in the form of a more customer-focused and socially responsible organization. That outlook may persuade some of the employees involved to exhibit the desired behaviour as they understand that a direct, increased material reward is waiting. The 'salience bias' is another example. This bias teaches us that it may be more effective to limit the arguments for a desired change to only a few factors that are particularly relevant to the employees involved. In other words, change actors may reach their goal sooner by emphasizing the two benefits of the desired change that are relevant to employees rather than providing a correct but drawn out and *uninteresting* presentation of the change.

Standing on the shoulders of giants

Kahneman, Tversky, Rijsman, and other scientists have conducted considerable valuable research and shown us that human behaviour is irrational. Their research refuted the prevalent dominant assumption of humans as rational agents who objectively weigh the outcome of their choices in their decision-making. These pioneering scholars founded behavioural economics and paved the path for thousands of scholars to delve even deeper into the irrational minds of humans. This became even clearer during our research as we sifted through an extraordinary number of scientific studies. We believe this vast amount of knowledge is amassed from a variety of biases that were only partially understood in relation with each other. Furthermore, we found that several biases lacked valid scientific backing and practical advice regarding the use or prevention of certain biases. For this book, we have selected the biases that were represented with a reasonable amount of evidence (meaning more than a few standalone studies) in scientific literature (primary biases). We structured them into a coherent model, analysed the available knowledge, and made this knowledge applicable for organizations and change. We believe that all biases must be viewed with both a practical and holistic outlook so that organizational frameworks and behaviours can be changed in an effective and adequate manner. Nevertheless, we want to stress that this book would have never possible without the exemplary work of all scientific researchers who laid the bases for all the different biases. We therefore want to express our gratitude to all scholars that added to the knowledge of biases with a quote inspired by Isaac Newton: "We, the authors of this book, could only expand the existing knowledge on biases by standing on the shoulders of giants."

Social motives underlying biases

While standing on these shoulders, providing you with the latest insights from scientific literature and connecting biases to the change management practice is one thing, but structuring biases into a practical and comprehensible framework, we believe, will make application of or intervention on biases more accessible and adequate. We have organized the different types of biases with the help of the core social motives by Fiske (2010): "Fundamental, underlying psychological processes that impel people's thinking, feeling, and behaving in situations involving other people." This pertains to the following five motives: belonging, understanding, controlling, trusting, and enhancing self. The model gives the relative position, relationship, or interaction and interdependency of the five core social motives and the underlying biases. By combining these motives with the types of biases that may appear in organizations and its employees, we want to gain more insight into possible distortions and understand what they can mean for change processes in organizations. In chapter 2, we elaborate about the model and the methodology we used, but before doing so, we provide you with a brief overview (see chapters 3–7 for an extensive discussion on the examples of biases):

- *Belonging*, the central core social motive, pertains to the idea that people want stable relationships with others to enable them to survive both psychologically and physically. The need for social belonging is the building block for good collaboration and decision-making, but it can also be an obstacle. A strong, very cohesive team can move mountains when it cooperates effectively. The social bonds in such teams are sometimes so intense that it can be described as a team of friends or a family culture. However, this may lead to minimizing conflict (including fruitful conflict), a lack of criticism and feedback within the team, and a hostile attitude towards the outside world and things that are different (in-group vs. out-group). The status quo bias and groupthink are examples of biases connected to the need to belong.
- *Understanding* refers to the motivation people need to understand, predict, and give meaning to their environment. This means that people want to understand the rationale behind a proposed organizational change: What is the (strategic) reasoning and the ultimate goal of the organization or the change? Biases related to understanding show us that not all of it is rational but that more cognitive processes play a large part in comprehending and accepting change. Attentional bias and framing effect are cognitive biases related to understanding.
- *Controlling* is the need for perceived contingency between behaviour and outcomes. A certain sense of control urges people to improve or learn from past or present situations to increase their control even further. In times of organizational change, people may feel that their existing sense of control and competence is being challenged or threatened. Here, perception is reality. It often revolves around the immediate (personal) costs of the change. Controlling often relates to tangible results related to specific stakeholders, or related assessments, uncertainties,

and perceptions. The illusion of control and hyperbolic discounting are examples of biases related to controlling.

- *Trusting* is the need to see 'the world' or personal context as a benevolent, safe place. In organizational terms, trusting refers to faith in the organization and its participants, especially when there is an upcoming change. Unlike understanding and controlling, trusting has an affective character. People generally want a social environment that can be characterized as sympathetic, good-natured, reliable, and open. In situations of change, the fulfilment of that need may be frustrated. The existing 'psychological contract,' or any current and past expectations no longer provide security, but are at risk. Trust takes years to build, but only a second to shatter. The mere exposure effect and the optimism bias are examples of biases related to trusting.
- *Self-enhancing* is the need to view the self as basically worthy or improvable and refers to self-confidence, a positive self-image, or being motivated to develop and improve the self. Furthermore, self-enhancement helps maintain the position in the group, and the group has the potential to enhance the self as well. This motive contributes to people being able to feel good about themselves. Within the organizational and change contexts, self-enhancement can be impactful in not only increasing the effectiveness of individuals on their own but also that of teams and organizations. Relevant biases in this regard are the sunk-cost fallacy and the overconfidence effect.

The approach and structure of the book

This book is a mutual reach-out between the world of cognitive and social biases and those of organizational behaviour and change management. The reach-out is formed by presenting 29 so-called primary biases. These biases are called primary because they are potentially relevant in the context of organizational behaviour and change management, are well-researched, and are related to a relatively sound foundation of scientific evidence. The primary biases are structured by using the five core social motives that form the backbone of the five relevant chapters. In addition, we have gathered, analysed, and described a collection of secondary biases. Compared to the primary biases, they lack the same evidence-based foundation. However, in a lot of cases they show relatively strong similarities with the concepts of primary biases. In addition, they provide language, definitions, and possible insights that are worth reflecting upon. Therefore, the secondary biases are explicitly distinguished from the primary ones and used in addition to the primary biases.

For the disciplines of organizational behaviour and change management and its scientists and practitioners, the biases described are without exception inspiring, sometimes thought-provoking, insightful, informative, helpful, and hence relevant. This book is evidence-based. The focus of it is on scientific research and evidence resulting from it. Its purpose is to feed further research and applications in the context of organizational behaviour and change management.

The next chapter focuses on the model and methodology used. We introduce the core social motives, the change methodology, and the evidence-based perspective and method. After this, we present the primary biases and related evidence per core social motive. Chapter 3 focuses on understanding, chapter 4 on controlling, chapter 5 on trusting, chapter 6 on self-enhancing, and chapter 7 on belonging. Chapter 8, the last one, is dedicated to integration and reflection: What are the lessons and insights and their relationships from all the biases for the field of organizational behaviour and change management and what does a more evidence-based, systematic, and integrative approach contribute to practice and research?

Bibliography

Bower, J. L. (2000). The purpose of change, a commentary on Jensen and Senge. In M. Beer & N. Nohria (Eds.), *Breaking the code of change*. Harvard Business School Press.

Festinger, L. (1957). *A theory of cognitive dissonance*. Stanford University Press.

Fiske, S. T. (2010). *Social beings: Core motives in social psychology*. John Wiley & Sons.

Furber, S. (2012). To build a brain. *IEEE Spectrum, 49*(8), 44–49.

Harris, J. J., Jolivet, R., & Attwell, D. (2012). Synaptic energy use and supply. *Neuron, 75*(5), 762– 777.

Janis, I. L. (1972). *Victims of groupthink: A psychological study of foreign-policy decisions and fiascoes*. Houghton Mifflin Company.

Kahnemann, D. (2011). *Ons feilbare denken: Thinking, fast and slow*. Uitgeverij Business Contact.

Pronin, E., Lin, D. Y., & Ross, L. (2002). The bias blind spot: Perceptions of bias in self versus others. *Personality and Social Psychology Bulletin, 28*(3), 369–381. https://doi.org/10.1177/0146167202286008

Rolfe, D. F., & Brown, G. C. (1997). Cellular energy utilization and molecular origin of standard metabolic rate in mammals. *Physiological Reviews*, 77(3), 731–758.

Rosenzweig, P. (2007). *The halo effect . . . and the eight other business delusions that deceive managers*. Simon and Schuster.

Sibony, O. (2019). *You are about to make a terrible mistake! How biases distort decision making-and what you can do to fight them*. Swift Press.

Tobena, A., Marks, I., & Dar, R. (1999). Advantages of bias and prejudice: An exploration of their neurocognitive templates. *Neuroscience & Biosal Reviews, 23*(7), 1047–1058.

Vroon, P. (1989). *Tranen van de krokodil*. Ambo/Anthos Uitgevers.

Weick, K. E. (1979). *The social psychology of organizing*. McGraw-Hill.

2 Model and methodology

Wouter ten Have, Cornell Vernooij, and Judith Stuijt

Introduction

The focus of this book and our research is on the study and consequent evidence related to the application of biases in the field of organizational behaviour and change management. This book forms a mutual reach-out between social psychology and change management. In summary, the purpose of our research and this book is threefold. The first aim is to assess the available cognitive and social psychological biases and research and fuel change management with the evidence and insights we find (evidence-based, scientific). The second is to present, categorize, and integrate the biases and findings by using a framework based on the five core social motives (Fiske, 2004) and our change management methodology: cohesive, systemic, and practical.

The overarching goal, however, inspired by the ideas and perspective of leading thinkers like Kurt Lewin, James Q. Wilson, Susan T. Fiske, and Daniel Kahneman, is to make the world a better place.

Social psychologists (being social scientists) study practical social issues. In our case, issues related to change management and the application of social psychological knowledge to real-world problems is a key goal. As Fiske (2004) states: "Social psychologists believe that if we understand how people influence one another, then perhaps we can understand and ameliorate some of the negative influences. Social psychology is in some ways a field for idealists" (p. 33). In addition, Fiske emphasizes that in the end, social psychology searches for wisdom, not just knowledge. This provides valuable extra guidance for the way in which social psychology has to be applied to the set of social issues we call change management: "Wisdom may be considered knowledge about people and the world combined with enduring moral, intellectual and societal concerns, that makes sense in the context of people's lived experience" (p. 33).

In this chapter, we describe and explain the model based on the five core social motives, the selection of cognitive and social psychological biases, and the evidence-based methodology we used to describe the biases and their contribution to organizational behaviour and change management.

DOI: 10.4324/9781003288237-2

A dynamic and integrative model of social motives

Fiske's (2004) essential idea is that "a small number of essential, core social motives enhance people's survival in groups" and that this "offers a unifying framework for understanding the field of social psychology" (p. 15); we add: and for making social psychology (better) available and (more) accessible from the perspective of organizations in general and change management in particular. In addition to the introduction of these five 'categories,' we have introduced our own visualization to combine categorization and integration; the five motives are related perspectives.

In our earlier research, 'The Social Psychology of Change Management,' we investigated the importance and relevance of social psychology to change and change management. The main ingredients or bricks were more than 100 selected social psychological theories. With regard to impact on specific change and change management, we have judged these ingredients to be fit for purpose. But from both a knowing and a learning perspective, not to mention application in practice, more than 100 theories were, to say the least, not that manageable. We have therefore chosen to categorize and model them. This categorization was based on Fiske's (2004) the social core motives belonging, understanding, controlling, trusting, and enhancing self. The model that structures this book is also based on these five core motives and their relative position, relationship or interaction, and interdependency. But before we explain the model further, we elucidate the value and functions of models and discuss these as learning aids.

The use of models as learning aids has two primary benefits (Gage & Berliner, 1992)—(1) they provide "accurate and useful representations of knowledge that is needed when solving problems in some particular domain" (p. 314) and (2) they make the process of understanding a domain of knowledge easier because they are the visual expression of the topic. Research (Gage & Berliner, 1992) shows that students who study models before a lecture may recall as much as 57 percent more on questions concerning conceptual information. This is compared with students who receive instruction without the advantage of seeing and discussing models. Other studies, like that by Alesandrini (1981), who studied different pictorial-verbal strategies for learning, came to similar conclusions. A model can be seen as a 'mnemonic.'

A mnemonic is any learning technique that aids information retention or retrieval in the human memory. A mnemonic enables people to remember and mobilize long lists of information (Gazzaniga & Heatherton, 2006), such as approximately 100 social psychological biases. The use of visual imagery is an especially effective mnemonic. A historical variant is related to monks placing specific knowledge in a systematic way in certain spaces in their monastery. This is the method of loci—placing objects like categories, subcategories, or ideas in familiar locations and retrieving them by going back to these locations. A similar technique is learning a list of key words, or pegs, and then categorizing new words with these pegs by visualizing them together. Mnemonics help original information become associated with something more accessible or meaningful, which, in turn, provides better retention of the information. In this book, Fiske's social core motives are the five spaces in which, or the umbrellas under which, the approximately hundred biases are organized in a meaningful and accessible way. In addition, these spaces are visualized and, in a way, construct a 'monastery' full of categorized and interrelated social psychological biases.

According to Fiske (2004), the underlying principle of the model is oriented towards the (better) survival of 'the social animal.' "All five motives orient toward making people fit better into groups, thus increasing their chances for survival" (p. 16). From this perspective, the chance of survival or the chance for change (in order to adapt to changing circumstances, contexts, conditions, or demands) could be defined as the sum of its parts. The parts are the five social core motives: belonging, understanding, controlling, trusting, and enhancing self. However, one can also see it as more (or even less) than the sum of its parts.

Core-motive synergies and trade-offs

The motives can be seen as interrelated, in positive or negative ways, in terms of synergies or trade-offs and antagonisms and form a dynamic system in which they interact and have (causal) relationships and dependencies (like the issues and topics they address and the social psychological biases to which they relate). For example, understanding can positively influence controlling, trusting can be a precondition for self-enhancing, a lack of trust can hamper a feeling of belongingness, and that there could be a trade-off between controlling and trusting.

From the perspective of the social animal and its biotope, the group (a family, a team, etc.) or organization (a company, a society, etc.), the motives cannot be separated in real life. They are interrelated and interdependent, together constituting the connective being that the social animal is in a dynamic way defining its biotope, or its social environment in maybe even a more dynamic way. Fiske (2004) also addresses the interactions and combinations of motives. She makes use of these to address important psychological concepts. For example, she uses three motives to discuss compliance and introduces it as "strategies to understand self, maintain belonging and control resources. She defines her idea as a unifying framework for understanding the field of social psychology. In describing the relationships among core social motives, Fiske positions belonging as the principal motive and defines understanding and controlling as relatively cognitive motives and trusting and self-enhancing as relatively affective motives (Table 2.1).

In a schematic way, one could envisage a cognitive and an affective axis, with belonging as the principal motive of the social animal or the quintessence at the very heart or crossing. To illustrate the interrelatedness or

Table 2.1 Relationships among Core Social Motives (Fiske, 2004)

Belonging *Need for strong, stable relationships*			
Relatively Cognitive Motives		*Relatively Affective Motives*	
Understanding	*Self-enhancing*	*Controlling*	*Trusting*
Need for shared meaning and prediction	Need for viewing self as basically worthy or improvable	Need for perceived contingency between behaviour and outcomes	Need for seeing others as basically benign

connectivity between the motives and the continuous interaction among the five motives and between the motives and specific contexts, one could introduce dynamism by using the lemniscate instead of the axis. The lemniscate shape bears an intrinsic dynamic component and entails continuously returning movements instead of linear lines. The uninterrupted lines, without a start and end point, can be equated to the iterative process that characterizes the positive or negative development of the social animal and its social relationships. The five social core motives and their mutual interconnectivity can be shown through two lemniscates and a connecting circle, a magnification of the central social motive, belonging (Figure 2.1).

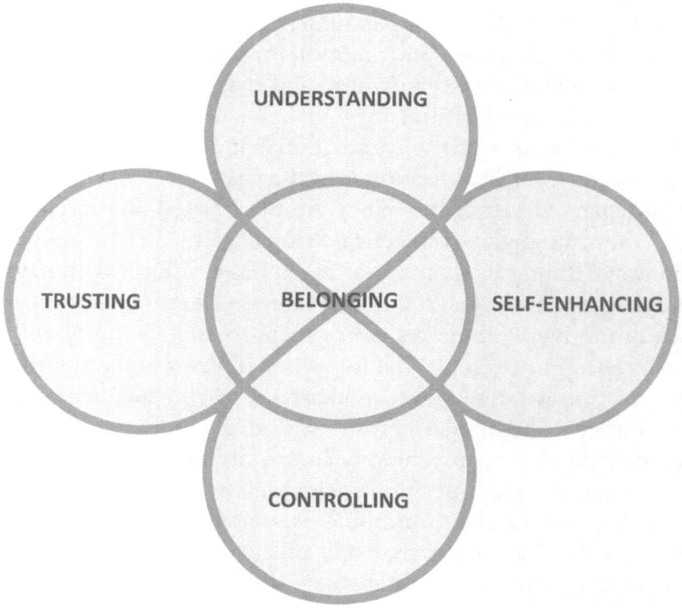

Figure 2.1 The Five Motives Ordered Using the Lemniscate

In this way, we categorize and connect the motives and hence the biases. In the subsequent five chapters, we elaborate on each of the core social motives by relating them to 29 primary biases that are most relevant from a change management perspective.

There is an additional reason for using the introduced visualization or modelling. The basic, dynamic form was initially developed for and applied and tested in the field of change management (Ten Have et al., 2015). This change-competence model for purposive change is aimed at helping to answer the core question when addressing 'purposive change': What should it be, and how should it be accomplished? (Bower, 2000). The first part is about the direction, idea, or change vision, and the second part about the execution, the feasibility, or change capacity (Figure 2.2). Change vision is visualized as the vertical axis or lemniscate and is defined as the key factor for change rationale and effect in connection. Change capacity, the horizontal part, is construed in terms of focus and energy in connection.

The combination of the two models—the social psychological model based on the five social motives and the change-competence model based on the five key factors for change—which share at least the schematic, visual, and conceptual similarities, provide additional insights and learnings with regard to (towards) the social psychology of change management. For an elaboration on these insights and learnings, we refer to the concluding

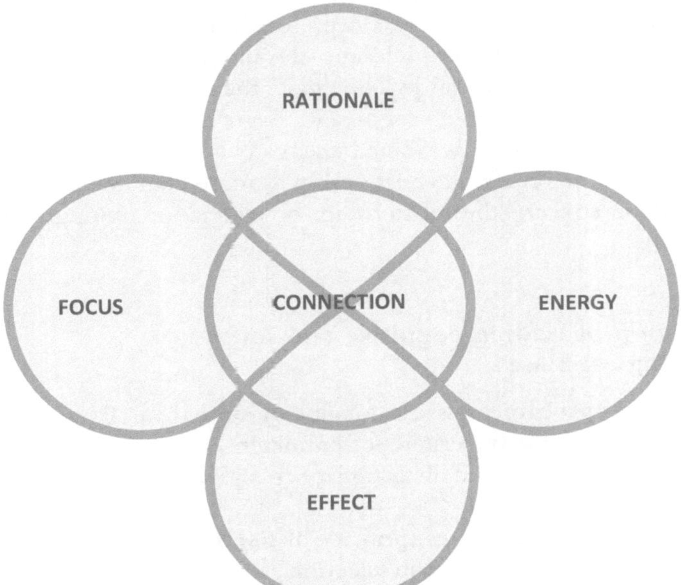

Figure 2.2 Change-Competence Model

chapter of this book. In this chapter, 29 primary biases are categorized and positioned in Fiske's model, and Fiske's model and the change-competence model are used as frameworks to describe the relevance and importance of the biases for change management.

In addition to the categorization and positioning of the biases, each bias is assessed with the help of the most relevant and best available scientific evidence ('rapid evidence assessment,' REA). For each bias and its evidence, we describe the relevance, consequences, and learnings for change management. In the chapters 3–7, the 29 primary biases are combined with other relevant (secondary) biases, social psychological theories, insights from the change management field, and its most popular books.

We begin in chapter 3 with the social psychological biases relating to the motive of understanding. As we described in the first chapter, biases help to quickly assess and respond in (social) situations without using too much of the brain's valuable processing power. Attentional bias, or the tendency to focus on certain elements while ignoring others, is the main bias that helps us assess our surroundings in a fast and efficient way. This seemingly basic function can be seen as a precursor to all other cognitive functions such as understanding, remembering, and learning. Therefore, we start with this overarching bias that is crucial in our motivation to understand our environment, to predict it, and to give meaning to it.

Understanding is followed by controlling, the other relatively cognitive motive. We also illustrate and envisage the domains of the affective motives, trusting and self-enhancing, and lastly belonging, the principal motive. In the following chapters, we provide a static categorization and description of biases. Where relevant, the interaction or dynamics with other related biases or social psychological theories is mentioned or discussed. The social psychological biases are attributed to the motive with the best or most relevant fit. Some biases can be related to more than one motive. For some others, the relationship to more than one is in fact illustrative; these concern the relationships or interaction among core social motives.

A selection of leading cognitive and social psychological biases

For this book, we have assessed a 'longlist' of more than 100 social psychological biases by using the criteria of prominence, relevance, and evidence. We selected 29 primary and 69 secondary cognitive and social psychological biases.

We present those 29 biases (primary biases) for which we could find a reasonable amount of evidence in scientific literature. We selected the biases, structured them in a coherent model, analysed them, and made them applicable for organizations and change. The secondary biases, despite lacking sufficient scientific evidence, show strong theoretical similarities to the 29 primary biases and can help to illustrate them. Therefore, when relevant, we have incorporated the secondary biases in the chapters.

To thoroughly map the field of social psychology and all the cognitive and social psychological biases, we extracted the biases from fundamental and overarching articles. To further bolster our list of biases, we ran a thorough search across books, the Internet, social psychological glossaries, and popular articles for the history of the field. This included the following bestsellers:

- *Thinking, Fast and Slow* by Daniel Kahneman
- *Biased: Uncovering the Hidden Prejudice That Shapes What We See, Think, and Do* by Jennifer L. Eberhardt
- *Judgement Under Uncertainty: Heuristics and Biases* by Kahneman, Tversky, and Slovic
- *Biases and Heuristics the Complete Collection of Cognitive Biases and Heuristics That Impair Decisions in Banking, Finance and Everything Else* by Henry Priest
- *Biased: 50 Powerful Cognitive Biases That Impair Our Judgment* by Henry Priest

The search resulted in a list of 98 social psychological biases.

Table 2.2 List of All Included Biases Categorized Using the Five Core Social Motives

Understanding	
1. Attentional bias	
—	Frequency illusion
—	Focusing effect
—	Distinction bias
2. Availability bias	
—	Availability cascade
—	Illusory correlation
—	Apophenia
—	Pareidolia
—	Well-travelled road effect
3. Conjunction fallacy	
—	Representativeness heuristic
—	Base- rate fallacy
4. Framing effect	
—	Projection bias
—	Unit bias
5. Priming effect	
—	Anchoring
—	Conservatism bias
—	Semmelweis effect
—	Law of the instrument
6. Recency effect	
7. Halo effect	
—	The law of small numbers
8. Similarity bias	

Table 2.2 (Continued)

Controlling	
1. Illusion of control	
—	Illusory superiority
—	Self-serving bias
—	Planning fallacy
2. Hindsight bias	
—	Outcome bias
3. Information bias	
—	Zero-risk bias
—	Ambiguity effect
—	Parkinson's' law
4. Risk compensation	
—	Reactance
5. Prospect theory	
—	Disposition effect
—	Dread aversion
—	Pseudo certainty effect
—	The neglect of probability
—	Sunk-cost fallacy
6. Delay (Hyperbolic) discounting	
—	Money illusion
Trusting	
1. Mere exposure effect	
—	Illusory truth effect
—	Rhyme-as-reason effect
—	Automation bias
2. Negativity bias	
—	Truthiness
—	Subjective validation
—	Diclinism
—	Pessimism bias
3. Optimism bias	
—	Normalcy bias
—	Pro-innovation bias
4. (Hostile) attribution bias	
—	Fundamental attribution error
—	Actor– observer bias
—	Third-person bias
—	Empathy gap
—	Hostile attribution bias
Self-enhancing	
1. Egocentric bias	
—	Self-serving bias
—	Spotlight effect
—	Forer effect
—	Zero-sum bias
—	Reactive devaluation
—	Not- invented- here syndrome
—	Curse of knowledge

2. Overconfidence effect	
—	Restraint bias
—	Moral credential effect
—	Ostrich effect
—	Choice-supportive bias
—	Bias blind spot
3. Confirmation bias	
—	Continued influence effect
—	Congruence bias
—	Illusion of validity
—	Backfire bias
—	Selection bias
4. Experimenter bias	
—	Funding bias
5. Endowment effect	
6. Sunk-cost fallacy	
Belonging	
1. Conformity	
2. Groupthink	
—	Bandwagon effect
3. Social desirability bias	
—	Courtesy bias
4. Status quo bias	
—	Omission bias
—	Inertia
5. System-justification bias	
—	Authority bias

Based on these inclusion criteria, 29 primary biases were included. These biases were categorized using the five core social motives of Fiske (2004) (Figure 2.3).

After selecting and categorizing the biases, we applied a rapid evidence assessment (REA) to each of them. Based on this and the bias itself, we have described the importance of, relevance to, and the potential of each bias in the field of change management. We discussed the bias itself within our team to define the possible contribution to the field of change and organization. This was primarily a deductive process of consensual validation carried out by experienced practitioners and scientists. The REA was focused on specific research on the biases applied to the field of change and organization. This was primarily an inductive process carried out by a team of analysts that delivered the REAs to the team of authors.

The definitive list of biases was categorized by using the five core social motives of Fiske (2004). This categorization is not 'absolute'; we have looked for the best fit. Several biases are relevant to or related to more than one core social motive. For example, the system-justification bias is placed

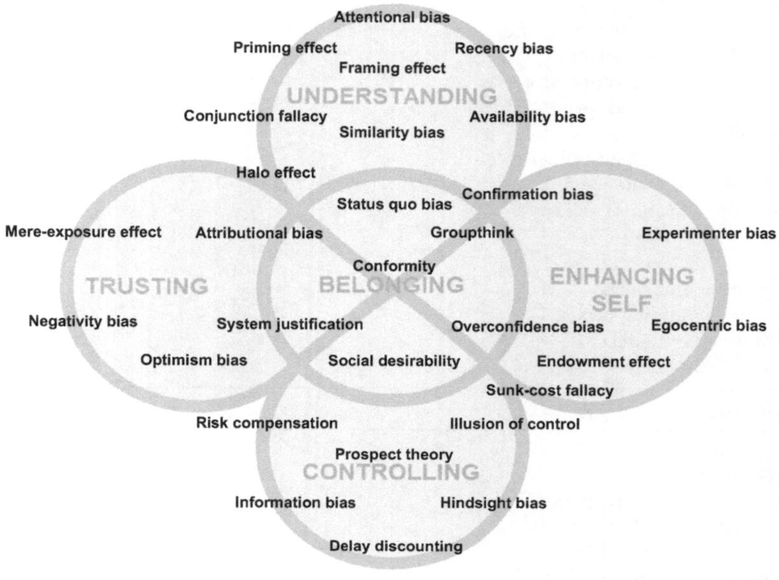

Figure 2.3 Primary Biases Categorized by the Five Core Social Motives

in the chapter on belonging, but it clearly also strongly relates to trusting. This interrelatedness, this interdependency, and these possible synergies and trade-offs between both core social motives and the related biases are also addressed by the dynamic modelling or visualization we introduced in the first chapter and further explain in this chapter. In the final chapter (chapter 8), we reflect on the 'interrelatedness' and the potential for and relevance (and possible complications) to the (further) development of the social psychology of change management.

Most of the selected primary cognitive and social psychological biases are based on well-founded empirical research. For practical reasons, we had to *limit* the selection of primary social psychological biases with assessed relevance to and potential for the organizational context, the field of change management, to around 30. We may have missed or left out relevant biases (from or outside the longlist). We will identify these biases or their 'offspring' in the organizational context and analyse and unleash them as well for the field of organization and change in the near future. In the coming chapters, we see and experience that with regard to the specific evidence on the almost 30 biases in the organizational context, the quantity and quality (level of evidence) as well as the relevance (what it contributes to the field and practice) will vary between the biases. Without doubt, future research will provide more such evidence to the field and practice. We will follow up this progress and include and integrate it in future versions, as we have with our earlier research and publications (Ten Have et al., 2016, 2018).

The importance of evidence-based practice and methodology

We need substantial evidence to assess the existence of the social psychological biases. Evidence can be described as information, facts, or data supporting a certain claim, belief, or assumption. There are four diverse sources of evidence: scientific literature, professional experience, internal data from the organization, and values and concerns by stakeholders. An important premise of evidence-based practice (EBP) is that all these types and sources of evidence—whether they relate to professional experience, organizational data, or scientific research findings—must be critically appraised for reliability and trustworthiness. This critical appraisal of evidence is at the heart of EBP. In our research, we applied the evidence-based methodology and more specifically the REA method to generate the evidence available with regard to the application of social psychological biases in the field of change and organization. In the following section, we provide a more detailed description of the evidence-based methodology (REA).

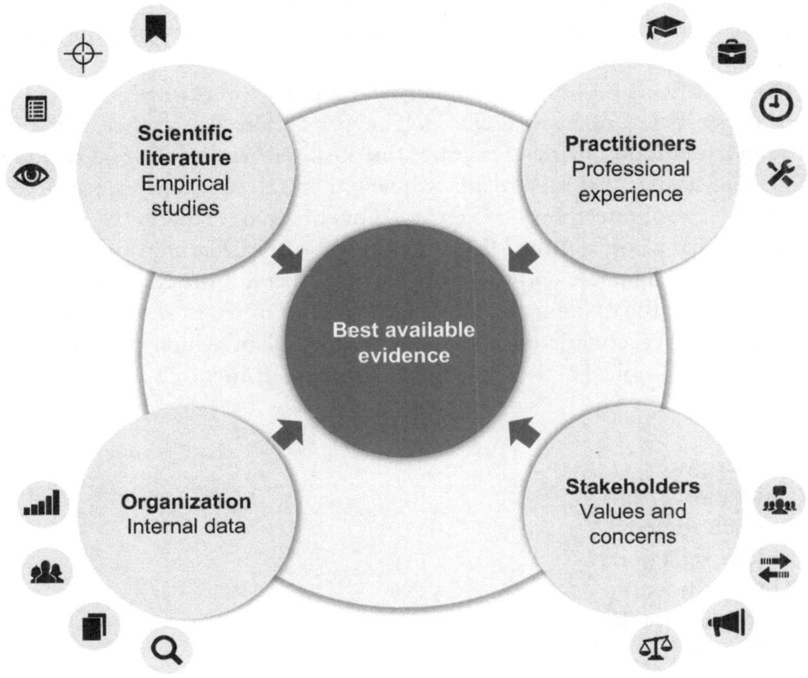

Figure 2.4 Sources Contributing to the Best Available Evidence

In advance, we must mention the following important disclaimer: The aim of this research was to find scientific evidence for the most prominent cognitive and social psychological biases in academic and popular literature. However, evidence in the scientific literature alone is insufficient to draw definite conclusions about the existence of social psychological biases. This means that biases lacking enough scientific evidence are not necessarily non-existent, as the underlying claim of these biases could very well be backed up by substantial evidence from other sources, such as professional experience or internal organizational data. The total of 29 primary social biases in our research thus should not be regarded as a complete or exhaustive list, as other sources of evidence could lead to other or additional prominent social psychological biases.

Rapid evidence assessment (REA)

Evidence summaries come in many forms. One of the best known is the conventional literature review, which provides a general overview of the relevant scientific literature published on a given topic. However, a conventional literature review is not always entirely trustworthy. Studies are often selected on the basis of the researcher's preferences rather than on explicit and objective criteria, and the research results are generally not subject to critical appraisal (Antman, 1992; Bushman & Wells, 2001; Chalmers et al., 1993; Fink, 1998). Most conventional literature reviews are therefore prone to severe bias and are considered unsuitable for answering questions about the effectiveness of strategies or interventions.

This is why REAs are the preferred method for reviewing evidence in evidence-based management. Such reviews address a focused question through a methodology that identifies the most relevant studies and includes only those studies that meet explicit quality and relevance criteria as determined by several researchers (Higgins & Green, 2006; Petticrew & Roberts, 2006). Unlike a conventional literature review, an REA is transparent, verifiable, and reproducible and therefore less biased and more relevant.

To examine the evidence base of the 29 biases in relation to change and organization, we conducted a series of REAs, all of which we have presented in this book. Each of the REAs conducted involved the following nine steps:

1. Description
2. Inclusion criteria
3. Search strategy
4. Study selection
5. Data extraction
6. Critical appraisal
7. Main findings
8. Conclusion
9. Practical reflections

1. *Description: What is the bias about and what is the basic assumption?*

This section describes bias (e.g., the availability bias or information bias) and its basic assumptions. We have used both popular and academic literature to explain and illustrate the bias and its underlying assumptions.

2. *Inclusion criteria: Which studies to include?*

This section specifies the criteria and justification for the inclusion (or exclusion) of particular studies. We applied the following inclusion criteria to all REAs:

- Type of publication: only articles published in peer-reviewed scholarly journals
- Language: only articles in English
- Type of studies: only quantitative studies
- Measurement: only studies that measured an effect of the bias
- Context: focus on studies relating the theory to organizations and/or change management
- Level of trustworthiness: only studies graded level D or above

Remark: To ensure thorough descriptions of the biases that made the long-list, we included a wider range of articles. From the main findings and beyond, we used the inclusion criteria just stated.

3. *Search strategy: How was the research evidence sought?*

For our first search, we combined the bias with change management. We limited the search to the following three bibliographical databases:

- ABI/INFORM Global from ProQuest
- Business Source Premier from EBSCO
- PsycINFO from Ovid

If the first search yielded an insufficient number of studies, we carried out a second, broader search only including the name of the bias. To find relevant studies in other disciplines (beyond social psychology and change management), we searched databases related to disciplines such as health care (e.g., PubMed) and education (ERIC). In addition, we used generic databases like Google Scholar. The search steps are summarized in Figure 2.5.

4. *Study selection: How were the studies to be included selected?*

In most cases, the search yielded many studies, sometimes several hundred. Some of these were not directly relevant to the research question. Hence,

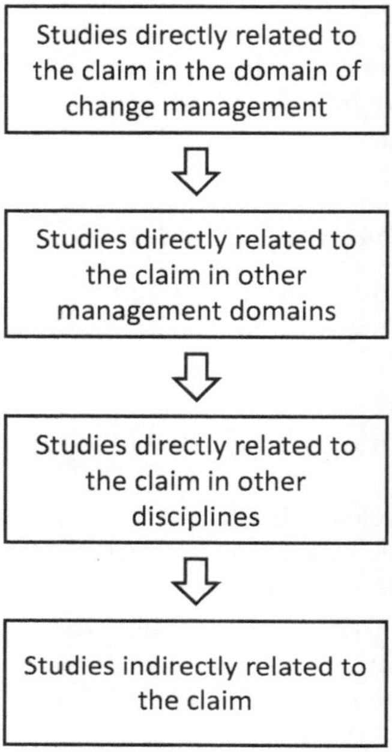

Figure 2.5 Overview of the Research Steps

two reviewers independently screened the titles and the abstracts of the studies identified for their relevance of the theory in relation to organizations. In the event of doubt, lack of information, or disagreement, they included the study. They then selected the remaining studies for inclusion based on the full text of the article. The reviewers excluded studies that failed to meet the inclusion criteria. Again, two reviewers worked independently to identify the studies to be included or excluded. If both reviewers disagreed on the inclusion of a study, a third reviewer, with no prior knowledge of the initial reviewers' assessments, evaluated it. The decision of this reviewer was final.

5. Data extraction

For data extraction, we collated the results of the studies included. In this phase, we extracted relevant data from the final set of studies—specifically data on the year of publication, research design, sample size, population (e.g., industry and type of employees), possible moderators or mediators, outcome measures, main findings, effect sizes, and limitations.

6. *Critical appraisal: How was the trustworthiness of the evidence appraised?*

we first determined a study's trustworthiness by assessing its methodological appropriateness. We rated the appropriateness high when the design reflected the best way to answer the research question. For cause-and-effect claims (i.e., if I do A, will it result in B?), we regarded a study that used both a control group and random assignment as the 'gold standard.' Nonrandomized studies and before-after studies came next in terms of appropriateness. Cross-sectional studies (surveys) were regarded as having the highest chance of reflecting bias in the outcome; therefore, we rated them lower down in terms of appropriateness. We rated meta-analyses that used statistical analysis techniques to pool the results of controlled studies as the most appropriate design. We used Campbell and Petticrew's classification system (Shadish et al., 2002; Petticrew & Roberts, 2006) to determine the methodological appropriateness of the research design of the studies included on the basis of a systematic assessment. We resolved any discrepancies through discussion or by consulting a third party where necessary. The following five levels of appropriateness were used for the classification (Table 2.3).

The methodological quality of study, or the method in which it was conducted, also affects its trustworthiness. To determine the methodological quality, the reviewers systematically assessed all the studies included based on explicit quality criteria, such as the PRISMA (Moher et al., 2009) and CONSORT statement, the CASP check lists, the checklists of the EPPI Center, and the critical appraisal criteria developed by the Center for Evidence-Based Management. On the basis of a tally of the number of weaknesses, the reviewers downgraded the trustworthiness by one or more

Table 2.3 Five Levels to Determine the Methodological Appropriateness of the Research Design of the Studies Included

Design	*Appropriateness*	*Level*
Systematic review and meta-analysis of randomized, controlled studies	Very high	A+
Systematic review and meta-analysis of controlled and/or before-after studies Randomized controlled studies	High	A
Systematic review and meta-analysis of cross-sectional studies Nonrandomized controlled before-after studies Interrupted time series	Moderate	B
Controlled studies without a pretest and uncontrolled studies with a pretest	Limited	C
Cross-sectional studies	Low	D

levels. To determine the final level of trustworthiness, they adopted the following rule of thumb:

- 1 weakness = no downgrade (i.e., we accept that nothing is perfect)
- 2 weaknesses = downgrade 1 level
- 3 weaknesses = downgrade 2 levels, etc.

Impact: Effect sizes

An effect (association or difference) can be statistically significant but may not necessarily be of practical relevance. Even a trivial effect can be statistically significant if the sample size is big enough. For this reason, we assessed the effect size—a standard measure of the magnitude (strength) of the effect—of the studies. To determine the magnitude of an effect, we applied Cohen's rule of thumb (Cohen, 1988). According to Cohen (1988), a small effect is only visible through careful examination, a medium effect is 'visible to the naked eye of the careful observer,' and a large effect is substantial, so anyone can easily see it.

7. *Main findings: What was found?*

This section provides an overview of the relevant main findings. We present the main evidence, the level of trustworthiness, and the effect size for each finding from the REA.

8. *Conclusion: What is the added value of the theory?*

This section presents the conclusions. The conclusion describes the added value of the bias in relation to organizations and the field of change management. The added value was based on the overall methodological appropriateness, quality of the studies that were included and the practical relevance of the effect sizes found.

9. *Practical reflections*

As we state in the introduction, evidence-based practice is based on four sources of evidence. Evidence in the scientific literature alone is insufficient. We need the experience and expertise of practitioners to be able to determine whether the research findings will apply in a particular situation. Practitioner expertise is also necessary when the evidence is contradictory or lacking. This section, therefore, shows how the findings of the REA relate to the daily practice of change managers and discusses their implications in practice.

Limitations

A REA provides a balanced assessment of what is known in the scientific literature about a bias by applying a systematic review method to search and critically appraise primary studies. However, for it to be 'rapid,' we have made concessions in terms of the breadth and depth of the search process for the REAs in this book. These include the exclusion of unpublished research, the use of a limited number of databases, and focus on meta-analyses and primary studies published over the past 20 years. As a consequence, some relevant studies may have been omitted. The critical appraisal also did not always include a comprehensive review of the psychometric properties of the tests, scales, and questionnaires used in the studies included. Given these limitations, care must be taken not to accept the findings presented in this book as conclusive.

Report and format per bias

The REA format as described previously is fully applied to each of the selected social psychological biases. However, given the purpose of this book and for practical reasons, we have partly redesigned the format used to report on each bias. To start with, four of the nine steps or parts of the procedure are general and only described in this chapter: (2) inclusion criteria, (4) study selection, (5) data extraction, and (6) critical appraisal. For this research and this book, one subsection has been added (2: 'relevance'). The format used for the social psychological biases in chapters 3 to 7 is:

1. What is (for example) availability bias?
2. What is the relevance of availability bias to organization and change?
3. Search strategy
4. Main findings
5. Conclusion
6. Practical reflections

The first section describes the bias, its history, background, and development primarily from a social psychological perspective. Section 2 is about the relevance of a bias in the context of organization and change. The bias is related and translated to the organizational context, management, and change. In this part, we may have used quotes from popular change management literature for illustration purposes. After the search strategy (section 3) and the main findings (section 4), we present the conclusion (section 5). On the basis of (organizational) context-relevant (main) findings, the conclusion describes what the contributions and insights for the practice of management and change are or can be. In the conclusion, we often relate to relevant change management topics. On the basis of evidence, paragraph 6 provides practical reflections and guidelines for the practice of management and change. For all biases addressed, we have based the conclusion on empirical evidence, that is, the main findings (section 4). However, we may also have based the conclusion partly on deductive elements, the (projected) relevance, the potential, and the logical and theoretical explanatory power of the bias. For practical considerations, we also have provided warnings or possible consequences of the findings and insights related to bias in the organizational context. In some cases, we have provided further illustration of the ideas and insights by making use of (popular) management literature. Each search strategy led to a matrix in which we describe the characteristics and findings of the included studies. In addition, a short description of excluded studies is part of the matrix. For practical reasons, we have not included the complete set of matrices in the book. However, we have included a bias plus matrix in Appendix B for each core social motive, leading to five examples.

*3.*Based on Ten Have, S., Ten Have, W. D., Huijsmans, A. B., & Otto, M. (2016). *Reconsidering change management: Applying evidence-based insights in change management practice.* New York, NY: Routledge, and Ten Have, S., Rijsman, J., Ten Have, W. D., & Westhof, J. (2019). *The social psychology of change management: Theories and an evidence-based perspective on social and organizational beings.* New York, NY: Routledge.

Bibliography

Alesandrini, K. L. (1981). Pictorial—verbal and analytic—holistic learning strategies in science learning. *Journal of Educational Psychology, 73*(3), 358–368. https://doi.org/10.1037/0022-0663.73.3.358

Antman, E. M. (1992). A comparison of results of meta-analyses of randomized control trials and recommendations of clinical experts. *JAMA, 268*(2), 240. https://doi.org/10.1001/jama.1992.03490020088036

Bower, J. L. (2000). The purpose of change, a commentary on Jensen and Senge. In M. Beer & N. Nohria (Eds.), *Breaking the code of change*. Harvard Business School Press.

Bushman, B. J., & Wells, G. L. (2001). Narrative impressions of literature: The availability bias and the corrective properties of meta-analytic approaches. *Personality and Social Psychology Bulletin, 27*(9), 1123–1130. https://doi.org/10.1177/0146167201279005

Chalmers, I., Enkin, M., & Keirse, M. J. N. C. (1993). Preparing and updating systematic reviews of randomized controlled trials of health care. *The Milbank Quarterly, 71*(3), 411. https://doi.org/10.2307/3350409

Cohen, J. (1988). *Statistical power analysis for the behavioral sciences* (2nd ed.). Lawrence Erlbaum Associates Inc.

Fink, A. (1998). *Conducting research literature reviews: From the Internet to paper*. Sage Publications, Inc.

Fiske, S. T. (2004). *Social beings: Core motives in social psychology*. John Wiley & Sons.

Gage, N. L., & Berliner, D. C. (1992). *Educational psychology* (5th ed.). Houghton Mifflin Company.

Gazzaniga, M. S., & Heatherton, T. (2006). *Psychological science: Mind, brain, and behavior* (2nd ed.). Norton & Company Inc.

Higgins, J. P. T., & Green, S. (2006, September). *Cochrane handbook for systematic reviews of interventions 4.2.6*. Retrieved September 1, 2015, from http://community.cochrane.org/sites/default/files/uploads/Handbook4.2

Moher, D., Liberati, A., Tetzlaff, J., & Altman, D. G. (2009). Preferred reporting items for systematic reviews and meta-analyses: The PRISMA statement. *PLoS Medicine, 6*(7), 1–6, e1000097. https://doi.org/10.1371/journal.pmed.1000097

Petticrew, M., & Roberts, H. (2006). *Systematic reviews in the social sciences: A practical guide*. Blackwell Publishing.

Shadish, W. R., Cook, T. D., & Campbell, D. T. (2002). *Experimental and quasi-experimental designs for generalized causal inference*. Houghton Mifflin Company.

Ten Have, S., Ten Have, W. D., Huijsmans, A.-B., & Otto, M. (2016). *Reconsidering change management: Applying evidence-based insights in change management practice*. Routledge.

Ten Have, S., Ten Have, W. D., Huijsmans, A. B., & Van der Eng, N. (2015). *Change competence: Implementing effective change*. Routledge.

Ten Have, S., Ten Have, W. D., & Rijsman, J. (2018). Naar een sociale psychologie voor gedragsverandering in organisaties. *Holland Management Review*, *177*, 67–75.

3 Understanding, biases, organizational behaviour, and change

Judith Stuijt, Cornell Vernooij, and Flore Louwers

A First Short Story of Understanding, Biases, and Change

Understanding is the need for shared meaning and prediction. People are naturally motivated to understand, predict, and give meaning to their environment, as this enables their functioning and survival in groups. This also applies to people within the organizational and change context. Understanding relates to several important topics, such as organizational mission and culture, change vision, and resistance to change. In an urge to understand the world around them, people rely on mental shortcuts. People tend to be selective about the information they attend to and focus specifically on things that are emotional, arousing, and relevant to them (attentional bias). In forming judgements about probabilities or frequencies, people seem to rely on comparable instances that come to mind (availability bias). People also falsely assume that multiple specific conditions are more probable than a single generic one (conjunction fallacy). The way a message is framed influences perceptions, evaluations, and decisions, and people are specifically influenced when messages contain emotional information (framing effect). Priming is a valid phenomenon in social interactions. When people are primed with certain stereotypical information, they rapidly form a mental categorization of the other and make social judgements according to that social category (priming effect). People generally give more weight to recent information than preceding information when forming judgements (recency effect). Specifically in social judgements, people perceived as physically attractive are generally evaluated more positively than those that are not (halo effect). Lastly, there are signs that people evaluate those they perceive as similar to themselves in a more favourable light (similarity bias).

Introduction

Understanding—the need for shared meaning and prediction—is the second core social motive (the first is belonging) and one of the two cognitive motives (the other one is controlling). Understanding refers to the motivation of people to understand their environment, predict it, and give meaning to it. Humans have a fundamental need to form shared meaning, which is instrumental in decision-making and helps coordinate with other group members (Fiske, 2004). Having an understanding of themselves and their surroundings enables humans to make decisions (and consequently, guide

DOI: 10.4324/9781003288237-3

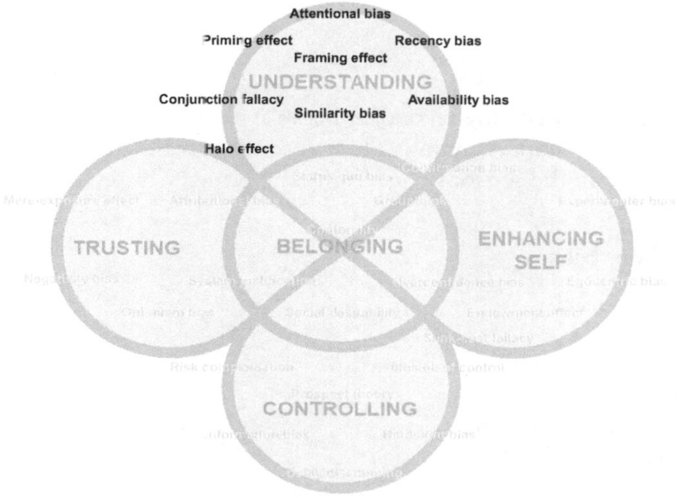

Figure 3.1 Primary Biases Related to the Core Social Motive of Understanding

behaviour) on the basis of accurate predictions and estimations and helps them to communicate and socialize with other people. From an evolutionary perspective, shared understanding is advantageous as it enables the functioning and survival of groups and the individuals within groups (Fiske, 2004).

In the organizational context, this motive can be understood as what the organization is, must do, and wants, and what organizational change means. In organizations, understanding is present or visible in, for example, 'a sense of mission,' the way people 'strategize,' the organizational culture, and values. Leaders, managers, and change agents must be aware of the need to understand and its importance in organizations and change. For example, shared understanding may impede change when a current 'joint view of reality' is in conflict with a new 'reality' related to the change. Understanding is related to change and management topics such as mission, leadership, organizational culture, change vision, and resistance to change (Ten Have et al., 2019).

We have identified eight primary biases related to the social motive of understanding:

Primary biases

Attentional bias
Availability bias
Conjunction fallacy
Framing effect

Priming effect
Recency effect
Halo effect
Similarity bias

In addition, the following secondary biases are identified to be related to the social motive of understanding. These secondary biases are (when relevant) incorporated in the sections concerning the primary biases.

Secondary biases

Affect heuristic
Anchoring
Conservatism bias
Semmelweis effect
Law of the instrument
Availability cascade
Present bias
Frequency illusion
Well-travelled road effect
Representativeness
Law of small numbers
Distinction bias
Base- rate fallacy
Unit bias
Focusing effect
Apophenia
Illusionary correlation
Pareidolia

This chapter first discusses the overarching primary bias—the 'attentional bias'—which is concerned with one, if not the most, critical element in the process of understanding: attention. Attention, albeit a seemingly basic function, can be seen as the precursor to all other cognitive functions such as understanding, remembering, and learning. Throughout the ages, philosophers have been interested in attention and have investigated it extensively. In 1674, in his book *The Search After Truth,* French philosopher Nicolos Malebranche described attention as crucial for human understanding and, simply, keeping our thoughts organized. This idea soon sparked interest among other great thinkers. Throughout the eighteenth and nineteenth centuries, various philosophers including German thinkers Gottfried Wilhelm Leibniz and Johann Friedrich Herbart made contributions to the field of attention studies. This led to the introduction of the study of attention to the field of psychology at the end of the nineteenth century. Psychologist John Ridley Stroop, whom we discuss later in this chapter, was the first to empirically test attention in 1935. To this day, attention remains a critical area of inquiry in the field of education, social psychology, and neuroscience. For this reason, we regard the attention-centred bias—attentional bias—as the most prominent of the biases in this chapter.

Various other biases, all of which emerge from the need to understand, fall under attentional bias. These biases can be categorized as (1) biases relating to probability or frequency judgements and (2) biases concerning the formation of social impressions or judgements about others. In the first part of this chapter, we focus on biases related to probability and frequency judgements followed by biases concerning the formation of social impressions.

Biases related to probability and frequency judgements

Humans tend to rely on mental shortcuts to understand the world around them. One of these shortcuts is the tendency to make judgements about the probability or frequency of an event by relying on how many comparable instances come to mind (availability bias). Another mental shortcut is the tendency to falsely assume that multiple specific conditions are more probable than a single generic one (conjunction fallacy).

Biases related to social impression formation

As a form of sense-making, people frame issues in socially recognizable ways and assign mental categories and stereotypes to themselves and to others. When evaluating objects or people, they are influenced by preceding, specifically recent, information. A positive impression about something or someone in one area positively influences perceptions or feelings in other areas. Lastly, people prefer those they perceive as being similar to them. Primary biases related to social impression formation about those being assessed are as follows: priming effect, recency effect, halo effect, and similarity bias. As mentioned previously, prior to zooming in on the biases related to the probability and frequency judgements and social impression formation, we will focus on the overarching attentional bias.

Attentional bias

What is attentional bias?

Attentional bias is the human tendency to focus on certain elements while ignoring others. Several factors from external events and stimuli (such as a perceived threat) to internal states (such as hunger or anger) can bias attention. American psychologist John Ridley Stroop was the first to empirically test attentional bias. In 1935, Stroop conducted the now-famous Stroop task in which he presented participants with the names of colours written in different colours of ink. Each word belonged to one of three groups: neutral (written in black ink), congruent (the colour name matched the colour of the ink), or incongruent (the colour name did not match the colour of the ink). He asked the participants to simply read aloud the written colour name, ignoring the colour of the ink. He found that people were slower to name the colour when the name and ink colours were incongruent. So, what cognitive processes lie beneath these findings? According to the selective attention theory, colour recognition requires more attention than reading a word, so the human brain instinctually pays attention to (and subsequently processes) the written information instead of the colours themselves. Overriding this instinctual attentional bias takes time, which explains for the delayed responses for incongruent words and colours.

According to a study by Cohen et al. published in the *Psychological Review* (1990), the Stroop task very clearly shows this selective attention process. The study states: "The effects observed in the Stroop task provide a clear illustration of people's capacity for and the ability of some stimuli to escape attentional control."

In the 1980s, a modified version of the Stroop task, known as the emotional Stroop (ES) task, became famous. In this version, participants received words with a certain emotional value: neutral (e.g., 'book'), positive (e.g., 'party'), or negative (e.g., 'war'), all written in certain ink colours. Participants were asked to say aloud the colour in which each word was written. Slower reaction times indicated deeper processing of a given word, and thus a possible attentional bias.

This bias towards emotionally related words is associated with clinically relevant symptoms such as anxiety and depression. Research has revealed that individuals who are depressed are more likely to say the colour for a negative word slower than that for a neutral word (Gotlib & McCann, 1984). This could be explained by people being more likely to pay attention to information that fits into their existing schemas, while ignoring that which does not (confirmation bias, chapter 6, Self-enhancing). People with depression, for example, usually have negative schemas about the world and are, therefore, biased about paying attention to negative information. More recently, researchers have investigated the relationship between attentional bias and health anxiety during the COVID-19 pandemic. Primary results of these studies indeed seem to indicate a positive relationship between health anxiety (e.g., the perceived risk of getting infected by the virus and the perceived consequences of contagion) and an attentional bias towards virus-related stimuli (Cannito et al., 2020).

Various theories mention attention as an important factor in social psychological processes. The social learning theory states that most of the behaviours that people display is the result of social learning, either deliberately or inadvertently, through modelling or the influence of example (Bandura, 1971). According to this theory, attention is the first step towards learning modelled behaviour. It is influenced by the characteristics of the observer (e.g., cognitive abilities, arousal, and personal history) and that of the behaviour or event that provides the modelling context (e.g., relevance, novelty, and functional value).

Another theory shining light on attention is the attribution theory, which is about the assigning of causes to your behaviour and that of others. Austrian psychologist Fritz Heider introduced the attribution theory in 1958. In explaining someone else's behaviour, Heider stated that people are motivated to specifically focus on certain types of stimuli, disregarding other information.

As a result, people (falsely) assume behaviours are caused either by factors outside one's own control (external attributions) or are the result of the person's own doing (internal attributions).

Attentional bias explains the human failure to consider alternative possibilities when occupied with an existing train of thought. In this train of thought, people end up directing their focus towards a single option or stimulus at the expense of other options. This fixation, in turn, can influence perceptions and opinions, decisions, and behaviour. For example, you may have experienced that as soon as you start paying attention to something, you start to notice it more often. This phenomenon is called the 'frequency illusion' or the 'Badder-Meinhof phenomenon,' referring to someone who learned about a West German militant group called the Badder-Meinhof gang and then suddenly seemed to hear about Badder-Meinhof everywhere. This is believed to be caused by the process of selective attention. By being fixated on a certain stimulus, an illusion is created that it appears more often. The frequency illusion is an example of secondary biases that are identified to be related to the social motive of understanding, specifically attentional bias.

Secondary biases related to attentional bias

Frequency illusion—the tendency to notice something more often after having noticed it once, leading to the belief that it has a high frequency

Focusing effect—the proneness to magnify the importance of something because of heightened attention to it

Distinction bias—the tendency to over-value the distinctions between two options when evaluating them simultaneously

Another example of how attentional bias influences perceptions is the 'focusing effect,' which is the magnification of importance of something because of heightened attention to it. Daniel Kahneman was the first to coin this bias. In a 2006 study, Kahneman his coauthors found that when people have a selective focus on their own income before rating their well-being, it misleads them into believing that more money makes them happier (Kahneman et al., 2006). In addition, attentional bias also exerts its influence on human judgements when comparing two options. For example, when people directly compare two options, they tend to focus on specific details instead of judging each option holistically. As a result, they view the two options as more distinctive than they are. This is called 'distinction bias.'

Attentional bias can also have an impact on memories. Since people can become overly focused on a single stimulus, they might become inattentive to other aspects of a situation. When recollecting the event later, their memories may be distorted, inaccurate, or incomplete. Attentional bias also carries implications for many institutions. One important example pertains to law enforcement. One study conducted in 2012 (Nieuwenhuys et al.) showed that police officers who had high levels of anxiety during a training were more likely to shoot at suspects, suggesting that the officers were attentionally biased towards threat-related information.

What is the relevance of the attentional bias to organizations and change?

As mentioned in the introduction, attentional bias is highly relevant in our everyday lives. When the bias shows up, people narrowly focus on one or two things and end up assigning them greater importance in decision-making, which eventually influences decisions. Translating this to the organizational context, attentional bias could have a large impact on decision-making processes of employees and leaders in organizations; for example, a company executive might focus too much on a particular measurement of employees' productivity and end up ignoring other valuable indicators of their performances. This could lead to either overestimating or underestimating the employees' total performance, with all the consequences that it entails.

Search strategy

Relevant databases were searched using the term 'attentional bias' both separately and in combination with the terms 'organisation*,' 'work,' 'employ*,' 'leader*,' and 'chang*.' This search yielded more than 500 results. After removing the duplicates and thorough examination, 1 meta-analysis, 0 systematic reviews, and 7 studies were included.

Main findings

1. *People tend to focus more on emotionally positive stimuli, especially when these are arousing and highly relevant to them (Level A).*

   According to a meta-analysis by Pool et al. (2016) in which the occurrence of attentional bias was studied among nearly 10,000 participants, people show an attentional bias for emotionally positive stimuli in comparison to neutral stimuli. Furthermore, the study showed that this bias was larger when the emotional stimuli were relevant to specific concerns (e.g., being presented food-related stimuli when hungry) of the participants compared with other positive stimuli that were less relevant to the participants' concerns.

2. *When people are in a happy mood, they shift their attention to salient information, which is positively related to future well-being. Reversely, when in a mood of fear, they shift attention to threatening cues (Level A).*

 A study from 2011 by Cavanagh et al. showed that shifts in attention to potentially salient (threatening and pleasant) cues after the induction of a happy mood were associated with higher levels of well-being three weeks later. Conversely, the induction of a fear mood shifted attention to threatening cues and was associated with increases in state anxiety. This finding is consistent with Fredrickson's broaden-and-build theory of positive emotion (Fredrickson, 1998, 2001), which suggests that in contrast to negative emotions, which are associated with specific thought-action repertoires, positive emotions generally broaden cognition. This allows for creativity and the building of resources required for well-being and resilience. Interpreted in view of this theory, broadening one's attention to both threatening and pleasant stimuli in one's environment may allow for the detection of resources and information that could be important for well-being.

3. *Several strategies have proven to be effective in shifting our attention from negative to positive stimuli, such as stress reappraisal and distraction techniques and moderate physical workouts (Level B).*

 Over the years, research has repeatedly shown that a focus on positive instead of negative information leads to improved well-being and overall functioning (Cummins & Nistico, 2002; Fredrickson & Joiner, 2002). Following this finding, several researchers have looked into methods to alter attentional bias, shifting attention from negative to positive information. In their 2018 study, Cai et al. (2018) deployed a five-day attentional bias modification (ABM) training. The ABM consisted of a dot probe test, a computerized attention task in which participants are trained to avoid a threat. After the training, the researchers concluded that participants started to pay more attention to the positive words than threatening words. In a 2017 experimental study, Crum et al. explored if stress responses could be altered by changing individuals' mindsets about the nature of stress in general and if this was related to attentional bias. A stress mindset was induced by letting the participants watch a three-minute video that either emphasized the enhancing properties of stress (stress-is-enhancing condition) or the deleterious properties of stress (stress-is-debilitating condition). The results indicated that a 'stress is enhancing' mindset produced heightened attentional bias towards positive stimuli when being given positive feedback. In contrast, those with a 'stress is debilitating' mindset experienced worse cognitive flexibility and less attention to happy faces when being given positive feedback. The study concluded that "whenever possible, people should attempt to evaluate stressors as challenging as opposed to threatening" (p. 13). More importantly, as this study shows, stress-reappraisal techniques could be useful in shifting our attention towards positive instead of negative stimuli.

Another study by Jamieson et al. (2012), examined whether reappraising arousal could decrease attentional bias for emotionally negative information. In this experimental study, they instructed one-third of the participants to think about their physiological arousal during a stressful task as functional and adaptive. The other participants were either instructed to ignore the source of the stress by purposefully looking away from it or were given no instructions at all. The study revealed that the participants who reappraised their arousal showed decreased attention to emotionally negative information compared to the participants who didn't. These results confirm the aforementioned finding that stress-reappraisal techniques are helpful in shifting our bias away from negative stimuli.

Lastly, an experimental study by Tian and Smith (2011) explored how attentional bias to emotional stimuli is altered when people simultaneously perform physical exercise. The study showed that when compared with rest, moderate-intensity exercise may promote a shift in attention towards pleasant emotional stimuli and away from unpleasant emotional stimuli. This, in turn, may help promote improved mood.

4. *In highly stressful situations, people could be less prone to fall prey to attentional bias (Level C).*

   Research by Jiang et al. (2017) investigated the influence of acute stress on attentional bias to threatening stimuli. The results suggested that acute psychosocial stress impairs attentional bias. This could be explained by the fact that acute stress leads to disruptive selective processing of information, thereby preventing attentional bias. So, whereas moderate-intensity exercise seems to promote attention towards positive stimuli (see the finding by Tian & Smith, 2011), it might not be the case for high-intensity exercise, as it activates the same systems involved in responding to an external threat (e.g., increased heart rate, blood pressure and levels of cortisol).

Conclusion

Several high-quality studies have found empirical evidence for attentional bias. These studies mainly show that people tend to focus on positive stimuli. Interestingly, high-quality empirical evidence on attentional bias towards negative stimuli is not yet available. In a way, this narrow focus on the 'positive attentional bias' in the scientific field might be seen as a manifestation of the bias itself. Several factors influence our proneness to attentional bias.

It appears that people are more likely to fall prey to the bias when the perceived information is arousing and highly relevant to them. Also, several strategies have proven to be effective in altering attentional bias, such as stress reappraisal techniques, distraction techniques, and moderate physical workouts. Lastly, as opposed to moderate physical workouts, when doing extreme exercise (as a form of a very stressful situation), humans are less prone to fall prey to attentional bias since they are prevented from selecting their attention to specific conditions.

Practical reflections

Attentional bias has several practical implications for organizations, including decision-making processes and communicating organizational change. As Pool et al. (2016) illustrated, people pay more attention to emotional information that is highly relevant to them compared to neutral, nonrelevant information. So, when communicating organizational change, managers and leaders should use positive, powerful language and make sure that their word usage fits in with the actual world and interests of their employees. In this way, they capture their employees' attention and can in turn positively influence employees' attitude towards change. *Storytelling*, which is the technique of incorporating inspiring stories and story structures in communicating organizational change, might be a powerful tool to do this. Also, paying more attention to positive information instead of negative information is associated with improved long-term well-being and overall functioning. Therefore, it would be advisable to deploy methods or techniques that either help reduce focus on negative information or strengthen a focus on positive information. As scientific research shows, stress reappraisal techniques and distraction techniques might be promising tools. Investing in trainings or workshops in which employees are being taught to reappraise stressful sources or learn how to adopt a 'stress is enhancing' mindset, might be an effective strategy for managers to shift their employees' focus more towards positive information, thereby improving their long-term well-being and overall functioning.

Availability bias

What is the availability bias?

Tversky and Kahneman (1973) introduced the availability bias, also known as the availability heuristic, in their article "Availability: A Heuristic for Judging Frequency and Probability." They describe the availability bias as "a persuasive heuristic in human judgement in which people judge the frequency of prevalence of some events by the ease with which relevant instances come to mind" (Tversky & Kahneman, 1973). In the academic literature, there seems to be consensus on the definition of the availability bias, as most of the studies use the Tversky and Kahneman's definition. The availability bias occurs in a lot of different domains of society: media, health, economy, education, and criminal justice. Media coverage can enhance a person's estimation of the likelihood of certain events. One example of the media influence on availability bias is people's perceived likelihood of dying from a shark attack versus their perceived likelihood of dying from falling airplane parts. Since the last is not as extensively covered by media as shark attacks, people mistakenly assume deaths caused by shark attacks are much more common than they are (Read, 1995). This is linked to a bias called 'availability cascade,' which is a self-reinforcing process where a certain idea, stance, or position triggers a chain reaction and therefore gains popularity in public discourse, which increases its availability to people. This heightened availability, in turn, makes this idea, stance, or position more plausible to the public.

Secondary biases related to the availability bias

Availability cascade—the self-reinforcing process where a certain perception or stance gains increasing plausibility in public discourse through its rising its availability

Illusory correlation—the proneness to perceive a relationship between variables (events, people, or actions) even when no such relationship actually exists

Apophenia—the tendency to perceive a meaningful connection or pattern between unrelated objects or ideas based on the recognition of a few components or stimuli

Pareidolia—a certain type of apophenia concerning the perceived connection between (usually) visual stimuli (e.g., the perception of a face within an inanimate object)

Well-travelled-road effect—the tendency of 'travellers' to appraise the time taken to cross routes differently depending on their familiarity with those routes

To illustrate how availability bias impacts probability and frequency judgements, we refer to a phenomenon called 'illusory correlation.' This is the tendency to perceive a relationship between variables, even when they aren't associated. The illusory correlation is suggested to be caused by the availability bias: People might perceive a relationship because some combinations are easily recalled, even though they are not especially frequent. In this vein, the secondary biases 'apophenia' and a certain type of apophenia called 'pareidolia' are also considered to be related to the availability bias. The biases, both describing the human tendency to perceive meaningful connections or patterns between unrelated stimuli, are also suggested to be caused by availability bias. By combining several unrelated stimuli to match a certain image that is mentally available, people falsely assume a relationship between these stimuli.

It must also be noted that the availability heuristic is not necessarily a bad thing per se. The assumptions that arise from this heuristic can result in correct estimations. However, the availability bias is highly error prone and must therefore be 'used' with caution (MacLeod & Campbell, 1992). Another phenomenon illustrating how the availability bias can exert its influence on our perceptions is the 'well-travelled-road effect.' The well-travelled-road effect is a cognitive bias in which 'travellers' estimate the duration to cross a route depending on their familiarity with that route. It is suggested that drivers put more cognitive effort when traversing unfamiliar routes, which makes them perceive the journey to be longer than it is. Conversely, when traversing familiar routes, they put less cognitive effort, making them perceive the trip as shorter.

What is the relevance of the availability bias to organizations and change?

The proposition that people tend to rely on available tools, knowledge, or experiences holds relevance in organizations and change. People, as also managers, often choose solutions that have proven to be successful during previous organizational changes and that they associate with or relate to the (top) management positions they have reached. However, in new situations, alternative approaches may be required. For example, because a project-based approach to a change has worked well on previous occasions, a manager could consider this approach to be the only road to success and thus be inclined to turn the next change initiative into a project. However, the specific circumstances of the current change may benefit from a more open, process-based approach. The suggested impact of the availability bias on decision-making does not apply solely to individual managers, but also to groups. "Group judgements, an important component of organizational decision-making, are not immune to this type of bias." (Sniezek & Henry, 1989; Stasson et al., 1988). Juries, legislators, board of directors, and project teams are just a few examples of groups that have to make important decisions together (Benbasat & Lim, 2000). A recurring theme within organizations is how employees and stakeholders are affected by the decision-making of these groups. Specifically, unethical decision-making has received much attention in the last few decades since it has resulted in many corporate scandals. It is self-explanatory that scandals are to be avoided at all costs. Nowadays, many managers seek guidance and information about the route to more ethical decision-making in organizations. Therefore, it would be prudent to learn more about biases such as the availability bias and their influence on decision-making in organizations.

Search strategy

Relevant databases were searched using the terms 'availability bias' and 'availability heuristic' both separately and in combination with the terms 'organisation*,' 'work,' 'employ*,' 'leader*' and 'chang*.' This search yielded 67 results. After removing the duplicates and thorough examination, 0 meta-analyses, 0 systematic reviews, and 4 studies were included.

Main findings

1. *Memories of a certain event lead to a higher perceived probability in the future (Level D).*

   A study by Macleod and Campbell (1992) put the availability bias to the test in an experimental setting where subjects made probability judgements concerning the occurrence of future events. Their main finding was that there was a positive significant correlation between the recollection of memories and the perceived probability of experiencing a similar event in the future, which means that more memories of a certain event led to a higher perceived probability in the future.

2. *The availability bias could be used in reinforcing ethical decision-making within organizations (Level D).*

   Hayibor and Wasieleski (2008) explored the impact of the availability bias on the decision-making process and on ethical behaviour in organizations. In their study, they found that the availability bias influences ethical decision-making through perceptions of moral intensity.

   Moral intensity can be described as the degree to which a moral imperative exists in relation to an issue. The study found that the perceived availability of consequences associated with an act and the perceived availability of others who believe that an act is morally acceptable are positively related to perceived moral intensity. Perceptions of moral intensity, in turn, positively affect how moral issues are viewed and ultimately resolved, leading to an increased likelihood of ethical decisions being made (Hayibor & Wasieleski, 2008).

3. *Electronic brainstorming and communication could reduce the presence of the availability bias in group decision-making (Level D).*

   In 2000, researchers Benbasat and Lim (2000) set up an experimental study that investigated the effects of electronic brainstorming and communication on the presence of the availability bias in group decision-making. The research showed that both were instrumental in reducing the availability bias—the presence of these systems caused the participants to be increasingly focused on low-availability items.

Conclusion

The availability bias as described by Tversky and Kahneman is a persuasive heuristic in human judgement in which people judge the frequency of prevalence of some events by the ease with which relevant instances come to mind. The main findings shed light on the bias itself, its impact on human decision-making, and promising tools to reduce the availability bias. Although the availability bias is not backed by a large amount of evidence, some interesting - initially intuitive- conclusions can be drawn. Firstly, the availability bias seems to have an influence on human thinking and decision-making because memories of a certain event lead to a higher perceived probability in the future. Secondly, it could impact ethical decision-making by its influence on perceived moral intensity (Hayibor & Wasieleski, 2008). Lastly, electronic brainstorming and communication seem to be promising tools to reduce availability bias in group decision-making (Benbasat & Lim, 2000).

Practical reflections

In general, the aforementioned main findings can be used to make managers aware of the availability bias. Creating awareness can be the first step towards the realization of an environment where it is easier to think outside the box and where organizational members are less tempted to simply rely on available instances when making judgements. Specifically, when trying to achieve the desired change, managers are often inclined to choose habitual and familiar paths they consider most effective. However, since organizations are dependent on both the internal and external context, change initiatives and approaches should be tailored to this context. Therefore, it would be prudent for managers to first take a moment to step back and evaluate the organizational context thoroughly and base change strategies accordingly. Consultation with other professionals to collect different perspectives might also be a good starting point for managers to create openness towards new approaches.

The main findings and corresponding conclusions also have practical implications. Firstly, according Hayibor and Wasieleski (2008), managers can achieve a greater likelihood of ethical decision-making within their organization by offering programmes, policies, or procedures that increase the belief that a certain act is morally wrong for employees. In their article, the researchers do not specify the exact content of the mentioned programmes. However, it would be prudent for managers to tailor these programmes, policies, and procedures to suit their own organization by aiming them at specific behaviours that are either desired or undesired in their organization. Secondly, although Benbasat and Lim (2000) mention that more research is necessary for the practical use of electronic brainstorming and communication tools to become clearer, the usage of these tools has some practical implications for organizations. Managers could experiment with electronical tools for communication to reduce the presence of availability bias within their organization. This has become undeniably more relevant due to the considerable increase of digital meetings as a result of the COVID-19 pandemic.

Conjunction fallacy

What is the conjunction fallacy?

Perhaps the simplest and most fundamental principle of probability is the inclusion rule: the probability of two events occurring together is always less than or equal to that of either one occurring alone. This principle can also be expressed as the 'conjunction rule.' However uncomplicated this rule seems to be, applying it turns out to be quite difficult. In fact, people usually assume that several specific conditions occurring together are more probable than a single general one. This is called the 'conjunction fallacy.'

Tversky and Kahneman (1983) first demonstrated the conjunction fallacy through the 'Linda problem'—a puzzle that is, till today, the most cited example of this fallacy. While Tversky named the fallacy after Linda Covington, his secretary at Stanford, the description and person depicted are fictitious.

> *Linda is 31 years old, single, outspoken, and very bright. She majored in philosophy. As a student, she was deeply concerned by the issues of discrimination and social justice, and even participated in antinuclear demonstrations.*

Which is more probable?

1. Linda is a bank teller.
2. Linda is a bank teller and is active in the feminist movement.

It is a robust observation that most people confronted with the Linda problem choose option 2. However, as stated above, the probability of two events occurring together (being a bank teller and being active in the feminist movement) must be less than or equal to the probability of one event occurring alone (being a bank teller).

Tversky and Kahneman argue that most people get this problem wrong because they use the 'representativeness heuristic' to make this kind of probability judgement. This heuristic is a mental shortcut that people are considered to utilize on a daily basis to make judgements by comparing novel situations and information to familiar mental concepts, social categories, or 'internal stereotypes.' Mental concepts, social categories, or internal stereotypes are well-known concepts in social psychology, and reliance on these concepts lies at the foundation of various social psychological theories. For example, the social identity theory states that people classify themselves and others in diverse social groups based on the prototypical characteristics of the members of the groups. Classifications could be organizational membership, religious conviction, gender, or age (Ten Have et al., 2019, p. 50). Social categories also are important in the attribution theory, which states that people use stereotypes, mental models, and 'benchmarks' to evaluate others and stimuli (Ten Have et al., 2019, p. 79).

Applying the representativeness heuristic to the Linda problem based on the description of Linda, option 2 seems more 'representative' of her (even though it is clearly mathematically less likely) and so people falsely assume Linda is more likely to be a bank teller and an activist. The human brain thus seemingly prefers representativeness over logic. This is illustrated by the famous American naturalist Stephen Jay Gould, who described his struggle with the Linda problem as follows:

> I am particularly fond of this example because I know that the conjoint statement is least probable, yet a little homunculus in my head continues to jump up and down, shouting at me—"but she can't just be a bank teller; read the description."
>
> (Gould, 1989)

The conjunction fallacy is also related to another phenomenon, the so-called 'base-rate fallacy.' This bias describes the tendency to rely on specific information over statistics. As a result, people make predictions and probability judgements based purely on individuating information, disregarding the base-rate information.

Secondary biases related to conjunction fallacy

Representativeness heuristic—a mental shortcut used to come to judgements by comparing novel situations and information to familiar mental concepts or 'internal stereotypes'

Base-rate fallacy—the tendency to rely on specific information rather than statistics

What is the relevance of the conjunction fallacy to organizations and change?

As stated earlier, one reason why people are prone to the conjunction fallacy is because they make use of the representativeness heuristic. Perhaps unsurprisingly, the conjunction fallacy and the representativeness heuristic are also seen in organizations and change, thereby influencing employees' perception, behaviour, and decision-making. A study from 2019 found that managers made biased decisions more than 50 percent of the time, many of which were based on representativeness (AlKhars et al., 2019). The conjunction fallacy specifically could have serious repercussions. For example, employees might hear separate rumours about possible layoffs and that the senior executive of their division is considering a career move. Employees judge each of these events on their own as unlikely—perhaps a 30 percent chance of layoffs and a 25 percent chance of the executive leaving. However, in view of the conjunction fallacy, people tend to overestimate the likelihood of specific co-occurring events. So, when employees hear both rumours jointly, they could judge the probability of both events occurring as high as 50 percent or more. As a result, employees experience more psychological stress, leading to negative health consequences such as exhaustion and burnout complaints.

However, organizations can also turn the conjunction fallacy to their advantage. For example, marketing strategies could subtly craft marketing messages in such a way that two different stereotypes are activated simultaneously; commercial brands could make their consumers believe their products have multiple benefits in conjunction with each other. One example of this is the skincare brand Neutrogena. Neutrogena has built a platform that equates health with beauty (while these concepts are in fact not always synonymous). By using a statement or tagline that is related to health (for example, "Recommended by dermatologists"), the brand activates a representation of healthy skin. By pairing this tagline with a photograph of a celebrity with beautiful skin, the consumers are prompted to think of beauty, and so the two concepts become linked in their minds. This way, the brand convinces the consumers that they will derive health as well as beauty benefits from its products.

Considering the relevance of the conjunction fallacy to organizations, it seems wise for managers and organizational leaders to take note of the possible origins, manifestations, and consequences concerning this fallacy.

Search strategy

Relevant databases were searched using the terms 'conjunction fallacy' and 'conjunction error' both separately and in combination with the terms 'organisation*,' 'work,' 'employ*,' 'leader*' and 'chang*.' This search yielded 80 results. After removing the duplicates and thorough examination, 0 meta-analyses, 0 systematic reviews, and 5 studies were included.

Main findings

1. *Scientific evidence supports the claim that people have the tendency to fall prey to the conjunction fallacy (Level B).*

   In their original 1983 experimental study, Tversky and Kahneman let undergraduate students solve the Linda problem to explore the occurrence of the conjunction fallacy. The results showed that 85 percent of the participants fell prey to the conjunction fallacy (reporting that the statement "Linda is a feminist bank teller," was more likely than the statement "Linda is a bank teller"). Moreover, the researchers reported similar rates of violations of the conjunction rule in several variations of the question, including introducing more choice options and using a different fictitious character. So, according to this study, people are usually prone to commit the conjunction fallacy. The results of Tversky and Kahneman's study were confirmed by various other studies. In most of these studies, the original method by Tversky and Kahneman, e.g., the Linda-problem or a variation of this problem, was replicated. In 2003, Moutier and Houdé examined the prevalence of the conjunction fallacy amongst psychology students. Results of this study showed that the incidence rate of the conjunction fallacy was extremely high: All (!) participants exhibited biased reasoning and fell prey to the conjunction fallacy. Additionally, de Neys et al. (2011) studied the occurrence of the conjunction fallacy amongst undergraduate students and found that, in line with previous findings, the vast majority of participants (no less than 76 percent) committed the conjunction fallacy on classic problems such as the Linda problem. Lastly, an experimental study by Aczel et al. in 2016 confirmed the previous results. In their study, in which variations of the Linda problem were used, the researchers found that a high number of participants committed the fallacy (percentages between 55 and 90).

2. *Even highly intelligent, statistically sophisticated people seem to be susceptible for the conjunction fallacy (Level C).*

In their 1983 experimental study, Tversky and Kahneman tested whether statistical education would eradicate the conjunction fallacy. They compared a 'naïve' group of undergraduate students with no background in probability or statistics to a 'sophisticated' group consisting of PhD students with advanced courses in probability, statistics, and decision theory to their credit. Results showed that even in the 'sophisticated' group, although the majority did obey the conjunction rule, the number of participants committing the conjunction fallacy was still high. Additionally, Oechssler et al. (2009) examined if people with relatively high cognitive abilities would be less prone to commit the conjunction fallacy than people with lower cognitive abilities. The results of their study showed that, even though incidence rates of the conjunction fallacy were lower for people with higher cognitive abilities, they were substantial. In other words, even intelligent, cognitively skilled people commit the conjunction fallacy. The finding that even highly intelligent people advanced in probabilities and statistics commit the fallacy suggests that people might not commit it out of a lack of understanding of the fundamental rules of probabilities but more because they don't perceive the Linda problem as a task that requires an application of these principles (or, for that matter, probabilistic reasoning). Instead, they rely on intuitive reasoning. As one of Tversky and Kahneman's participants illustrates, *"I thought you only asked for my opinion"* (1983, p. 300).

3. *Inhibition trainings could be promising in decreasing the prevalence of the conjunction fallacy (Level C).*

   In their 2003 experimental study, Moutier and Houdé trained participants to inhibit the conjunction bias by teaching them not to solely concentrate on specific elements of the event presented to them but to use the rules of propositional logic. After the training, the number of participants committing the conjunction fallacy was reduced by a mere 50 percent. These results suggest that, through training, the human brain can overcome reasoning biases like the conjunction fallacy.

4. *People might be less likely to commit the conjunction fallacy in decision-making when they consult other people (Level D).*

   Charness et al. (2010) explored the occurrence of the conjunction fallacy among university students through a series of experiments. In this study, they found that communication between participants influenced the incidence rate of the conjunction fallacy. When they allowed the subjects to consult with other subjects before giving their answers, the proportions fell dramatically. This was particularly the case when the size of the group rose from two to three persons. According to Charness et al., "the presence of a third person in a group may create a 'cascading effect,' in which the person who finds the correct answer has a better chance of persuading one other member of the group and the weight of the two maybe sufficient to make the third member accept their conclusion even if not persuaded" (p. 555).

5. *Priming people with systematic processing skills might reduce their proneness to the conjunction fallacy (Level D).*

   In an experimental study, Huntsinger and Ray (2016) observed the influence of emotions and processing styles on the conjunction fallacy. Results showed that participants in a positive mood primed with heuristic processing were more likely to commit the conjunction fallacy than similarly primed sad participants. However, when participants in a good mood were primed with a systematic processing style, they were less likely to commit the conjunction fallacy. According to Huntsinger and Ray, happy people tended to adopt a more top-down, global style of thinking and reliance on stereotypes (e.g., heuristic processing style), making them more prone to commit the conjunction fallacy. This contrasts with a more bottom-up, detailed style of thinking (e.g., systematic processing style), which could act as a buffer against the conjunction fallacy. So, priming people with systematic processing styles could reduce the occurrence of the conjunction fallacy.

Conclusion

Scientific evidence supports the claim that people tend to commit the conjunction fallacy, thereby falsely assuming that several specific conditions are more probable than a single generic one (Tversky & Kahneman, 1983). Even highly intelligent people advanced in probabilities and statistics commit the fallacy (Tversky & Kahneman, 1983; Oechssler et al., 2009), which suggests that committing conjunction fallacy is not necessarily because of a lack of understanding of the fundamental principles governing probabilities but instead because we are being governed by heuristics such as representativeness, which cloud our judgements and causes us to rely on internal stereotypes. However, it is not impossible for the human brain to overcome the conjunction fallacy. Simply making people aware of the fallacy and training them to inhibit it seems to be a good starting point (Moutier & Houdé, 2003). Moreover, consultation might be an effective strategy to minimize the occurrence of the conjunction fallacy in decision-making (Charness et al., 2010).

Practical reflections

Following these conclusions, we made some practical reflections for managers and organizations.

Firstly, like many biases and heuristics, awareness is key when it comes to the conjunction fallacy. Both managers and employees should be aware of the fact the people are tended to rely on heuristics and internal stereotypes, which causes them to make judgemental errors. Making the causal mechanisms that underlie the conjunction fallacy (such as representativeness) explicit might be an effective approach for managers to buffer against the conjunction fallacy in their organization (Moutier & Houdé, 2003).

Secondly, research shows that consultation might be an effective strategy to inhibit the conjunction fallacy (Charness et al., 2010). In this vein, it would be advisable for managers to stimulate consultation in formal decision-making processes. Moreover, managers can go one step further and encourage their employees to consult each other on a daily basis in individual decision-making situations. In communicating this to their employees, managers might even suggest forming groups of three persons instead of pairs, since three persons are even less likely to commit the conjunction fallacy than two ("three heads are better than one"). Lastly, we suggest that managers target the mental context in which emotions are experienced to prevent employees from falling prey to biases like the conjunction fallacy (Huntsinger & Ray, 2016). Specifically, it would be prudent for managers to promote employees' systematic processing skills, which will deter them from relying solely on internal stereotypes and heuristics (as Huntsinger & Ray illustrate it: "a focus on the forest") and feel encouraged to use a more bottom-up, detailed style of thinking instead ("a focus on the trees").

Framing effect

What is the framing effect?

Tversky and Kahneman (1981) first observed the framing effect—a bias that suggests that even when the outcome of two options is equal, our response to those options could differ depending on the way the option is presented to us (e.g., which features of the option are highlighted). Levin et al. (1998) distinguished three types of framing: risky-choice framing, attribute framing, and goal framing.

Risky framing refers to the decision-making process when confronted with a choice based on risks and probabilities. This is equivalent to the prospect theory, in which people prefer the sure option in a positive frame and the risky option in a negative frame (see chapter 4 Controlling—prospect theory). Tversky and Kahneman (1981) used the Asian disease problem to demonstrate how frames influence decision-making. In this problem, subjects had to choose between two separate statistically equal binary options described in a positive frame (lives saved) and negative frame (lives lost). Similar to the prospect theory, the subjects chose the riskier option when confronted with a negative frame (e.g., 400 out of 600 lives will be lost) and the less risky option when confronted with a positive frame (e.g., 200 out of 600 lives will be saved).

Attribute framing refers to the tendency of making more positive evaluations of stimuli framed positively and more negative evaluations of stimuli framed negatively. For example, Levin and Gaeth (1988) found that ground beef is rated as tastier when labelled in a positive valence (75 percent lean) than when labelled in a negative valence (25 percent fat).

Goal framing refers to the difference in persuasive impact between messages set out from a positive frame of 'gaining' or 'avoiding a loss' and messages from a negative frame of 'not gaining' or 'suffering a loss.' So, whereas attribute framing describes the stimulus from a positive or negative valence, goal framing describes the outcome of a certain event in either a positive or negative way. Goal framing provides people with the motivation to take action when confronted with a possible 'loss' rather than a possible 'gain.'

The framing effect is considered to be related to the 'affect heuristic/projection bias,' which states that current emotions and not the long term-effects of their decisions influence people in their decision-making. Following this reasoning, framing information in an emotionally appealing way should be effective in influencing behaviour. In fact, research has shown that framing relies on emotional appeals and can be designed to have specific emotional reactions (Yacoub, 2012).

The framing effect is also proposed to relate to the 'unit bias,' which relates to people's tendency to want to complete a unit of a given item or task. A 2006 study by Geier et al. explored the unit bias in the consumption of soft pretzels. Results of this study indicated that participants' consumption was influenced by the unit bias. When whole pretzels were offered, people ate an entire pretzel. However, when the pretzels were cut in half, people only ate half. The subjects thus perceived whatever portion they were given as a unit and felt the urge to eat up this unit. This is just one example of how people could be influenced in their behaviour by framing the unit of some entity.

Framing can also be linked to the 'stress-appraisal theory,' which states that peoples' emotions to certain information or events are extracted from their evaluations of that information. Following this reasoning, framing information in a positive way leads to a positive evaluation of that information, thereby evoking positive emotions and responses accordingly.

In short, according to the framing effect, the way a message is framed (i.e., gain or loss, positive or negative) likely influences human perceptions, evaluations, and decisions. By overvaluing *how* something is said (the 'frame' of the message) at the expense of valuing *what* is being said, the framing effect can trigger irrational behaviour and cause people to choose worse options that are more effectively framed over better options framed badly.

One example of how the framing effect can influence decisions concerns patients' preference regarding treatment. In 1989, O'Connor explored the influence of framing on patients' preferences about cancer chemotherapy. In the study, she asked participants to choose between two cancer treatments. While the first treatment option was toxic, the second was nontoxic, but less effective than the first option. She framed the options in either a positive way (e.g., probability of living) or a negative way (e.g., probability of dying). Results showed that when she used a negative frame to present the options, patients were less likely to choose more toxic yet more effective treatment options (O'Connor, 1989).

The effect is also likely to exert its influences in the field of media and politics. Journalists, for example, often use different 'frames' surrounding an issue to alter the reader's perception without having to change the facts. Media channels deliberately choose certain words and images to cover a story (e.g., disaster vs. setback) (Bryant et al., 2013). In the field of politics, members of political parties use framing in their communication to emphasize certain characteristics or consequences of an issue or policy to the exclusion of other features. By increasing the accessibility of those characteristics in people's judgements, individuals can be swayed between supporting and opposing a policy depending on the valence of the highlighted feature (Chong, 2019).

Last, but not least, many well-known, global companies have used the framing effect to their advantage. For example, the multinational coffeehouse chain Starbucks has used its inviting interior, soothing background music, and special Italianized beverage names to successfully 'frame' its products in such a way that it enhances people's perception of its product quality. Through this clever packaging, the company differentiates itself from its competitors in the coffee market and creates the idea among consumers that Starbucks coffee is the best. However, when the frame or 'background' is removed, the result will be a bare product (e.g., 'just' coffee), which doesn't seem to differ that much from other products anymore.

Secondary biases related to framing effect

Affect heuristic/projection bias—type of mental shortcut in which people make decisions influenced by their current emotions

Unit bias—the tendency to want to complete a unit of a given item or task

What is the relevance of the framing effect to organizations and change?

Within organizations, decisions are often made based on a particular flow of information. Information can be factual but not necessarily neutral. Whenever information is processed or a choice is presented, the way in which that information is presented matters. For instance, the framing of a particular organizational change or a project might influence whether the organization actually embarks on this change. The rationale, the big 'why' of the change, is essential to the success of organizational change (Ten Have et al., 2015). The frame in which a proposal is presented can help persuade managers or employees about the desirability of the change. However, the framing effect increases the subconscious focus on irrational ques rather than on the rational arguments, which could lead to suboptimal decision-making. Therefore, organizations need to be aware of this effect to not let it cloud their judgement and use it to their advantage where possible and ethical.

Search strategy

Relevant databases were searched using the term 'framing effect' both separately and in combination with the terms 'organisation*,' 'work,' 'employ*,' 'leader*,' or 'chang*.' This search yielded 891 results. After removing the duplicates and thorough examination, 5 meta-analyses, 0 systematic reviews, and 3 studies were included.

Main findings

1. *People can be influenced by (risky, attribute, and goal) frames during decision-making processes (Level B).*

   In a meta-analysis of 136 studies, Kühberger (1998) found scientific evidence that the framing effect influences people in their decision-making. Twenty years later, Steiger and Kühberger re-evaluated Kühbergers' dataset (2018). Both studies found that the magnitude of the framing effect differed across studies, because no clear conceptualization and methodologies are used throughout the literature. In their meta-analysis of 51 studies, Piñon and Gambara (2005) acknowledged this as well. In order to solve this issue, they distinguished three types of framing based on the taxonomy of Levin et al. (1998). In their study, they found that the magnitude of the impact differed across the different types of frames—the impact of the risky framing effect and the goal framing effect was medium, while the impact of the attribute framing effect was small. In this way, the authors disentangled the conceptual overlaps, showing that the impact of the framing effect can differ for the specific types of framing effects.

2. *Gain frames induce positive emotions, while loss-frames induce negative emotions, and stronger emotions increase the effectiveness of the framing effect (Level B).*

   In their meta-analysis of 25 studies with a total of 5,772 participants, Nabi et al. (2020) investigated the relationship between emotions and loss/gain framing. According to their findings, gain frames tend to induce positive emotions, while loss frames induce negative emotions. Furthermore, these frames are more effective or persuasive when they induce more intense positive and negative emotions, respectively. Following this line of reasoning, emotions thus play a role in mediating the influence of framing effects. If these frames are to be used effectively, or conversely, if one wants to mediate their effects, the role of emotions and their intensity is then of considerable importance.

3. *The effectiveness of framing messages depends on a complex interaction of dispositional, situational, and individual factors (Level B).*

   In their meta-analysis of 27 studies, Xu and Huang (2020) found a minimal effect size when it came to charity advertising and framing. Because the framing had no influence on the effect of the advertising, they point out that the persuasive impact of framing is highly dependent on a complex interaction of dispositional, situational, and individual factors. Building on the previous main finding, pertaining to emotions, one can imagine that the effectiveness of framing has many moderators. To optimally understand and leverage the framing effect, more research on the possible moderator variables is necessary.

4. *Loss framing is more effective than gain framing in altering behaviour (level C).*

   In their systematic review of 47 articles, Homar and Cvelbar (2021) investigated the importance of loss aversion in environmental decisions. According to the authors, when it comes to environmental decisions, people are more likely to change to pro-environmental behaviour if an environmental problem such as climate change is framed as a loss that must be prevented. They argue that policy makers should therefore continuously stress the losses of not performing pro-environmental behaviour and not the gains of performing said behaviour.

Conclusion

The various findings seem to indicate the existence of some sort of overall framing effect, with the magnitude of the impact varying from small to medium. In addition, there is evidence of the existence of the different types of frames—risky framing, attribute framing, and goal framing. The studies show that different frames have different effects and that both positive and negative frames can influence people's behaviour. The more intense emotions a frame evokes, the more persuasive the message is. The varying power of the frames could, in part, be caused by the way the bias is measured and conceptualized (Piñon & Gambara, 2005). It would be beneficial to test the different forms of the framing effect separately in disparate studies. This would give a more valid and complete view of the framing affect. Furthermore, different scholars argue that more framing research is needed to identify possible moderators. When there is a larger understanding of the moderators on the effects of framing, the framing effect can be better leveraged or mitigated when necessary.

Practical implications

The framing effect is associated with loss aversion from the prospect theory. When designing a particular message for persuasive effect, organizations ought to take insights from prospect theory into account (i.e., "losses loom larger than gains"). When used in combination, framing something as a loss that needs to be prevented could be leveraged. At the same time, it must be noted that positive or gain frames can also have a persuasive effect. As Nabi et al. (2020) argue, loss and gain frames induce negative and positive emotions, respectively. The more intense the emotion evoked, the more effective the respective framing messages become. This finding is consistent with the 'affect heuristic.' However, despite the link between loss aversion and the framing effect, it is not always advisable to use a negative or a loss frame within organizations, especially not in the long run. Negative frames can help create urgency and can help incite people to take action; however, in the long run this can also create a negative atmosphere in the organization. Positive frames, on the other hand, can help and stimulate people to improve performances for a longer period.

In addition, organizational leaders must be aware of the framing effect and its impact on their employees to possibly prevent their organization to become too influenced by frames. Frames do partly remove rationality from decision-making, which makes decision-makers more prone to errors. In the literature, there is no proven method to mitigate the effects of framing but acknowledging its existence and being aware of frames is a good first step.

Priming

What is priming?

Priming (or the priming effect) is a phenomenon where the introduction of one stimulus influences how an individual perceives (and, subsequently, responds to) a subsequent stimulus. When people are being primed, a stimulus (an image, word, sound, or smell) in their environment unconsciously activates certain associations in their memory. This activation influences their response to the stimulus. For example, a moment after we see the word 'dentist,' we will be faster to recognize the word 'tooth' than an unrelated word like 'house' because the medical concepts are closely associated in our mind. This phenomenon is closely related to the recency effect, which pertains to better learning, storing, and retrieving recently presented information than information presented earlier.

Since the early 1980s, researchers have studied priming by considering how exposure to certain types of information can influence perceptions and thoughts. One of these researchers, social psychologist Bargh, defined priming as "the passive, subtle and unobtrusive activation of relevant mental representations by external, environmental stimuli, such that people are not and do not become aware of the influence exerted by those stimuli" (Bargh & Huang, 2014).

The concept of priming is strongly related to a secondary bias called 'anchoring,' which is the susceptibility to compare a certain stimulus to a particular reference point or 'anchor' presented earlier. People are prone to relying heavily on the first piece of information presented to them, and when they do, they filter all new information through this existing framework. This is the foundation of the 'social judgement theory' (Sherif & Hovland, 1961), which states that people perceive and evaluate an idea by comparing it with current attitudes or their 'anchor point.' The closer the idea is to their anchor point, the more likely they are to accept the idea.

Existing frameworks, called 'social representations' are fundamentally aimed at 'making the unfamiliar familiar' (Moscovici, 1984). This classification of new information into pre-established (social) categories makes us reluctant to make significant changes to our beliefs, ideas, plans, behaviour, and even the tools we use.

Secondary biases related to priming

Anchoring—the tendency to compare stimuli to a particular reference point ('anchor')

Conservatism bias—the tendency to revise one's belief insufficiently when presented with new evidence

Semmelweis effect—the tendency to reject new evidence or new knowledge because it contradicts established knowledge, norms, or standards

Law of the instrument—the tendency to over-rely on familiar tools

Although priming occurs without conscious awareness, it can have a significant impact on various aspects of everyday live. Priming has mostly been studied in the field of social psychology and has been linked to various social psychological concepts such as 'stereotypes' and 'social representations.' Accordingly, priming can exert its influence on social behaviour. An experimental study by Bargh et al. (1996) showed that people primed with words associated with impolite behaviour were more likely to show ruder behaviour themselves, such as interrupting another's conversation. This study also showed that priming people with certain stereotypes impacts behaviour. In the study, Bargh et al. primed one half of participants with words generally associated with stereotypes about elderly people. They did not provide the other half of the participants with a prime. Upon leaving the experiment site, people primed with the words related to older adults were more likely to walk more slowly than participants not primed (Bargh et al., 1996). Perhaps the best-known priming experiment was conducted in 1957 by American market researcher James Vicary, who primed cinema visitors by projecting the words 'eat popcorn' and 'drink Coke' onto the screen for such a short time it was barely visible to the naked eye. After this projection, however, popcorn sales rose by 58 percent (!) and Coke sales by 18 percent (Marhenke & Imhoff, 2020). Regardless of the absence of high evidence-level studies replicating these findings, this study is illustrative of how certain priming cues, even when people are unaware of it, can have an impact on (social) behaviour.

What is the relevance of priming to organizations and change?

Central to the concept of priming is the idea that people can be greatly influenced by previous information when making decisions. As such, while many people might perceive their decisions to be based on pure intuition and 'gut-feeling,' it is actually highly influenced by their memory and previous experiences. As Napoleon once wrote, "On the battlefield, inspiration is usually nothing but recollection." In other words, our choices are based on the rapid recognition of a situation that has readily been experienced and memorized, consciously or unconsciously. While past encounters can be a relevant source of information when making decisions, self-assured decision-making by those who place too much faith in their intuition run the risk of overseeing relevant information that could be beneficial in the current context. Therefore, organizational leaders and practitioners should be wary of the potential adverse effects of priming in decision-making processes.

As stated in the introduction, priming can also impact people's behaviour and social interactions. In that vein, priming can exert effects on employee's organizational behaviour in negative as well as positive ways. For example, linking priming to goal orientation and motivation—it is probable that priming employees with the concept of competitiveness makes them prone to behaving in a more competitive way. While this could improve job performance at an individual level, employees behaving competitively towards each other might result in a more hostile work environment. Similarly, organizational members primed with antisocial behaviour might consequently behave disrespectfully towards colleagues, thereby creating a negative social work environment. On a more positive note, priming is increasingly being utilized by educators as a learning tool for students with learning disabilities (Wexler et al., 2016). Likewise, priming could be used as an educational intervention in organizations. Certain employees (e.g., those with learning disabilities or concentration problems) might perform better when they know what they can expect. So, by presenting new material before it is taught in trainings, employees are allowed to grow comfortable with it, enabling them to pay better attention during the actual training. These examples illustrate why priming is of great importance to the study of organizations and change. Since priming generally happens unconsciously, it often goes unnoticed by organizational members. However, an increased awareness of priming enables managers and organizational leaders to both mitigate its negative impact and seize its advantages.

Search strategy

Relevant databases were searched using the term 'priming' both separately and in combination with the terms 'organisation*,' 'work,' 'employ*,' 'leader*,' or 'chang*.' This search yielded about 140 results. After removing the duplicates and thorough examination, 5 meta-analyses, 0 systematic reviews, and 0 studies were included.

Main findings

1. *People rely on stereotypical primes when forming judgements about others (Level B).*

   Kidder et al. (2017) performed a meta-analysis on stereotype priming. Results showed that stereotype priming effects are genuine. Priming people with stereotypical information regarding a target influences their subsequent judgements about this target. The effect of the priming relies on several factors, such as the type of judgement to be made (quick vs. complex) and the characteristics of the target (age, race, gender, etc.). Results also showed that race produced the largest stereotype priming effects, suggesting that when forming judgements about others, people are more likely to be influenced by stereotypical information concerning race than, for example, gender.

2. *Scientific evidence shows that priming influences attitudes and behaviour (Level B).*

   In 2012, Cameron et al. performed a meta-analysis of more than 150 studies examining the relationship between priming and behaviour. Results all pointed towards the same direction: Priming participants (using different stimuli such as names, images, or words) influenced behaviour—from behavioural intentions to actual behaviours such as eating, drinking, and smoking. Furthermore, priming influenced participants' explicit attitudes such as political views, trait judgements, and beliefs about sexuality.

3. *Primed goals influence organizational behaviour, especially if these goals are valued highly by employees (Level A).*

   A meta-analysis by Chen et al. (2020) of 23 studies with a total of more than 3,000 participants examined the effect of primed goals on several outcomes such as performance, creativity, need for achievement, and persistence. Results showed that priming organizational members with achievement goals had an overall positive effect on their job performance and the need for achievement. Additionally, primed goals as well as consciously set goals both had positive effects on organizational behaviour, and the effect of these two types of goals was shown to be additive. Another meta-analysis by Shantz and Latham (2011) reached more or less the same conclusion. In this study, call centre employees primed with a photograph of a woman winning a race raised significantly more money from donors than those who were not primed. On the basis of these findings, Shantz and Latham concluded that employees primed to reach a certain goal exhibit better performance. Priming employees with goals seems to have the most impact when they value these goals highly. Weingarten et al. (2016) conducted a meta-analysis on the effects of primed goals on organizational behaviour and found that priming effects were stronger if people inherently valued the outcome (e.g., students with a high achievement motivation attempting a graded intelligence test) or because value was manipulated to be high, such as in the use of incentives (e.g., money or a gift) in exchange for accurate responses.

Conclusion

In conclusion, scientific evidence consistently shows that priming influences human perceptions, attitudes, and behaviour. Stereotype priming is a valid phenomenon in social interactions. Research suggests that when people are primed with certain stereotypical information, they rapidly form a mental categorization of the other and make social judgements according to that social category. This in turn is likely to influence their social treatment (Kiddler et al., 2017). Additionally, priming not only influences individual behaviours such as drinking and smoking, it also impacts beliefs about politics and sexuality (Cameron et al., 2012). In addition, we can draw relevant information from research in the organizational context. For example, priming employees with goals can have a positive effect on job achievement and job performance (Chen et al., 2020; Shantz & Latham, 2011), especially when these goals are valued highly by organizational members. However, this does not only apply to goals that are inherently valued. Creating a valued goal by using incentives yields the same results (Weingarten et al., 2016). This last finding is in line with the conclusions from our earlier research on whether financial incentives are an effective way to encourage change and improve performance (Ten Have et al., 2016). A first and important finding was that there is strong evidence that, overall, financial incentives have a moderate positive effect on performance (e.g., Cerasoli et al., 2014; Weibel et al., 2009). This positive effect is often referred to as the 'price effect'—the financial incentive increases the intention to perform well because of the monetary benefit. However, this effect differs among forms of incentives, types of motivation, and performance outcomes. Additionally, our research from 2019 showed that monetary incentives had a positive effect only when large or significant enough; small incentives can have a negative effect on job satisfaction (Ten Have et al., 2019).

Practical reflections

The knowledge that priming influences human perceptions, judgements, and behaviour has some practical implications for organizations. Firstly, stereotype priming could have negative effects on the work floor, such as skewed social perceptions leading to undesired social behaviour. Therefore, it would be prudent for managers to organize trainings, seminars, or workshops for organizational members in which the effects of stereotype priming and the underlying causal mechanisms are made explicit. On a more positive note, priming effects could also be beneficial for organizations. One example is the finding that higher valued goals yield stronger priming effects, eventually resulting in better performance. Managers might make use of this by looking into the goals that employees value intrinsically and use priming techniques accordingly. Monetary rewards could also be promising in guiding employee behaviour. Caution is warranted though, since the usage of bonuses or other monetary incentives may foster a competitive spirit in the workplace that undermines other values such as cooperation. Also, as our earlier research demonstrated, only large monetary incentives have a positive effect on job satisfaction. Since small incentives can lead to negative effects on job satisfaction, managers should either pay enough or not pay at all (Pouliakas, 2010).

Recency effect

What is the recency effect?

The recency effect is a cognitive bias in which recently presented information is better learned, stored, and retrieved over previously presented information. Researchers describe the recency effect as "an occurrence that happens when the information that is presented last in a series of information units, has a particularly marked influence on a person's subsequent judgments" (Fang et al., 2018), or as "more weight that is put on the latest information by a decision-maker when he or she is requested to evaluate a short series of mixed information" (Yang et al., 2018). German psychologist Hermann Ebbinghaus discovered the recency effect during his memory experiments in which participants were asked to recall items from a list of words. Ebbinghaus found that the location of a word on the list had a pronounced influence on the participants' ability to accurately recall that word. Specifically, they recalled items at the end of the list best (the recency effect). During these experiments, Ebbinghaus also discovered that participants recalled the first few items better than those in the middle. This is called the 'primacy effect.' The recency and primacy effect are often named simultaneously and are together considered serial-position effects—the tendency for people to better learn or remember facts, impressions, or items presented at the beginning or end of a sequence than that presented in the middle of it. Media and communication strategists often refer to the serial position effects and use them to enhance the effectiveness of their communication strategies. For example, a frequently repeated piece of advice for presenters, which is commonly seen as the framework for any successful presentation, is "Tell them what you're going to tell them, tell them, and then tell them what you've told them." This advice actually is rooted in ancient Greek philosopher Aristotle's philosophy and is referred to as the 'Aristotelian triptych.' By emphasizing the message at the beginning and repeating it at the end, speakers assure that their messages are better remembered by the audience. This structure has been adopted by many coaches, trainers, and news channels.

The recency effect has been studied in various domains and sectors. Particularly in the commercial field, the proposition that the most recently displayed information has a particular marked influence on recollection and, ultimately, consumption behaviour has fascinated marketers. Commercial companies have designed their selling strategies according to this principle; for example, making sure advertisements usually end in a positive and appealing way. The recency effect is also suggested to influence the legal field, since it assumes that a jury's ultimate decision concerning a certain case might be mostly dependent on a lawyer's closing argument. Another example where the recency effect can exert its influence is the stock market: investors might falsely believe a rising market will continue to appreciate or that a declining market or stock is likely to keep falling, merely based on the most recent market information they've received.

What is the relevance of the recency effect to organizations and change?

The recency effect can have great influence on the organizational and change context. If employees are pronouncedly influenced by recent information, the effectiveness of change communication might thus be partially dependent on the communication structures and storylines used by managers and change leaders. The recency bias might also have repercussions on social perceptions and employee behaviour towards colleagues. For example, when managers base professional judgements of their colleagues solely on their most recent performance instead of their longer-term professional development, it could result in skewed perceptions and judgements concerning their professionalism and capabilities and ultimately their behaviour. The recency bias relates to organizational concepts such as change communication, social judgements, and decision-making. Understanding the relationship between the recency effect and these concepts can provide managers with tools to better understand, and ultimately manage, organizational behaviour.

Search strategy

Relevant databases were searched using the term 'recency effect' and 'recency bias' both separately and in combination with the terms 'organisation★,' 'work,' 'employ★,' 'leader★,' and 'chang★.' This search yielded about 45 results. After removing the duplicates and thorough examination, 2 meta-analyses, 0 systematic reviews, and 5 studies were included.

Main findings

1. *The information presented last, in a series, is remembered more clearly and influences people's subsequent judgements (Level B).*

   A meta-analysis of Holbrook et al. (2007) explored the results of more than 500 experiments on the recency effect. The analysis showed significant recency effects across the experiments. Another meta-analysis across 158 experiments exploring the recency effect by Bishop and Smith (2001) showed that 15 percent reflected significant recency effects. The 1990 study by Tubbs et al. to explore the relation between the recency effect and decision-making by auditors indicated that the information presented last to auditors had a marked influence on their eventual judgements. A similar study by Yang et al. (2018) on investors drew the same conclusion: presenting investors with positive information last resulted in a higher chance of them investing.

2. *The recency effect is more likely to occur when people receive information that is relatively long, difficult to understand, preceded by other information, or communicated orally (Level B).*

   Bishop and Smith (2001) found that, if information is transferred orally and the message is long, people are more likely to be influenced by the recency effect. Furthermore, Holbrook et al. (2007) found that questions that were hard to understand together with full-sentence answer choices also increased recency effects. Additionally, Holbrook et al.

found a positive relation between the number of questions answered previously and the recency effect.

3. *Indications are found that teamwork could temper the severity of the recency bias (Level D).*

   One of the main conclusions of a study executed by Ahlawat (1999) was that teamwork could have a decreasing effect on recency effects. According to Ahlawat (1999), using audit teams causes superior comprehension and recall of evidence and results in judgements that are less biased. An important note: This study was done on auditors, and the results should therefore not be generalized without corresponding caution.

4. *The recency effect might influence the perceived traits of others (Level D).*

   Fang et al. (2018) studied the influence of the recency effect on perceived traits. They found that the final emotion an individual showed had a more pronounced impact on how others perceived the traits of that individual compared to preceding emotions. These findings suggest that when making trait judgements about others, observers weigh heavily on the most recently displayed emotions in dynamic expressions. Apparently, these leave an 'imprint' on observers, causing them to draw trait inferences from these emotions.

Conclusion

Recency effect—the bias in which people weigh recent information more heavily than preceding information—has been studied in various domains, from social settings to the organizational context. Meta-analytical evidence shows that recency effect influences human judgements and behaviours. Less high-quality scientific evidence has been found regarding social judgements; however, the available (albeit low-quality) research does point out that the recency effect could influence trait judgements. Several factors have an influence on the recency effect. Studies have shown that when information is relatively long, difficult to understand, is preceded by other information, or communicated orally, the recency effect is more likely to occur. Furthermore, the recency effect might be tempered by teamwork. However, considering the low evidence levels of the study included, some caution is warranted in generalizing this finding.

Practical reflections

For organizations and change, the proposition that people are profoundly influenced by the recency effect could hold significant relevance. For example, when communicating an upcoming organizational change, managers are advised to end their stories with positive and uplifting messages since employees are likely to rely on this information when forming opinions and judgements about the change. Furthermore, an important implication can be drawn from the study by Ahlawat, suggesting that teamwork tempers the severity of the recency bias. According to Ahlawat, a group discussion may enhance cognitive involvement and causal reasoning, leading to a more complex problem analysis. So, it would be advisable for managers and leaders to form groups to arrive at (strategic) organizational decisions.

Halo effect

What is the halo effect?

The halo effect is a type of cognitive bias in which positive impressions of a stimulus in one area positively influence perceptions or feelings of that stimulus in other areas. The halo effect is also referred to as the 'physical attractiveness stereotype' or the 'beauty-is-good stereotype.' However, this effect doesn't just affect people's perceptions of others or objects based on their attractiveness. It can cover other assumed traits as well. People who are socially skilled or kind, for example, may also be seen as more likeable and intelligent. Perceptions of one quality or trait thus leads to biased judgements about other qualities or traits.

The term 'halo effect' refers to the religious concept of 'halo' (derived from the Greek ἅλως, meaning glory or aureole), which is a crown of light rays around or above a saint's head, bathing the individual in a heavenly light to show their goodness. The effect was originally identified by the American psychologist Frederick L. Wells (1884–1964) in 1907. However, psychologist Edward Thorndike was the first to coin the term 'halo effect' in a 1920 paper titled "The Constant Error in Psychological Ratings." In his study, Thorndike asked two commanding officers to evaluate their soldiers in terms of physical qualities, intellect, leadership skills, and personal qualities. Thorndike's goal was to see how the ratings of one quality would affect other qualities. Results of the study showed that high ratings of one quality, such as physique, correlated with high ratings of other characteristics, such as leadership. When Thorndike originally coined the term 'halo effect,' he was referring only to people; however, its use has been greatly expanded to other areas. In marketing, the halo effect exerts itself when perceived positive features of one product extend to the whole brand. An example is the popularity of Apple's iPod causing great public enthusiasm for Apple's other products such as the iPad, iMac, etc.

The halo effect is suggested to have detrimental effects on various fields and domains, such as education, the judicial context, politics, and leadership. For example, one study by Harari and McDavid (1973) found that teachers gave the highest grades to pupils with the most attractive names. A more recent study from 2016 found that teachers' judgements of academic performance were influenced by their students' attractiveness (Talamas et al., 2016).

Lastly, a 2010 study found that attractiveness is a strong predictor of decisions regarding who is put in a position of leadership (Verhulst et al., 2010).

A bias that is considered to be related to the halo effect is the 'the law of small numbers.' This is the tendency to generalize about all members of a certain group based on knowledge about just one or very few people (*see the frame containing related biases*). Stated bluntly, people tend to generalize, and they do it based on very little evidence. Like the halo effect, the law of small numbers has been a popular subject of study over the last few decades. The most noticeable difference lies in the fact that the halo effect is studied mostly in the domain of social psychology, while the law of small numbers is linked to mathematics and statistics. Nevertheless, since both biases concern the formation of hasty generalizations based on one or a few pieces of information, the main findings concerning the halo effect in the section below might also be applicable to the law of small numbers.

Secondary biases related to the halo effect

The law of small numbers—the tendency to generalize about all members of a certain group based on information about just one or very few people

What is the relevance of the halo effect to organizations and change?

The halo effect can be of high relevance to organizations and change as it applies not only to people but also to organizations. As financial performance is one of the most available characteristics of an organization, companies with outstanding financial success can become the subject of the halo effect and consequently turn into popular objects of imitation. One example is General Electric (GE) in the late 1990s when Jack Welsh was CEO. The company's highly favourable position on the stock market urged many companies to copy GE's practices, methods, and approaches, the most well-known of which was the 'forced ranking' system. This evaluation system ranked employees' performance based on mutual comparison by putting employees in one of three categories (top 20 percent, middle 70 percent, and the lowest-performing 10 percent). However, while many companies initially adopted this system, most quickly gave it up because of its presumed negative consequences on team cohesion and motivation. This illustrates how under the influence of the halo effect, organizations can be misled in their strategic decision-making by blindly copying their competitors' best practices.

In addition, the halo effect is considered one of the most common biases affecting performance appraisals and reviews. Supervisors may evaluate subordinates based on the perception of a single characteristic rather than their entire performance. For example, employees with high enthusiasm and a positive attitude but lacking the required knowledge or ability to perform their job successfully may receive better ratings from their colleagues than their performance deserves. The halo effect could also play a role in recruitment and selection. If future employers perceive applicants as attractive or likeable, they could more likely perceive them as intelligent and qualified. Researchers also suggest that the halo effect could have an impact on income. A study by Parret (2015) published in the *Journal of Economic Psychology* found that, on average, food servers perceived as attractive earned approximately $1,200 more per year in tips than their other counterparts. A study by Judge et al. (2009) found that physical attractiveness had a positive effect not only on people's self-confidence but also on their overall income and financial well-being. The halo effect could also apply to organizations. High-performing organizations such as Google are thus attributed with a brilliant strategy or excellent leadership, even though this has not necessarily been proven.

Search strategy

Relevant databases were searched using the terms 'halo effect' and 'physical attractiveness stereotype' both separately and in combination with the terms 'organisation*,' 'work,' 'employ*,' 'leader*,' or 'chang*.' This search yielded 701 results. After removing the duplicates and thorough examination, 2 meta-analyses, 0 systematic reviews, and 8 studies were included.

Main findings

1. *People perceived as physically attractive are generally evaluated more positively than those who are not (Level B).*

   A meta-analysis of 78 experiments concluded that people perceived as physically attractive were also seen as more sociable, dominant, sexually warm, mentally healthy, intelligent, and socially skilled than others. However, people perceived as physically attractive were not perceived as possessing greater character (e.g., being an honest, trustworthy, or kind person) and were seen as less modest than others (Feingold, 1992). This meta-analysis also looked at whether (and to which extent) those perceived as physically attractive possess these characteristics associated with physical attractiveness (e.g., sociability, dominance, etc.). In other words, are those considered good-looking really what people think them to be? The short answer to this question was no. No notable relationships were found between physical attractiveness and basic personality traits such as sociability or dominance.

   A meta-analysis of 76 studies concerning the physically attractiveness stereotype by Eagly et al. (1991) reached the same conclusion:

   People perceived as good-looking were also perceived as being more socially competent than others. They were also perceived as being vainer and less modest. Importantly, the researchers found that the strength of the halo effect differed across perceived personality traits. For example, where good looks induced strong inferences about social competence, they caused weaker judgements about intellectual competence and had almost no impact at all on beliefs about integrity and concern for others. Therefore, Eagly et al. concluded: "Although the consensus among social psychologists has been that the beauty-is-good stereotype is extremely strong and robust, this meta-analysis found there was considerable variation in the strength of the beauty-is-good effect from study to study and from measure to measure within studies" (p. 121).

2. *The halo effect is stronger when women are targeted compared to men, and the effect is weaker when one receives personal information about the individual (Level B).*

In his meta-analysis, Feingold (1992) not only found that physically attractive people were perceived as more sexually warm, but he also found that this effect was stronger when the targets concerned physically attractive women compared to men. In the meta-analytic study by Eagly et al. (1991), results showed that the halo effect was weaker when subjects received individuating information about the target. According to the study, looks should thus be relatively less important in the perceptions of friends, acquaintances, family members, and colleagues than in perceptions of strangers because perceivers have extensive information about these people in addition to their physical appearance.

3. *The halo effect could be related to organizational reputation management (Level C).*

Coombs and Holladay (2006) investigated the halo effect in light of an organization's reputation and crisis management through an experimental study. Results indicated that when an organization has a very favourable public reputation, this can create a halo effect that protects it during a crisis. When this is the case, the halo effect might work as a shield that deflects the potential reputational damage following a crisis. However, this was only the case for organizations with highly favourable reputations. When an organizations' reputation was only moderately favourable, the halo effect was not strong enough to protect the organizational reputation. In 2015, Pitsakis et al. also investigated the halo effect in the field of organizational reputation management. In a cross-sectional study of over a hundred English and Scottish universities and their 1,117 spinoff firms, they found empirical evidence that the reputation of an organization's secondary activities can influence public perception of that organization's main activities. Thus, according to this study, venturing into peripheral activities, which is a common organizational endeavour, can generate positive spill overs for established activities through the halo effect. Furthermore, Cui et al. (2019) examined how congruence between a sports sponsorship and an organization's public image was related to the customers' attitude towards it through the halo effect. The results of their experiment indicated that when consumers remember a sponsorship they perceive to be congruent with the sponsoring company's public image, the memory produces a strong halo effect, provoking positive company attitudes. This implies that when organizations want to establish a positive reputation, they should consider how the halo effect influences customers' organizational attitude formation and match their marketing strategies accordingly.

4. *The halo effect might be stronger when people are aroused or in a positive mood and have low social interaction anxiety (Level D).*

In 1996, Bagozzi studied the halo effect in the context of attitudes towards blood donation. He found arousal to be a moderating factor in the occurrence of the halo effect. Specifically, when people had positive attitudes towards giving blood and received physical arousal, this led them to more strongly believe that positive consequences of giving blood would occur. So, according to this study, when someone perceives an action to be positive and when that person is also physically aroused, the more likely it is that the halo effect occurs, causing them to expect more positive consequences.

Furthermore, an experimental study by Forgas (2011) found that mood can either strengthen or decrease the halo effect. According to this study, a positive mood enhances the halo effect, while a negative mood can eliminate it. Lastly, Y. Li et al. (2019) conducted an experimental study to explore the physical attractiveness stereotype in service encounters. The results indicated that physical attractiveness of service providers positively affects customer citizenship behaviour. Customers were friendlier towards service providers they considered physically attractive and were more willing to share helpful ideas with them in the future than with other employees. However, the effect only existed for customers with low social interaction anxiety. People who were anxious to interact with the attractive service providers did not show greater customer citizenship behaviour. According to this study, being physically attractive is thus no longer advantageous when the perceiver is anxious to interact with them.

5. *The halo effect might be important in customer–employee interactions (Level D).*

Several experimental studies have explored the halo effect in organizational settings. As mentioned, the study by Y. Li et al. (2019) found that the physical attractiveness of service providers positively affects customer citizenship behaviour. Another study by Reingen and Kernan (1993) explored the halo effect in the personal-selling context. Participants in an experimental setting were asked to rate the selling skills of attractive and unattractive salespersons based on their pictures. As expected, more favourable selling skills were attributed to physically attractive salespersons compared to their unattractive counterparts. In addition, participants yielded to a request to donate money significantly more if the one making the request was attractive compared to their less attractive colleagues. Another experimental study on the halo effect in customer service was conducted by Dagger et al. (2013). Frontline employees of a medical clinic were trained to improve their interpersonal skills. The improvement of frontline employees' interpersonal skills led to a more positive overall service evaluation by customers through the halo effect. However, the trainings not only increased customers' positive perceptions of these specific employees, these also led to more positive perceived service attributes of other medical personnel in the clinic. This study seems to demonstrate a manifestation of not necessarily the halo effect, but rather 'the law of small numbers' bias that was described in the introduction of this chapter. It shows that the evaluation of a whole group or organization can be influenced by the evaluation of one single member of that group.

Conclusion

Research into the halo effect shows us clearly that books will be judged by their covers. In general, people perceived as phyisically atractive are perceived as possessing more positive character traits than people perceived as less physically attractive. Specifically, they are seen as more sociable, dominant, sexually warm, mentally healthy, intelligent, and socially skilled. However, they are also generally seen as less modest and vainer. Several factors have been shown to moderate the physical attractiveness stereotype, such as sex and individuating information. Arousal, mood, and social interaction anxiety also might be moderating factors, although the level of evidence available is quite low. The halo effect seems to play a role in organizational reputation management. Also, studies have shown that the physical appearance of employees might influence customer–employee interaction and customers' behaviour, although some caution is warranted since the quality of these studies is not high. All in all, initial impressions can linger and, to the extent that they do, our behaviour is likely to be stereotypically governed. This conclusion makes the halo effect certainly relevant to organizations.

Practical reflections

Several practical reflections for managers and organizations can be made. When communicating organizational change, managers and leaders could make use of the halo effect. As Bagozzi's study (1996) illustrated, under arousal conditions, people are more prone to fall prey to the halo effect. According to Bagozzi, arousal could be simulated through the use of persuasive communications conjuring up emotionally charged memories or images. One suggestion for managers or leaders is to use inspiring stories and story structures in communicating organizational change, also called *storytelling*, to positively influence employees' attitude towards the change. Note, however, that for the halo effect to occur, employees' attitude towards the change has to be positive. When employees perceive the change to be negative or show resistance towards it, arousing them with emotionally charged stories is not likely to have the same impact through the halo effect. This doesn't necessarily mean that storytelling has no effect on employees when they hold negative attitudes towards the change. However, when this is the case, the halo effect doesn't play a role in changing their opinions.

Managers could also make use of the halo effect to strengthen their organizational reputation. According to Pitsakis et al. (2015), they could use the halo effect as a strategically managed tool to generate the popularity of the firm's core business. As the study showed, when organizations venturing into noncore activities clearly signal this to their customers, this could create a positive reputation of these activities. Through the halo effect, this could in turn positively influence the reputation of the organization's core business. A suggestion for managers and leaders is thus to not only 'step out of their comfort zone' and explore secondary activities that strengthen their reputation, but also to actively communicate these activities to their customers, thereby strengthening the popularity of their organization. Note, however, that the manner in which the organization is able to perform these secondary activities successfully is a crucial determinant in the customers' perception and, with this, the organization's popularity. So, managers are advised to focus on executing those secondary activities they believe will strengthen their reputation. Also, the study by Cui et al. (2019) pointed out that sports sponsorship that is highly congruent with a company can produce positive and amicable reactions from consumers through a halo effect. So, when attempting to establish a positive organizational reputation, managers should make use of the halo effect by matching the type of sponsorship with their type of company.

Even though the halo effect can be used to more effectively communicate organizational change and strengthen organizational reputation, managers should also be aware of the negative consequences of the halo effect, for example, in recruiting procedures. Studies have shown that, unlike what is common practice (that people are often unaware of), selecting people on the basis of their looks is not always a good human resource strategy when recruiting frontline employees. For example, as the study by Y. Li et al. (2019) suggests, if customers have high social interaction anxiety, they may prefer to interact with a service provider of average attractiveness to avoid creating a negative impression on the attractive provider.

Moreover, Forgas (2011) points to the importance of forming accurate impressions on the basis of limited information in the working field, especially in organizational, industrial, and clinical settings. The halo effect disturbs this formation of accurate impressions as it causes affective factors to influence social judgements. As Forgas's study illustrated, certain circumstances, like a positive mood, can increase the halo effect. According to Forgas,

> The possibility that positive affect may increase halo effects has important practical implications in areas where impression formation is important, such as in the legal, forensic, clinical, educational, counselling and human resources fields. Training programs for professionals working in these fields may be designed to increase people's awareness of such affectively induced biases.
>
> (p. 816)

Investing in training programmes might thus be a helpful first step for organizations to prevent the halo effect from influencing social judgements.

Similarity bias

What is the similarity bias?

The similarity bias (also called 'similarity heuristic' or 'affinity bias') occurs when individuals evaluate people they perceive as similar in a more favourable light than those they find less similar (Sacco et al., 2003). Stated bluntly, we prefer what is like us over what is different (in-group vs. out-group). The similarity-attraction paradigm (Byrne, 1997) posits that people tend to feel attracted to similar others. The notion that similarity is a crucial determinant of interpersonal attraction is well illustrated by well-known proverbs such as "birds of a feather flock together." The growing popularity of this phenomenon has given rise to extensive research on the similarity bias over the last few decades. Several social psychological theories are related to the similarity bias, such as the social impact theory, proposing that the amount of social influence an individual experiences in group settings is partly dependent on the presence of those they perceive as close to them. In other words, we are more influenced by people we think are more similar to us than people who (in our perception) are not.

Another related theory is the theory of cooperation/competition, which states that how people believe they are socially interdependent on others impacts their dynamics and performance. According to American social psychologist Morton Deutsch, who proposed the theory in 1949, "if you're positively linked with another, then you sink and swim together; with negative linkage, if the other sinks, you swim, and if the other swims, you sink" (Deutsch, 2012, pp. 278–279). Positive interdependence can result, for example, from the need to share a resource, but also from mutual sympathy for each other and the feeling of 'closeness' (Ten Have et al., 2019). The social exchange theory is the third social psychological theory related to the similarity bias. The theory states that people tend to form relationships with others whose values and opinions generally are in agreement with their own. Also, they are more likely to bond with others who are 'equal to them,' as viewed as the sum of abilities, performances, and characteristics. In short, people are more likely to form bonds with people they consider similar to them. For example, a study on college-dorm roommates showed that individuals with shared attitudes, values, backgrounds, and academic achievements usually became friends (Newcomb, 1961). Interestingly, it could also be the individual's perceived similarity to another person, rather than their objective similarity, which breeds liking. As such, research has found that individual's perceived similarity with another forms potential for attraction in romantic relationships, even when actual similarity is reported to be low (Montoya et al., 2008).

What is the relevance of the similarity bias to organizations and change?

The similarity bias could have a great deal of impact on various organizational processes, such as selection and recruitment. For instance, in interview evaluations, similarity-attraction may manifest in racial similarity bias when interviewers favour those of the same race over others (Buckley et al., 2007). Or interviewers may give the green light to candidates who went to the same university or sports club as themselves, being unconscious that their decision might not be based on very solid ground.

Indeed, consistent evidence supports the view that surface-level characteristics, such as race, gender, and other demographic variables, of both the applicant and the interviewer may influence the interviewer's evaluations (de Kock & Hauptfleisch, 2018, p. 138). So, hiring with unchecked similarity bias could impact the workplace by onboarding a narrow pool of candidates, who in many aspects resemble the employers of the organization, thereby possibly negatively affecting diversity in the workplace. It is, therefore, necessary to learn more about this bias, where it comes from, how it could affect employees and organizations, and to explore possible strategies effective in minimizing it.

Search strategy

Relevant databases were searched using the term 'similarity bias' and 'similarity heuristic' both separately and in combination with the terms 'organisation*,' 'work,' 'employ*,' 'leader*,' or 'chang*.' This search yielded about 36 results. After removing the duplicates and thorough examination, 0 meta-analyses, 0 systematic reviews, and 3 studies were included.

Main findings

1. *People could evaluate others they perceive to be similar to themselves (race or gender) in a more favourable light than those they perceive as less similar (Level D).*

   In a 2018 study, de Kock & Hauptfleisch investigated the occurrence of similarity bias in recruitment procedures. Specifically, the researchers examined if interviewers showed a racial similarity bias towards applicants (i.e., a preference for those racially similar to them). Results indeed indicated that when interviewers requested general responses from applicants (such as 'Tell me more about yourself") and evaluated responses using their own criteria, they assigned significantly higher scores to applicants from the same race group as compared with applicants from the opposite race group. Another study by Elkins et al. (2001) explored the existence of a gender-similarity bias in evaluations of gender discrimination allegations. Participants in the study were asked to read a scenario describing either a male (in one scenario) or a female employee (in the other scenario) who worked as pilots for a fictitious airline. Each had applied for a promotion to the supervisory position of chief pilot. Both scenarios also indicated that the nonrecipient of the promotion had filed a claim of gender discrimination against the company. The participants were then asked to evaluate the gender discrimination allegations. Results suggested that female evaluators tended to be favourably biased in favour of female plaintiffs, supporting the existence of a gender-similarity bias.

2. *Personal threat might affect our susceptibility to the similarity bias (Level D).*

   In 2002, Elkins at al. conducted a study comparable to their 2001 study in which they explored possible gender-similarity bias in evaluations of sex discrimination allegations. The results of the study confirmed the findings of Elkins et al.'s 2001 study: Women differentiated plaintiffs on the basis of gender, whereas men did not. At first glance, these findings suggest that men, for some reason, might be more objective observers than women, at least in this context. However, the researchers found that in another scenario involving a child-custody proceeding, men exhibited a similarity bias and thus seem to be equally susceptible to the bias. Elkins et al. point to the role of perceived threat. Their findings showed that in the context of sex-discrimination allegations, women fell prey to the bias because they perceived employment discrimination as personally threatening to themselves. Likewise, men found the child custody scenario to be more threatening than women did and subsequently exhibited a similarity bias.

3. *The use of highly structured interviews might be a possible way to suppress similarity bias during selection and recruitment procedures (Level D).*

   In the aforementioned study by de Kock and Hauptfleisch (2018), researchers examined if the similarity bias could be affected by the type of structure used in the interview. To test this, they compared low-structured interviews, consisting of broad questions requesting general responses from the applicant ("Tell me more about yourself"), to high-structured interviews containing specific "What would you do if. . ." questions that are informative of applicants' competencies and therefore widely used in interview practices. Findings indicated that interviewers favoured racially similar applicants less in high-structured interviews than in low-structured ones. According to de Kock and Hauptfleisch, this could be explained by the fact that imposing an interview structure guides interviewers' impression formation processes towards job-relevant information and away from irrelevant interviewee characteristics such as race, thereby suppressing automatic heuristics such as the similarity bias.

Conclusion

Despite the widespread use of the saying "birds of a feather flock together," the availability of scientific evidence for the similarity bias with high evidence level seems to be limited. The available research although does point to the direction that the bias exists and that people are affected by perceived similarity regarding gender and race. Some signs indicate that perceived personal threat affects our proneness to fall prey to the bias; however, more high-quality empirical research is needed to fully support this notion. Lastly, a possible method to minimize the similarity bias could be the use of highly structured interviews, presumably because imposing an interview structure influences interviewers' information processing and causes their attention to shift away from irrelevant characteristics and towards job-relevant information.

Practical reflections

The practical reflection for organizations with regard to the similarity bias predominantly concerns the selection and recruitment processes. Managers are first and foremost well advised to be aware of the similarity bias possibly influencing their hiring decisions. Furthermore, as the results of de Kock and Hauptfleisch' study (2018) suggest, it would be prudent for them to use structured interviews when selecting applicants for positions. According to de Kock and Hauptfleisch, practitioners who disregard research evidence of this nature and keep using low-structured interviews will continue to make poor selection decisions and might even risk exposing their organizations to equal-employment litigation (de Kock & Hauptfleisch, 2018, p. 149). Also, Elkins et al. (2002) suggest that, when being faced with allegations of discrimination managers and organization should ensure that the investigations regarding sex discrimination allegations are conducted by a panel of internal compliance officers from both genders. In this way, there would be the potential for an 'offsetting' effect of the gender-similarity bias (Elkins et al.,

2002, p. 290). Lastly, when trying to combat this bias, it is not sufficient to simply bring together people with diverse backgrounds. When people have worked long in the same organization, they will share the same experiences, successes, and obstacles. As a result, they will likely form the same attitudes, believe the same stories, and develop a preference for the same 'similar others.' Instead of merely recruiting people with diverse backgrounds, leaders should ensure 'cognitive diversity' (e.g., including people with diverse skills, perspectives, and areas of expertise). An example of this is a bank CEO giving legal experts, risk management specialists, and investment specialists a voice in strategic decision-making. By ensuring sufficient cognitive diversity, the board can make decisions based on the valuable contributions of different experts. This way, more alternative ideas and opinions are likely to be shared and evaluated than if decision-makers were very similar to each other.

Bibliography

Aczel, B., Szollosi, A., & Bago, B. (2016). Lax monitoring versus logical intuition: The determinants of confidence in conjunction fallacy. *Thinking & Reasoning*, *22*(1), 99–117. https://doi.org/10.1080/13546783.2015.1062801

Ahlawat, S S. (1999). Order effects and memory for evidence in individual versus group decision making in auditing. *Journal of Behavioral Decision Making*, *12*(1), 71–88. https://doi.org/10.1002/(SICI)1099-0771(199903)12:1<71::AID-BDM308>3.0.CO;2-Q

AlKhars, M., Evangelopoulos, N., Pavur, R., & Kulkarni, S. (2019). Cognitive biases resulting from the representativeness heuristic in operations management: An experimental investigation. *Psychology Research and Behavior Management*, *12*, 263–276. https://doi.org/10.2147/prbm.s193092

Bagozzi, R. P. (1996). The role of arousal in the creation and control of the halo effect in attitude models. *Psychology & Marketing*, *13*(3), 235–264. https://doi.org/10.1002/(SICI)1520-6793(199605)13:3<235::AID-MAR1>3.0.CO;2-D

Bandura, A. (1971). *Social learning theory*. New York: General Learning Press.

Bandura, A. (1972). *Socialization: Lexikon der Psychologie, Band III*. Herder.

Bargh, J. A., Chen, M., & Burrows, L. (1996). Automaticity of social behavior: Direct effects of trait construct and stereotype activation on action. *Journal of Personality and Social Psychology*, *71*(2), 230–244. https://doi.org/10.1037/0022-3514.71.2.230

Bargh, J. A., & Huang, J. Y. (2014). The selfish goal: Autonomously operating motivational structures as the proximate cause of human judgment and behavior. *Behavioral and Brain Sciences*, *37*(2), 121–135. https://doi.org/10.1017/s0140525x13000290

Benbasat, I., & Lim, J. (2000). Information technology support for debiasing group judgments: An empirical evaluation. *Organizational Behavior and Human Decision Processes*, *83*(1), 167–183. https://doi.org/10.1006/obhd.2000.2905

Bishop, G , & Smith, A. (2001). Response-order effects and the early gallup split-ballots. *Public Opinion Quarterly*, *65*(4), 479–505. https://doi.org/10.1086/323575

Bryant, J., Thompson, S., & Finklea, B. W. (2013). *Fundamentals of media effects*. McGraw-Hill Education.

Buckley, M. R., Jackson, K. A., Bolino, M. C., Veres, J. G., & Feild, H. S. (2007). The influence of relational demography on panel interview ratings: A field experiment. *Personnel Psychology*, *60*(3), 627–646. https://doi.org/10.1111/j.1744-6570.2007.00086.x

Byrne, D. (1997). An overview (and underview) of research and theory within the attraction paradigm. *Journal of Social and Personal Relationships, 14*(3), 417–431. https://doi.org/10.1177/0265407597143008

Cai, W., Pan, Y., Chai, H., Cui, Y., Yan, J., Dong, W., & Deng, G. (2018). Attentional bias modification in reducing test anxiety vulnerability: A randomized controlled trial. *BMC Psychiatry, 18*(1), 1–9. https://doi.org/10.1186/s12888-017-1517-6

Cannito, L., di Crosta, A., Palumbo, R., Ceccato, I., Anzani, S., La Malva, P., Palumbo, R., & di Domenico, A. (2020). Health anxiety and attentional bias toward virus-related stimuli during the COVID-19 pandemic. *Scientific Reports, 10*(1), 1–8. https://doi.org/10.1038/s41598-020-73599-8

Cameron, C. D., Brown-Iannuzzi, J. L., & Payne, B. K. (2012). Sequential priming measures of implicit social cognition. *Personality and Social Psychology Review, 16*(4), 330–350. https://doi.org/10.1177/1088868312440047

Cavanagh, S. R., Urry, H. L., & Shin, L. M. (2011). Mood-induced shifts in attentional bias to emotional information predict ill-and well-being. *Emotion, 11*(2), 241. https://doi.org/10.1037/a0022572

Cerasoli, C. P., Nicklin, J. M., & Ford, M. T. (2014). Intrinsic motivation and extrinsic incentives jointly predict performance: A 40-year meta-analysis. *Psychological Bulletin, 140*(4), 980–1008. https://doi.org/10.1037/a0035661

Charness, G., Karni, E., & Levin, D. (2010). On the conjunction fallacy in probability judgment: New experimental evidence regarding Linda. *Games and Economic Behavior, 68*(2), 551–556. https://doi.org/10.1016/j.geb.2009.09.003

Chen, X., Latham, G. P., Piccolo, R. F., & Itzchakov, G. (2020). An enumerative review and a meta-analysis of primed goal effects on organizational behavior. *Applied Psychology, 70*(1), 216–253. https://doi.org/10.1111/apps.12239

Chong, D. (2019). Competitive framing in political decision making. In *Oxford research encyclopedia of politics*. Oxford University Press. https://doi.org/10.1093/acrefore/9780190228637.013.964

Cohen, J. D., Dunbar, K., & McClelland, J. L. (1990). On the control of automatic processes: A parallel distributed processing account of the Stroop effect. *Psychological Review, 97*(3), 332–361. https://doi.org/10.1037/0033-295x.97.3.332

Coombs, W. T., & Holladay, S. J. (2006). Unpacking the halo effect: Reputation and crisis management. *Journal of Communication Management, 10*(2), 123–137. https://doi.org/10.1108/13632540610664698

Crum, A. J., Akinola, M., Martin, A., & Fath, S. (2017). The role of stress mindset in shaping cognitive, emotional, and physiological responses to challenging and threatening stress. *Anxiety, Stress, & Coping, 30*(4), 379–395. https://doi.org/10.1080/10615806.2016.1275585

Cui, G. Q., Lee, J. Y., & Jin, C. H. (2019). The role of sports sponsorship in negative new stories about a brand: Approach the halo effect. *Cogent Business & Management, 6*(1), 1–20. https://doi.org/10.1080/23311975.2019.1699284

Cummins, R. A., & Nistico, H. (2002). Maintaining life satisfaction: The role of positive cognitive bias. *Journal of Happiness Studies, 3*(1), 37–69. https://doi.org/10.1023/a:1015678915305

Dagger, T. S., Danaher, P. J., Sweeney, J. C., & McColl-Kennedy, J. R. (2013). Selective halo effects arising from improving the interpersonal skills of frontline employees. *Journal of Service Research, 16*(4), 488–502. https://doi.org/10.1177/1094670513481406

de Kock, F. S., & Hauptfleisch, D. B. (2018). Reducing racial similarity bias in interviews by increasing structure: A quasi-experiment using multilevel analysis. *International Perspectives in Psychology*, 7(3), 137–154. https://doi.org/10.1037/ipp0000091

de Neys, W., Cromheeke, S., & Osman, M. (2011). Biased but in doubt: Conflict and decision confidence. *PLoS One*, *6*(1), e15954, 1–10. https://doi.org/10.1371/journal.pone.0015954

Deutsch, M. (2012). A theory of cooperation—competition and beyond. In P. A. Van Lange, A. W. Kruglanski, & E. T. Higgins (Eds.), *Handbook of theories of social psychology* (Vol. 2). Sage Publications, Inc.

Eagly, A. H., Ashmore, R. D., Makhijani, M. G., & Longo, L. C. (1991). What is beautiful is good, but . . .: A meta-analytic review of research on the physical attractiveness stereotype. *Psychological Bulletin*, *110*(1), 109–128. https://doi.org/10.1037/0033-2909.110.1.109

Elkins, T. J., Phillips, J. S., & Konopaske, R. (2002). Gender-related biases in evaluations of sex discrimination allegations: Is perceived threat the key? *Journal of Applied Psychology*, *87*(2), 280–292. https://doi.org/10.1037/0021-9010.87.2.280

Elkins, T. J., Phillips, J. S., Konopaske, R., & Townsend, J. (2001). Evaluating gender discrimination claims: Is there a gender similarity bias? *Sex Roles*, *44*(1–2), 1–15. https://doi.org/10.1023/a:1011059131505

Fang, X., van Kleef, G. A., & Sauter, D. A. (2018). Person perception from changing emotional expressions: Primacy, recency, or averaging effect? *Cognition and Emotion*, *32*(8), 1597–1610. https://doi.org/10.1080/02699931.2018.1432476

Feingold, A. (1992). Good-looking people are not what we think. *Psychological Bulletin*, *111*(2), 304–341. https://doi.org/10.1037/0033-2909.111.2.304

Fiske, S. T. (2004). *Social beings: Core motives in social psychology*. John Wiley & Sons.

Forgas, J. P. (2011). She just doesn't look like a philosopher . . .? Affective influences on the halo effect in impression formation. *European Journal of Social Psychology*, *41*(7), 812–817. https://doi.org/10.1002/ejsp.842

Fredrickson, B. L. (1998). What good are positive emotions? *Review of General Psychology*, *2*(3), 300–319. https://doi.org/10.1037/1089-2680.2.3.300

Fredrickson, B. L. (2001). The role of positive emotions in positive psychology: The broaden-and-build theory of positive emotions. *American Psychologist*, *56*(3), 218–226. https://doi.org/10.1037/0003-066x.56.3.218

Fredrickson, B. L., & Joiner, T. (2002). Positive emotions trigger upward spirals toward emotional well-being. *Psychological Science*, *13*(2), 172–175. https://doi.org/10.1111/1467-9280.00431

Geier, A. B., Rozin, P., & Doros, G. (2006). Unit bias. *Psychological Science*, *17*(6), 521–525. https://doi.org/10.1111/j.1467-9280.2006.01738.x

Gotlib, I. H., & McCann, C. D. (1984). Construct accessibility and depression: An examination of cognitive and affective factors. *Journal of Personality and Social Psychology*, *47*(2), 427–439. https://doi.org/10.1037/0022-3514.47.2.427

Gould, S. J. (1989). The streak of streaks. *Chance*, *2*(2), 10–16. https://doi.org/10.1080/09332480.1989.10554932

Harari, H., & McDavid, J. W. (1973). Name stereotypes and teachers' expectations. *Journal of Educational Psychology*, *65*(2), 222–225. https://doi.org/10.1037/h0034978

Hayibor, S., & Wasieleski, D. M. (2008). Effects of the use of the availability heuristic on ethical decision-making in organizations. *Journal of Business Ethics*, *84*(S1), 151–165. https://doi.org/10.1007/s10551-008-9690-7

Holbrook, A. L., Krosnick, J. A., Moore, D., & Tourangeau, R. (2007). Response order effects in dichotomous categorical questions presented orally. *Public Opinion Quarterly*, *71*(3), 325–348. https://doi.org/10.1093/poq/nfm024

Homar, A. R., & Cvelbar, L. K. (2021). The effects of framing on environmental decisions: A systematic literature review. *Ecological Economics*, *183*, 1–18. https://doi.org/10.1016/j.ecolecon.2021.106950

Huntsinger, J. R., & Ray, C. (2016). A flexible influence of affective feelings on creative and analytic performance. *Emotion*, *16*(6), 826–837. https://doi.org/10.1037/emo0000188

Jiang, C., Buchanan, T. W., Yao, Z., Zhang, K., Wu, J., & Zhang, L. (2017). Acute psychological stress disrupts attentional bias to threat-related stimuli. *Scientific Reports*, 7(1), 1–11. https://doi.org/10.1038/s41598-017-14138-w

Jamieson, J. P., Nock, M. K., & Mendes, W. B. (2012). Mind over matter: Reappraising arousal improves cardiovascular and cognitive responses to stress. *Journal of Experimental Psychology: General*, *141*(3), 417–422. https://doi.org/10.1037/a0025719

Judge, T. A., Hurst, C., & Simon, L. S. (2009). Does it pay to be smart, attractive, or confident (or all three)? Relationships among general mental ability, physical attractiveness, core self-evaluations, and income. *Journal of Applied Psychology*, *94*(3), 742–755. https://doi.org/10.1037/a0015497

Kahneman, D., Krueger, A. B., Schkade, D., Schwarz, N., & Stone, A. A. (2006). Would you be happier if you were richer? A focusing illusion. *Science*, *312*(5782), 1908–1910. https://doi.org/10.1126/science.1129688

Kidder, C. K., White, K. R., Hinojos, M. R., Sandoval, M., & Crites, S. L. (2017). Sequential stereotype priming: A meta-analysis. *Personality and Social Psychology Review*, *22*(3), 199–227. https://doi.org/10.1177/1088868317723532

Kühberger, A. (1998). The influence of framing on risky decisions: A meta-analysis. *Organizational Behavior and Human Decision Processes*, *75*(1), 23–55. https://doi.org/10.1006/obhd.1998.2781

Levin, I. P., & Gaeth, G. J. (1988). How consumers are affected by the framing of attribute information before and after consuming the product. *Journal of Consumer Research*, *15*(3), 374–378. https://doi.org/10.1086/209174

Levin, I. P., Schneider, S. L., & Gaeth, G. J. (1998). All frames are not created equal: A typology and critical analysis of framing effects. *Organizational Behavior and Human Decision Processes*, *76*(2), 149–188. https://doi.org/10.1006/obhd.1998.2804

Li, Y., Xie, L., Gao, T., & Guan, X. (2019). Does being beautiful always help? Contingency effects of physical attractiveness of the service providers on customer response. *Journal of Services Marketing*, *33*(3), 356–368. https://doi.org/10.1108/jsm-05-2018-0140

MacLeod, C., & Campbell, L. (1992). Memory accessibility and probability judgments: An experimental evaluation of the availability heuristic. *Journal of Personality and Social Psychology*, *63*(6), 890–902. https://doi.org/10.1037/0022-3514.63.6.890

Marhenke, T., & Imhoff, R. (2020). Increased accessibility of semantic concepts after (more or less) subtle activation of related concepts: Support for the basic tenet of priming research. *The Journal of General Psychology*, *147*(2), 186–211. https://doi.org/10.1080/00221309.2019.1665489

Montoya, R. M., Horton, R. S., & Kirchner, J. (2008). Is actual similarity necessary for attraction? A meta-analysis of actual and perceived similarity. *Journal of Social and Personal Relationships*, *25*(6), 889–922. https://doi.org/10.1177/0265407508096700

Moscovici, S. (1984). The phenomenon of social representation. In R. Farr & S. Moscovici (Eds.), *Social representations*. Cambridge University Press.

Moutier, S., & Houdé, O. (2003). Judgement under uncertainty and conjunction fallacy inhibition training. *Thinking & Reasoning*, *9*(3), 185–201. https://doi.org/10.1080/13546780343000213

Nabi, R. L., Walter, N., Oshidary, N., Endacott, C. G., Love-Nichols, J., Lew, Z. J., & Aune, A. (2020). Can emotions capture the elusive gain-loss framing effect? A meta-analysis. *Communication Research*, *47*(8), 1107–1130.

Newcomb, T. M. (1961). *Acquaintance process*. Holt, Rinehart and Winston.

Nieuwenhuys, A., Savelsbergh, G. J. P., & Oudejans, R. R. D. (2012). Shoot or don't shoot? Why police officers are more inclined to shoot when they are anxious. *Emotion, 12*(4), 827–833. https://doi.org/10.1037/a0025699

O'Connor, A. M. (1989). Effects of framing and level of probability on patients' preferences for cancer chemotherapy. *Journal of Clinical Epidemiology, 42*(2), 119–126. https://doi.org/10.1016/0895-4356(89)90085-1

Oechssler, J., Roider, A., & Schmitz, P. W. (2009). Cognitive abilities and behavioral biases. *Journal of Economic Behavior & Organization, 72*(1), 147–152. https://doi.org/10.1016/j.jebo.2009.04.018

Parrett, M. (2015). Beauty and the feast: Examining the effect of beauty on earnings using restaurant tipping data. *Journal of Economic Psychology, 49*, 34–46. https://doi.org/10.1016/j.joep.2015.04.002

Piñon, A., & Gambara, H. (2005). A meta-analytic review of framing effect: Risky, attribute and goal framing. *Psicothema, 17*(2), 325–331. https://www.researchgate.net/publication/28108507_A_meta-analytic_review_of_framing_effect_Risky_attribute_and_goal_framing

Pitsakis, K., Souitaris, V., & Nicolaou, N. (2015). The peripheral halo effect: Do academic spinoffs influence universities' research income? *Journal of Management Studies, 52*(3), 321–353. https://doi.org/10.1111/joms.12119

Pool, E., Brosch, T., Delplanque, S., & Sander, D. (2016). Attentional bias for positive emotional stimuli: A meta-analytic investigation. *Psychological Bulletin, 142*(1), 79–106. https://doi.org/10.1037/bul0000026

Pouliakas, K. (2010). Pay enough, don't pay too much or don't pay at all? The impact of bonus intensity on job satisfaction. *Kyklos, International Review for Social Sciences, 63*(4), 597–626. https://doi.org/10.1111/j.1467-6435.2010.00490.x

Read, J. D. (1995). The availability heuristic in person identification: The sometimes misleading consequences of enhanced contextual information. *Applied Cognitive Psychology, 9*(2), 91–121. https://doi.org/10.1002/acp.2350090202

Reingen, P. H., & Kernan, J. B. (1993). Social perception and interpersonal influence: Some consequences of the physical attractiveness stereotype in a personal selling setting. *Journal of Consumer Psychology, 2*(1), 25–38. https://doi.org/10.1016/s1057-7408(08)80073-3

Sacco, J. M., Scheu, C. R., Ryan, A. M., & Schmitt, N. (2003). An investigation of race and sex similarity effects in interviews: A multilevel approach to relational demography. *Journal of Applied Psychology, 88*(5), 852–865. https://doi.org/10.1037/0021-9010.88.5.852

Shantz, A., & Latham, G. (2011). The effect of primed goals on employee performance: Implications for human resource management. *Human Resource Management, 50*(2), 289–299. https://doi.org/10.1002/hrm.20418

Sherif, M., & Hovland, C. I. (1961). *Social judgment: Assimilation and contrast effects in communication and attitude change*. Yale University Press.

Sniezek, J. A., & Henry, R. A. (1989). Accuracy and confidence in group judgment. *Organizational Behavior and Human Decision Processes, 43*(1), 1–28. https://doi.org/10.1016/0749-5978(89)90055-1

Stasson, M. F., Ono, K., Zimmerman, S. K., & Davis, J. H. (1988). Group consensus processes on cognitive bias tasks. *Japanese Psychological Research, 30*(2), 68–77. https://doi.org/10.4992/psycholres1954.30.68

Steiger, A., & Kühberger, A. (2018). A meta-analytic re-appraisal of the framing effect. *Zeitschrift Für Psychologie, 226*(1), 45–55. https://doi.org/10.1027/2151-2604/a000321

Talamas, S. N., Mavor, K. I., & Perrett, D. I. (2016). Blinded by beauty: Attractiveness bias and accurate perceptions of academic performance. *PLoS One, 11*(2), e0148284, 1–18. https://doi.org/10.1371/journal.pone.0148284

Ten Have, S., Rijsman, J., Ten Have, W., & Westhof, J. (2019). *The social psychology of change management: Theories and an evidence-based perspective on social and organizational beings*. Routledge.

Ten Have, S., Ten Have, W., Huijsmans, A., & Van der Eng, N. (2015). *Change competence: Implementing effective change*. Routledge.

Ten Have, S., Ten Have, W., Huijsmans, A.-B., & Otto, M. (2016). *Reconsidering change management: Applying evidence-based insights in change management practice*. Abingdon: Routledge.

Tian, Q., & Smith, J. C. (2011). Attentional bias to emotional stimuli is altered during moderate- but not high-intensity exercise. *Emotion, 11*(6), 1415–1424. https://doi.org/10.1037/a0023568

Tversky, A., & Kahneman, D. (1973). Availability: A heuristic for judging frequency and probability. *Cognitive Psychology, 5*(2), 207–232. https://doi.org/10.1016/0010-0285(73)90033-9

Tversky, A., & Kahneman, D. (1981). The framing of decisions and the psychology of choice. *Science, 211*(4481), 453–458. https://doi.org/10.1126/science.7455683

Tversky, A., & Kahneman, D. (1983). Extensional versus intuitive reasoning: The conjunction fallacy in probability judgment. *Psychological Review, 90*(4), 293–315. https://doi.org/10.1037/0033-295x.90.4.293

Verhulst, B., Lodge, M., & Lavine, H. (2010). The attractiveness halo: Why some candidates are perceived more favorably than others. *Journal of Nonverbal Behavior, 34*(2), 111–117. https://doi.org/10.1007/s10919-009-0084-z

Weibel, A., Rost, K., & Osterloh, M. (2009). Pay for performance in the public sector—benefits and (hidden) costs. *Journal of Public Administration Research and Theory, 20*(2), 387–412. https://doi.org/10.1093/jopart/mup009

Weingarten, E., Chen, Q., McAdams, M., Yi, J., Hepler, J., & Albarracín, D. (2016). From primed concepts to action: A meta-analysis of the behavioral effects of incidentally presented words. *Psychological Bulletin, 142*(5), 472–497. https://doi.org/10.1037/bul0000030

Wexler, B. E., Iseli, M., Leon, S., Zaggle, W., Rush, C., Goodman, A., Esat Imal, A., & Bo, E. (2016). Cognitive priming and cognitive training: Immediate and far transfer to academic skills in children. *Scientific Reports, 6*(1), 1–9. https://doi.org/10.1038/srep32859

Xu, J., & Huang, G. (2020). The relative effectiveness of gain-framed and loss-framed messages in charity advertising: Meta-analytic evidence and implications. *International Journal of Nonprofit and Voluntary Sector Marketing, 25*(4), 1–11. https://doi.org/10.1002/nvsm.1675

Yacoub, M. (2012). *Emotional framing: How do emotions contribute to framing effects?* [Master's thesis, University of North Carolina]. Carolina Digital Repository, 1–47. https://doi.org/10.17615/bgv2-bz55

Yang, W., Ma, J., Chen, H., Maglione, A. G., Modica, E., Rossi, D., Cartocci, G., Bonaiuto, M., & Babiloni, F. (2018). Good news or bad news, which do you want first? The importance of the sequence and organization of information for financial decision-making: A neuro-electrical imaging study. *Frontiers in Human Neuroscience, 12*, 1–14. https://doi.org/10.3389/fnhum.2018.00294

4 Controlling, biases, organizational behaviour, and change

Maarten Hendriks, Cornell Vernooij, and Ruben ten Have

A First Short Story of Controlling, Biases, and Change

Controlling is the need for perceived contingency between behaviour and outcomes. A certain sense of control urges people to improve or learn from past or present situations in order for them to increase their control even further. During organizational change, people may feel that their existing sense of control and competence is challenged or threatened. The replacement or adjustment of routines, habits, cultural patterns, and cognitive schemes necessary for change could lead to serious stress and resistance to change. To foster their sense of control, people tend to overestimate the degree of control over events that are in essence uncontrollable (illusion of control). The heightened perception of control and competence spans past, present, and future situations. For instance, people tend to overestimate their foresight knowledge of an event after the event has occurred, with the potential repercussions of overestimating the responsibility of others and limiting (organizational) learning (hindsight bias). The longing for control is also present in decision-making. People may tend towards seeking more and more information sometimes, even when it cannot affect the outcome of the decision (information bias). Furthermore, in most cases, people attach more weight to avoiding losses than to acquiring equivalent gains (prospect theory). Lastly, people tend to prefer smaller immediate rewards over larger later rewards, a tendency associated with impulsive, risk-taking, and procrastinating behaviour (delay discounting). Despite popular belief that people tend to display more risk-taking behaviour when safety measures are in place, scientific research has not found support for this claim (risk compensation).

Introduction

Controlling is the need for coherence between people's behaviour and the given outcomes. It is one of the two cognitive social motives (the other one is understanding). The social motive to exercise control over one's behaviour and one's circumstances makes people feel competent, effective, and in control of themselves and their environment. The absence of perceived control can lead to feelings of helplessness and cause stress and anxiety. In addition, it is evolutionarily advantageous to have an enhanced sense of control because it increases the ability to learn from situations. If a person

DOI: 10.4324/9781003288237-4

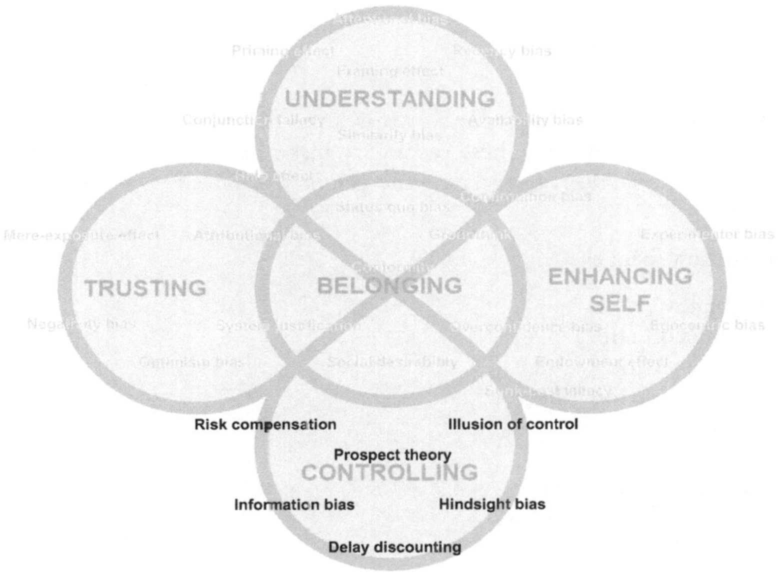

Figure 4.1 Primary Biases Related to the Core Social Motive of Controlling

has no control over certain outcomes, there is simply no reason to change or improve behaviour. If people feel like they can or could have changed the given outcome, they will learn more from their mistakes and successes. The increased perception of control, therefore, facilitates an advanced learning ability in humans and increases their survival odds.

In the context of organizations and, especially during change, the existing sense of control and competence may be challenged or threatened. Changing organizational circumstances could demand replacement or adjustment of routines, habits, cultural patterns, and cognitive schemes. In times of change, people may experience serious stress as a consequence of perceived loss of control. This could, therefore, result in resistance. Controlling is related to change and management concepts such as change capacity, culture, resistance to change, commitment, and performance management. Since controlling increases the survival odds of humans, the brain is programmed with several biases to increase one's perception of control (Fiske, 2004, p. 20). We have identified the following six primary biases that relate to the social motive of control:

Primary biases

Illusion of control
Hindsight bias

Information bias
Risk compensation
Prospect theory
Delay discounting

In addition, the following secondary biases are identified to be related to the social motive of control. These secondary biases are (when relevant) incorporated in the sections concerning the primary biases.

Secondary biases

Ambiguity effect
Disposition effect
Dread aversion
Pseudo-certainty effect
Default effect
Extension neglect
Neglect of probability
Exaggerated expectation
Zero-risk bias
Outcome bias
Hot hand fallacy
Impact bias
Money illusion
Reactance
Parkinson's law
Planning fallacy

The first primary bias this chapter discusses is the overarching bias that gives a heightened sense of control over situations in general—the illusion of control. However, people not only tend to cognitively attain control over their present situations but also over circumstances in the past and the future. We have, therefore, categorized the remaining six biases in chronological order based on the past, present, and future. First, we describe the bias that increases an elevated sense of control over past situations, the hindsight bias. We then illustrate the two biases that direct the present perception of control—the information bias and risk compensation. Finally, we will elaborate on the biases that yield the feeling of control over future events—the prospect theory, framing effect, and delay discounting.

Illusion of control

What is the illusion of control?

The term 'illusion of control' was originally coined by Langer (1975), who defined it as "the expectancy of a personal success probability inappropriately being higher than the objective probability would warrant." More generally, the illusion of control is the tendency to overestimate the degree of control over events that are in essence uncontrollable. The illusion of control can be linked to the expectancy theory, which states that the expectation of the given outcome affects people's behaviour. The illusion of control is shared under the larger set of positive illusions. These positive illusions consist of the three following biases: (1) overestimation of one's abilities compared to that of others (illusory superiority), (2) optimism about the future that is unrealistic (optimism bias, see chapter 5, Trusting), and (3) the illusion of control over things that cannot be controlled (i.e., illusion of control) (Kruger et al., 2009). The positive illusions are prime examples of self-serving biases, in which the perception of reality is distorted to maintain and enhance self-esteem or any other favourable perception of oneself.

The illusion of control can be seen in disparate situations in which people want to increase their extent of control. A striking example is the rainmaking rituals performed across the world throughout history. Various tribes and societies have tried to influence the uncontrollable weather with certain rituals to create optimal circumstances for their crops and other environmental benefits. Another example of the illusion of control is superstition. For instance, the five-time best football player in the world Cristiano Ronaldo is considered to be one of the hardest working players on and off the field. However, to maximize his feeling of control, he has unusual rituals, such as always entering the pitch with his right foot first, which do not objectively support his performance on the field. These unproven beliefs people follow to enhance their perception of control can be both conscious and nonconscious. The illusion of control is often visible when analysing behaviour of gamblers, stock traders, and medical patients. They all have the common belief that despite their situation not being controllable, any form of control could benefit their outcomes.

Secondary (nonscientifically researched) biases related to the illusion of control

Illusory superiority—the tendency to overestimate one's qualities and abilities compared to those of others

Self-serving bias—the tendency to hold a distorted perception of reality to maintain and enhance self-esteem or any other favourable perception of oneself

Planning fallacy—the tendency to make overconfident estimations about the duration of a future task and underestimation of the time needed

What is the relevance of the illusion of control to organizations and change?

The illusion of control can be of great importance in the organizational context. For example, at the individual level, the discrepancy between believed control and actual control of managers (over the behaviour of their employees) can influence how they set goals and objectives and interact with their employees. But also at the organization level, an overestimation of control could have a significant impact and lead to impervious goals and ambitions. Similar to the repeatedly researched application of the bias in gambling, the illusion of control could be used to understand organizational forecasts and investment decisions (Durand, 2003). The illusion of control is closely related to the workings of the planning fallacy, which defines that estimations about the duration of a future task are overconfident and underestimate the time needed. Mitigating the illusion of control could prevent risky investments, unrealistic forecasts, and unattainable goals. Also in times of organizational change, leaders might have a perception of enhanced control over their organization and employees, while in most cases a discrepancy exists between the perception of control and the true degree of control. Recognizing these discrepancies could lead to a better understanding of the extent of their organizational control. Leaders can, in that case, focus more on the things they have control over instead of wasting time on noncontrollable variables. A realistic perception of organizational control makes a positive outcome in the change context more plausible and will lead to attainable goals.

Search strategy

Relevant databases were searched using the term 'illusion of control' both separately and in combination with the terms 'organisation*,' 'work,' 'employ*,' 'leader*,' or 'chang*.' This search yielded 303 results. After removing the duplicates and thorough examination, 2 meta-analyses, 0 systematic reviews, and 2 studies were included.

Main findings

1. *People tend to overestimate the degree of control over events that are in essence uncontrollable (Level B).*

   Stefan and David (2013) found a consistent effect in their meta-analysis of 34 studies. This finding indicates the existence of the illusion of control as a psychological bias. They state that "the illusion of control appears constantly, to variable degrees, in association with numerous situational and psychological factors." Similar to the findings of Stefan and David, Presson and Benassi's (1996) meta-analyses of 53 studies suggest a lack of agreement in terms of the definition and measurement of the illusion of control in scientific research. Presson and Benassi (1996) stipulate that illusory judgement would be a more fitting term, mainly because the studies reviewed in their meta-analysis do not so much reflect the specific aspect of control as they do judgement. Nonetheless, when taking into account that different conceptualizations and measurement methods are used for the illusion of control, Stefan and David stress that the consistent effect they found is a strong indicator of the existence of the illusion of control. They underline the importance of clear conceptualization of the bias in future research to create more robust conclusions but are still quite confident to conclude that people tend to overestimate the degree of control over events.

2. *A strong perception of organizational control by the top management could lead to an overestimation of the success of their organization in forecasts (Level D).*

   Durand (2003) investigated the effect of organizations' illusion of control on their forecasting ability, with a survey taken by 785 French CEOs. He found that "a firm's illusion of control, manifested by higher relative investments in R&D and high self-perception, increases positive forecast biases." This means that organizational illusion of control leads companies to overvalue their resources but undervalue that of their competitors, which makes their own forecast wrongly positive and causes an inaccurate assessment of risks. Durand states that proper forecast ability is a competitive advantage, which in turn could lead to above-average performances. Durand presupposes that an organization that invests in legitimate market-information gathering and employee-capability management could mitigate these effects. This could lead to a firm being better aware of its environmental conditions (i.e., other players in the market) and provide an appropriate judgement of its own capabilities.

3. *Illusion of control is associated with a lower performance in stock trading (Level D).*

   Fenton-O'Creevy et al. (2003) analysed the role of the illusion of control in stock trading in four City of London investment banks with 107 stock traders. They found that traders with higher levels of an illusion of control performed worse than those less biased. The scholars suggest that traders with a high perception of control ignore feedback that reflects their lack of control and that they stick to their original investment strategy even if this strategy is not effective.

Conclusion

There is substantial empirical evidence for the illusion of control. The illusion of control appears constantly in various situations, even when we consider the different methods of measuring and the different conceptualizations. The scientific evidence presented in the meta-analyses by Presson and Benassi (1996) and Stefan and David (2013) confirms that there is a general effect pertaining to the illusion of control, meaning that there is evidence that people tend to think they have control over things they do not. However, the research regarding this phenomenon seems to be still in development. Further studies on the bias would need to find a clear definition of what the concept does and does not entail. This would build towards the operationalization of one unambiguous definition, which could increase the validity and reliability of the studies on the illusion of control. When the bias is systematically untangled, it will increase the knowledge about the extent of the effect of the illusion of control on people and organizations.

Practical reflections

The illusion of control has been shown to be present in the organizational context, together with the adverse consequences that come with it. The believe to be in control in a situation where little or no control can be exercised can lead to overconfident (organizational) forecasts in which risks are inaccurately assessed, which in turn could lead to ineffective goal-setting. Similar effects of the illusion of control are found in investment decisions. A stronger illusion of control leads to the impaired performance of investment bankers and possibly because of overconfidence and inadequate risk assessment. Following the adverse effects on forecasting abilities, risk-taking, and investment performances, organizations should counter the effects of the illusion of control. Keil et al. (2007) suggest that a possible solution could be a heightened level of awareness about the illusion of control through education, training, and discussion about potential situations the bias may appear. On the other hand, they argue that education could also aggravate the problem by making people overconfident in their 'control' over the illusion of control. It is clear that organizations would benefit from research with a clear conceptualization of the illusion of control and subsequently research on how to mitigate the illusion of control.

Hindsight bias

What is hindsight bias?

Hindsight bias causes people to overestimate their foresight knowledge of an event after the event has occurred, and they believe they 'knew it all along.' For instance, after the market crashed in 2008, people stated that the housing market was an economic bubble predestined to burst. However, till the market collapsed, very few people acted like they knew the market was based on a distortion. Hindsight bias is a retrospective illusion of control that can lead to impactful misjudgements of past events. It prompts people to overestimate the responsibility of others for a specific outcome because the consequences of their deeds occur to others as more foreseeable and controllable. The bias can also limit the opportunity to learn from experiences (Blank et al., 2007). If people believe that they knew it all along, they have no reason to question their previous analyses and decisions. A proper understanding of hindsight bias may help people recognize the bias and withstand its tendencies (Guilbault et al., 2004).

Despite the large number of studies concerning hindsight bias, the influence of different cognitive and motivational processes on hindsight bias is fairly unknown (Guilbault et al., 2004). Hawkins and Hastie (1990) have, based on prior research, come up with the frequently used conceptual theory that consists of four processes of hindsight judgement where hindsight bias plays a role. The first is the recall of the belief before the event. If this memory is not cognitively available, the second process is to rejudge the outcome to reconstruct the belief before the event. A proposed way of doing this is the third conceptual process—anchoring on the current outcome (Groß & Pachur, 2019). People adjust their current beliefs and attempt to imagine how they would have reacted without knowing the outcome before the event. This process is closely related to the outcome bias—the tendency to focus more on the outcome rather than on other available information at the time in deciding if a past decision was correctly made. The final proposed process is a motivational process. If people are motivated to be seen in a positive light, they will be more inclined to say that they knew it all along.

Secondary (nonscientifically researched) biases related to hindsight bias

Outcome bias—the tendency to focus primarily on the outcome rather than on other available information at the time in deciding if a past decision was correctly made

What is the relevance of the hindsight bias to organizations and change?

Hindsight bias has been demonstrated to affect people in a variety of (organizational) situations, such as in the workplace, courtroom, classroom, and clinic (Guilbault et al., 2004). Legal situations are one organizational context where hindsight bias specifically plays a large role. During a lawsuit, people always regard the case and the presented facts with outcome knowledge, which makes them especially prone to hindsight bias. Giroux et al. (2016) give a striking example of a 2009 Italian trial: "In 2009, six Italian scientists were asked to predict whether a large earthquake would strike L'Aquila, Italy, after a series of small tremors had frightened the city. These scientists concluded that it was impossible to predict a large earthquake. To their and many innocent victims' misfortune, an earthquake 6.3 in magnitude shook L'Aquila 6 days later, killing over 300 people. Because the scientists had failed to predict this large quake, they were convicted of manslaughter and sentenced to 6 years in prison for their 'criminally mistaken' assessment of risks" (p. 190). As can be seen from the example, judgements based on hindsight bias, which attributes greater predictability to certain events, can have a devastating impact on people's lives in legal settings. Luckily for the scientists, the charges were overthrown in appeal.

Hindsight bias has also been shown to be prevalent in medical settings. Radiologists who were cognizant of cancer in a patient could detect anomalies in earlier radiographs for 82 percent of the time, even though these radiographs were originally diagnosed as normal (Muhm et al., 1983). This could lead to an inflated perception of doctors' responsibility to diagnose patients with diseases. The financial sector is another organizational context where hindsight bias plays a role. Financial institutions often reward bonuses to their investors on the basis of hindsight bias. If a high-risk investment leads to a positive outcome, the investor is honoured with a bonus. If an investment with a similar risk assessment does not have a positive outcome, no bonus is granted to the investor, and the investor could even be disciplined. The bonuses are given based on the assumption that the investor made a good or bad prediction about the outcome of the investment. This line of reasoning attaches too much foreseeability to a volatile financial system. This foregoing reward system, based on hindsight bias, reinforces risk-taking behaviour, which can lead to taking unwanted financial chances. In addition to these specific work contexts, hindsight bias is a psychological effect that also frequently occurs in daily practice within a broader organizational context. As said earlier, hindsight bias may lead to an inability to learn from certain situations and could hinder the prevention of harmful situations.

Search strategy

Relevant databases were searched using the term 'hindsight bias,' 'knew-it-all-along phenomenon,' and 'creeping determinism' both separately and in combination with the terms 'organisation*,' 'work,' 'employ*,' 'leader*,' or 'chang*.' This search yielded 192 results. After removing the duplicates and thorough examination, 3 meta-analyses, 0 systematic reviews, and 0 studies were included.

Main findings

1. *In a substantial number of cases people tend to overestimate their foresight knowledge of an event after the event occurs (Level A).*

   The meta-analyses of Christensen-Szalanski and Willham (1991) of 122 studies, and Guilbault et al. (2004) of 252 studies, showed an overall small to medium effect of hindsight bias. This indicates that people generally can accurately establish former judgements, but in a substantial number of cases people tend to retrospectively enlarged their foresight knowledge of an event of which they know the outcome.

2. *The effect of hindsight bias is larger for neutral events than for positive or negative events (Level A).*

   Christensen-Szalanski and Willham (1991) and Guilbault et al. (2004) state that people show less retrospective judgement influenced by hindsight bias when the event, of which the outcome is known, is positive or negative. People tend to evaluate neutral events with more hindsight bias. The researchers presuppose that positive and negative events are more memorable and that it makes the recollection of the earlier assessment more accurate, which decreases hindsight bias. There was no difference found between the prevalence of hindsight bias with positive or negative events, which implies that they are both equally memorable.

3. *Experts and nonexperts are both equally susceptible to hindsight bias (Level A).*

   Guilbault et al. (2004) found no difference between hindsight bias in experts and nonexperts. They state that even the most experienced individuals are prone to hindsight bias. The scholars emphasize the importance of proper training to reduce hindsight bias in experts because their erroneous decisions can lead to highly undesirable outcomes. Christensen-Szalanski and Willham (1991) found a difference between people familiar with the task or event and those not familiar. Guilbault et al. (2004) argue that not everyone familiar with a topic is an expert. Also, in the meta-analysis from 1991, people assigned to the 'nonfamiliar' group were those who had participated in studies about word problems. Therefore, Guilbault et al. (2004) concluded that the comparison between 'familiar' and 'nonfamiliar' as methodized by Christensen-Szalanski and Willham (1991) was not a valid way to compare experts with nonexperts.

4. *There is no difference in hindsight bias regarding events that did occur or did not occur (Level A).*

   Guilbault et al. (2004) found in their meta-analysis no difference in the degree hindsight bias affects judgements about events that did occur or did not occur. This is an important finding for the legal context; for instance, in criminal law, both an unlawful omission and the perpetration of an offence are punishable and yet affected by hindsight bias. Christensen-Szalanski and Willham (1991) however found a significant difference between events that did or did not occur. Guilbault et al. (2004) tried to replicate these opposing findings from the 1991 meta-analysis. Nevertheless, the replication did not result in any noticeable differences between events that did or did not happen. They state that the meta-analysis from 1991 used a couple of unpublished articles to which they had no access, but that it would be very unlikely that adding these articles would result in a significant difference.

5. *There is no difference in hindsight bias between different age groups (Level B).*

   The meta-analysis from Groß and Pachur (2019), in which they evaluated nine studies that comprised a total of 366 young adults and 368 older adults, showed no difference in judgement accuracy between young adults and older adults. Both groups were equally affected by the hindsight bias. The study additionally found that older adults were less likely to correctly recollect their judgement before a specific event and, therefore, relied more on the process that reconstructs the former judgement. They call this the 'recollection bias.'

6. *No intervention supported by high-level scientific evidence exists that can reduce hindsight bias (Level A).*

Guilbault et al. (2004) show that studies that created a manipulation to reduce the effect of hindsight bias did not help reduce it. This is consistent with the aforementioned notion that it is unclear what underlying processes generate hindsight bias. Nevertheless, Guilbault et al. (2004) also showed that manipulations to increase hindsight bias were effective. These recent studies could create a more profound insight into the workings of hindsight bias. Clear knowledge of the underlying processes of hindsight bias can help create a technique to reduce these judgement errors in the future.

Conclusion

The three included meta-analyses including a large number of studies show that hindsight bias causes people to overestimate their foresight knowledge of an event after the event has occurred. The studies show only a small to medium effect of the bias. This leads to the assumption that people often can accurately establish former judgements. But in a substantial number of cases, hindsight bias has an undeniable effect on people's judgements and decision-making. Despite the small effect, hindsight bias can have detrimental consequences, as can be seen in the Italian trial example. Furthermore, in the cases hindsight bias affects people's cognitive processes, it can have far-reaching consequences in the organizational context. The studies show that a wide variety of people are affected by the bias. Accordingly, experts are as susceptible to hindsight bias as nonexperts, and different age groups are identically affected by the bias. The effects of the bias differ per situation. If the event has a positive or negative outcome, the recollection of the original judgement is more accurate than in a neutral situation. It is suggested that an emotional outcome is more memorable. For situations where a certain event did or did not occur, there is no difference found in the effects of the hindsight bias. The meta-analyses all show the inadequacy of earlier studies to identify the underlying processes of the hindsight bias. This absence has prevented scholars from coming up with a proper intervention to reduce the effects of the hindsight bias.

Practical reflections

As said earlier, hindsight bias has a small effect on judgements and decision-making but can have large consequences if the judgements and decisions are based on hindsight bias. The first organizational effect of hindsight bias is the overestimation of others' responsibilities following the belief that the outcome was foreseeable. In a lot of countries, the foreseeability of an outcome is used as a legal measure to assess the extent of responsibility to an outcome (Giroux et al., 2016). This distorted perception of responsibility due to hindsight bias can lead to a greater (legal) liability in personal and organizational contexts. Hindsight bias could also affect organizational reward systems due to the attribution of greater responsibility to the outcome of an event. This could lead to higher rewards and tougher disciplinary measures than objectively appropriate, which, in turn, could promote undesired organizational behaviours. The second effect of hindsight bias in an organizational context is the possible limiting effect on (organizational) learning. If people believe that they had correctly predicted the outcome, they have no reason to reevaluate their previous thought process, which would lead them to behave in the same way the next time they are in a similar situation.

The meta-analyses could not make a distinction in which people are more prone to the hindsight bias, but it did show that certain events are reviewed with more hindsight bias. This causes us to believe that most people are affected by the bias, but that the extent of hindsight bias differs per situation. Despite the difference in situations, the studies could not explain the inner workings of hindsight bias, which makes it harder to come up with an adequate intervention against the bias. Hence, future research should try to uncover a remedy for hindsight bias to lower its possible negative effects within organizations.

Information bias

What is information bias?

The information bias pertains to the "tendency to seek information even when it cannot affect the outcome" (Vaughan, 2013). This means that people tend to seek more and more information because they believe this will help them make educated decisions. The information bias relates strongly to the 'zero-risk bias' (the tendency to prefer the elimination of risks) and 'ambiguity effect' (the tendency to prefer options of which the odds of a favourable outcome are known). Accumulating information can heighten their present sense of control over their decision-making and the expected outcomes. This is in line with another well-known bias, 'Parkinson's law,' which dictates that people tend to increase the complexity or expand the duration of a task to fill the time available for its completion. The same happens when people seek information. If there is plenty of time available, all this time will be used to seek more information. However, more information does not always increase the quality of the decisions. After a certain point, new information does not consistently add value to the decision-making process and the favourability of the outcome of the decision. The information provided might be about irrelevant alternatives or irrelevant factors for the given choice (Baron et al., 1988). Remarkable about the information bias is that other biases that oppose the information bias, such as the 'confirmation bias' (chapter 6, Self-enhancing) and groupthink (chapter 7, Belonging). Both biases theorize that people search or discuss information they are already familiar with, instead of accumulating additional (unknown) information (Zhang et al., 2014).

Secondary (nonscientifically researched) biases related to Information bias

Zero-risk bias—the tendency to prefer the complete elimination of risks (and benefits) of certain elements, even when alternative options produce greater overall risk reduction
Ambiguity effect—the tendency to prefer an option for which the odds of a favourable outcome are known over one for which they are unknown
Parkinson's law—the tendency to increase the complexity or expand the duration of a task to fill the time available for its completion

What is the relevance of the information bias to organizations and change?

Although the body of work and the amount of research on the information bias is scarce, it is not hard to envisage how it could affect organizations and change. The tendency to seek more information could impede the efficiency of a decision-making process, assignment, or any other set of objectives. According to the information bias, employees and managers would constantly be looking for new, unknowingly irrelevant, information even when currently available information is sufficient for the given purpose. This would unnecessarily lengthen processes, increase costs, and possibly increase the risk of erroneous decision-making due to the pollution of the available information with an abundance of irrelevant information. Furthermore, if people would spend a substantial amount of time on searching for new (unnecessary) information, this leaves them with lesser time for their normal work, which could induce stress.

Search strategy

Relevant databases were searched using the terms 'mere exposure effect' and 'familiarity principle' both separately and in combination with the terms 'organisation*,' 'work,' 'employ*,' 'leader*,' or 'chang*.' This search yielded 202 results. After removing the duplicates and through examination, 0 meta-analyses, 0 systematic reviews, and 1 study was included.

Main findings

1. *People tend to incorporate information that does not affect the outcome in their decision-making (Level D).*

   Baron et al. (1988) found that people tend to consider information not relevant to their decision-making. In their experiments, they instructed subjects to diagnose a certain disease and either gave them information about irrelevant alternatives or gave them extra (relevant) information. The subjects evaluated this information, even if the information could not alter the outcome in terms of diagnosing the disease. Their finding pertained to testing for particular diseases. But the broader implication is that their evidence suggests that the information bias exists in that people seek more information even when unnecessary. The finding provided by Baron et al. (1988) is specific to the medical context. This poses a problem for the generalizability of this finding. When it pertains to medical experiments, people might be more inclined to prefer more information as it concerns their health.

Conclusion

The information bias, while initially intuitive, is not backed by a substantive amount of evidence. Baron et al. (1988) seem to be the only ones to have conceptualized this particular 'cognitive' understanding of the information bias.

Practical reflections

Although in the current world, with information flow being enormous, the information bias might still be quite influential and, therefore, seems relevant for scholars to investigate. Follow-up research is needed to be able to draw conclusions for the organizational and change context.

Risk compensation

What is risk compensation?

Risks of an unwanted outcome are always present. When driving a car you can get into an accident; when running a business, you can go bankrupt; or when going outside your house during a pandemic, you can get infected. People try to avoid these outcomes by mitigating these risks with safety regulations or measures. However, the bias of risk compensation possibly devaluates these safety measures. Risk compensation is a form of behavioural adaptation that causes people to display more risk-taking behaviours when safety regulations/measures are in place. Risk compensation could (partly) offset the positive effect of the safety measures taken. Risk compensation thus contravenes the zero-risk bias (the tendency to prefer the elimination of risks). In the light of controlling, (safety) regulations can feel like a restriction of one's autonomy, hence risk compensation can be seen as taking back autonomous control when other people impose boundaries and regulations. This bias is, therefore, very closely related to the bias of reactance (the tendency to respond when a person feels that someone or something is taking away their choices or limiting the range of alternatives).

Risk compensation played a large role in the discussion concerning the obligation to wear face masks in public locations due to the COVID-19 pandemic. It was said that face masks would give people a false sense of security, which would lead them to violate the social distancing rules. Therefore, it was hypothesized that mandatory face masks would increase the spread of the COVID-19 virus compared to the already effective distancing measures. Due to this bias, policymakers are often hesitant to introduce certain safety measures, because it is generally unclear if the measures do more good than harm. It is essential to understand the workings of this bias to stimulate effective safety measures or to reduce the bias if necessary.

Three possible outcomes follow risk compensation. One, a general risk is reduced after taking safety measures, but risk compensation partly reduces the total effect of the safety measure. Two, risk compensation behaviour levels out the benefits of the safety measure, so the safety measure has no effect on the overall risk. Three, due to risk (over)compensation, the safety measure has a counterproductive effect, which makes the situation worse than before the safety measure. In the first scenario, the safety measure is still expedient; in the latter two scenarios, the safety measure has no desirable outcome especially if perceived from a cost–benefit ratio.

Studies concerning risk compensation primarily focus on safety measures in traffic situations. A very popular subject is the effect of the bicycle helmet regulation on head trauma statistics (Hoye, 2018; Esmaeilikia et al., 2019). Other traffic-related studies include driving feedback applications (Reinmueller et al., 2020), railway crossing visibility (Ward & Wilde, 1996), and seatbelt regulations (Janssen, 1994). If the bias works as is hypothesized, these safety measures would have little to no effect on the actual safety of traffic participants. Another popular subject regarding risk compensation research is the use of protective measures to counter the spread of HIV (Liu et al., 2013; Ortblad et al., 2019).

Secondary (nonscientifically researched) biases related to risk compensation

Reactance—the tendency to respond when a person feels that someone or something is taking away their choices or limiting the range of alternatives

What is the relevance of risk compensation to organizations and change?

As mentioned previously, the main focus of scholars regarding risk compensation has been on traffic and sexual safety. We found no relevant studies that focused on risk compensation within organizations. However, it is very likely that risk compensation also has its influence within organizations. For instance, safety measures concerning manual labour could lead to employees being less attentive due to a false sense of security. This could hinder the workings of the prescribed measures. The same principle applies to risk-taking behaviour in the financial sector. After the market crash in 2008, various financial regulations were installed to prevent said events from happening again. However, if people in financial institutions develop a false sense of security due to these regulations, they could display increased risk-taking behaviour and initiate behaviours that could lead to a new crisis.

Furthermore, a considerable amount of medium to large companies has a risk and compliance department. This signals the importance of risk management within companies. Organizations acknowledge the negative outcomes of risks and try to mitigate risks till an acceptable level is reached. Proper risk management enables effective and safe governance and business processes. Risk compensation could interfere with proper risk management and should, therefore, be reduced to a bare minimum.

Search strategy

Relevant databases were searched using the term 'risk compensation,' 'risk homeostasis,' 'Peltzman effect,' and 'behavioural adaptation' both separately and in combination with the terms 'organisation*,' 'work,' 'employ*,' 'leader*,' or 'chang*.' This search yielded 281 results. After removing the duplicates and thorough examination, 2 systematic reviews of which one was also a meta-analysis, and 1 study were included.

Main findings

1. *The available literature shows minimal to no evidence for the effects of risk compensation (Level A).*

   The combined systematic review and meta-analysis of 21 studies by Hoye (2018) and the systematic review of 23 studies by Esmaeilikia et al. (2019) found no evidence for risk compensation with helmeted cyclists. They even found that helmeted cyclists displayed less risky behaviour than unhelmeted cyclists. Hoye (2018) states that this difference cannot solely be interpreted in terms of behaviour adaptation via risk compensation. Most reviewed studies in both Hoye (2018) and Esmaeilikia et al. (2019) did not directly measure the causal relationship between mandatory helmet use and risk compensation, which may lead to inaccurate results. Furthermore, several possible moderators are conceivable. Hoye suggests that this difference may be due to the general difference between people who wear and do not wear helmets. However, the majority of the used studies are based on real life data, and in real life other moderator variables are always at play. On the basis of these two studies, combined with the absence of other studies with a proper research design, we conclude that the effects of risk compensation in scientific research are either not shown or very limited.

2. *If risk compensation affects behaviour, it would likely still be beneficial to promote safety measures to mitigate unwanted risks (Level D).*

   Yan et al. (2021) investigated the effect of risk compensation of face-mask regulations on time spent at home during the COVID-19 pandemic. They found that the two weeks after the introduction of face-mask regulations, people spent on average 11–24 minutes less at home per day and increased visits to commercial locations. The scholars estimated that this increase was partly the result from social-distancing fatigue. A limitation of this study is that it does not measure, physical distance, handwashing, and face-mask wearing. Furthermore, it is unclear if COVID-19 infections increased to the decrease in time spent at home. This makes it hard to generate any evidence regarding risk compensation. If we were to evaluate risk compensation in light of the time spent at home, the risk of spending time outside increases by 1.1–2.5 percent of the total average time awake. This very small increase combined with the conclusion of the main finding 1, brings us to conclude that in the vast majority of cases it would still be beneficial to promote safety measures and that their effect will not be completely levelled out by risk compensation.

Conclusion

The effects of risk compensation are either not shown in scientific research or very limited. Both systematic reviews found counterintuitive results regarding risk-compensating behaviour when wearing a bicycle helmet. The face-mask study that found a very small effect of possible risk compensation could not control for other variables and could not test the actual outcome of the safety measure, which makes this study not the most robust for testing risk compensation. However, the study did show a small difference between the before and after measure, which could be explained by risk compensation. This small difference cannot be interpreted as a complete compensation of the risk, but more as a small decrease of the effectiveness of the safety measure. This small possible discount outweighs the negative outcomes when no safety measure is effective.

Practical reflections

Unwanted risks should be mitigated to increase the potential performance of an organization. The belief in the risk compensation theory threatens the introduction of effective safety measures. One of the main arguments opposing obligatory face masks during the COVID-19 pandemic was that people would gain a false sense of security when wearing a face mask, which would lead them to disregard other safety measures such as social distancing. It was argued that face masks would not reduce the spread of the coronavirus due to hypothesized risk-compensating behaviour. This argument lasted for a considerable amount of time in different parliaments, during which time more infections could have been prevented by adequate safety measures. As can be seen by this example, arguments that have no foundation in the scientific literature can lead to hazardous and ineffective situations. We, therefore, suggest that until further evidence appears in the scientific literature, the risk-compensation bias should not be included as an argument in discussions about safety measures. It hinders the process of the effective introduction of beneficial preventative measures. There is no clear evidence of the existence of risk compensation, but unnecessary risk should be mitigated. Therefore, it is wise to monitor the effectiveness of safety measures, and if risk compensating behaviour is detected, it should be investigated and tempered if possible.

Prospect theory

What is prospect theory?

The prospect theory was first conceptualized by Kahneman and Tversky (1979). It was formulated as a critique and alternative to the mainstream 'expected utility theory,' which was the standard model for decision-making. The quintessential phrase to typify the new contribution of the model, was "losses loom larger than gains." This phrase delineates the prospect theory, which suggests that when it comes to decision-making people attach more weight to losses than gains. When faced with a risky choice for a gain, people become risk-averse, but when faced with a risky choice for a loss, they become risk-seeking. People thus want to prevent a loss at all times, even when objectively the expected utility value attached to a particular choice is lower. This is most vividly illustrated by the value function shown in the next paragraph. The steeper function for losses than for gains illustrates that losses have a larger perceived impact on value than gains with a similar magnitude.

Kahneman and Tversky (1979) state that when people are faced with a choice, they prefer a sure win over a probable win, even when the expected value of the probable win is higher. For instance, when people are presented with the choice between A (you have a 100 percent chance on € 100 [expected value is € 100]) and B (you have a 50 percent chance on € 210 and a 50% on € 0 [expected value is € 105]), the majority of people will choose option A, implying they are risk-averse when faced with a risky gain even when option B has a statistically higher expected value. Conversely, when faced with the choice between a sure loss and a probable loss, the same people prefer the risky loss with lower expected value over the sure loss—A (you have 100 per cent chance to lose € 100 [expected loss is € 100]) and B (you have a 50 percent chance to lose € 210 or a 50 percent chance to lose € 0 [expected loss is € 105]). When faced with a loss, people tend to be more risk-seeking and thus loss averse. When people want to avoid losses more than they want to seek gains, it is called 'loss aversion.' A striking nonmonetary example of loss aversion is an example by Kahneman (2011) that mentions a study on golfers by Pope and Schweitzer. The objective in golf is to have the least points at the end of the day. A par is seen as 0 points and a birdie as −1. They found that golfers (unconsciously) try a little harder when putting for par (avoiding a loss) than for putting a birdie (acquiring a gain). Kahneman and Tversky (1979) stated at the time that prospect theory departs from the idea that people are rational economic agents, arguing that there is a degree of irrationality due to people basing their decisions on reference points and displaying loss aversion. This bias, therefore, contradicts the rational model of the theory of planned behaviour, which is a person's attitude towards behaviour, subjective norms, and perceived behavioural control in combination shape that person's behavioural intentions and behaviours.

The prospect theory is one of the overarching biases from Kahneman and Tversky (1979) and is therefore strongly related to several other decision-making biases. The focus on avoiding a loss or a negative situation is strongly related to the negativity bias (chapter 5, Trusting). As illustrated by the preceding example, people do not evaluate the expected value of their decision, which shows that they are also influenced by another bias, 'the neglect of probability' (the tendency of people to disregard probability when making a decision under uncertainty). Two other biases are apparent in the gain choice of this example—'the (pseudo) certainty effect,' which theorizes that people have the tendency to prefer an apparent certain option and 'the ambiguity effect,' which hypothesizes that people prefer a choice of which the odds of a favourable outcome are known. Based on 'dread aversion,' the fear of a loss is also apparent in people's perception of the future. This bias states that people generally attach more weight to possible negative future events as opposed to positive future events. Finally, loss aversion and the prospect theory are also linked to a more practical bias, 'the disposition effect.' This bias is based on the tendency of investors to sell assets that have increased in value and holding assets that have lost value. This bias shows that investors are not willing to take risks with assets that have gained value and are willing to take risks with already owned depreciated assets, which in turn is related to the 'sunk-cost fallacy.'

Secondary (nonscientifically researched) biases related to prospect theory

Disposition effect—the tendency of investors to sell assets that have increased in value while holding assets that have lost value

Dread aversion—the tendency to attach more weight to possible negative future events as opposed to positive future events

Pseudo-certainty effect—the tendency to prefer an apparent certain option even though it is factually uncertain

The neglect of probability—the tendency to disregard probability when making a decision under uncertainty

Sunk-cost fallacy—the tendency to follow through on an endeavour if time, effort, or money are already invested into it

What is the relevance of the prospect theory/loss aversion to organizations and change?

The prospect theory can be a factor in decision-making and risk-taking within organizations. Managers or decision-makers might often try harder to avoid possible losses than gaining possible benefits (Tversky & Kahneman, 1991). This means that an organization could be led by the fear of losing rather than by the ambition of gaining and growing. This could lead to smaller investments in innovations through R&D, which could induce the risk of being overtaken by innovative competitors and make the organization irrelevant. Another plausible example of the prospect theory can be found in the rationale behind hiring external expertise. Organizations are less likely to hire external expertise to increase growth or smoothen processes when they are doing well, but they would be more likely to hire external expertise when performances have been poor. However, oftentimes it would be wise to "repair the roof when the sun shines" and hire external expertise even when the organization is doing well to gain an advantage or to avoid future losses and augment growth. Furthermore, as can be seen from the simple experiment mentioned earlier, people tend to not choose the statistical better choice when it opposes the prospect theory, which leads to suboptimal decision-making.

Prospect theory is also relevant in explaining risky behaviour by and in organizations. People experience a general loss aversion, but their loss aversion might induce risk-seeking behaviour when it comes to sure losses and probable losses (Tversky & Kahneman, 1992). Risk-seeking under the prospect of sure losses is illustrative of the phrase "a drowning man will clutch at a straw." When faced with certain loss, firms might consider irrational or very risky investments, even when there is a high probability of an even greater loss than the sure loss.

Search strategy

Relevant databases were searched using the terms 'loss aversion' and 'prospect theory' both separately and in combination with the terms 'organisation*,' 'work,' 'employ*,' 'leader*,' or 'chang*.' This search yielded 6098 results. After removing the duplicates and thorough examination, 2 meta-analyses, 1 systematic review, and 1 study were included.

Main findings

1. *People tend to prefer avoiding losses to acquiring equivalent gains, specifically in decision-making concerning product choices and monetary gains (Level B).*

   In their meta-analysis of 33 studies Neumann and Böckenholt (2014) analysed the role of loss aversion in product choice. Their findings confirm that there is loss aversion among consumers when it comes to product choice, as loss aversion was significant across their 109 product-choice observations. At the same time, the existence of a loss aversion is dependent on contextual factors such as product type and consumer characteristics. For example, durable goods are, according to the findings of the Neumann and Böckenholt (2014), subject to more loss aversion than nondurable goods. The scholars state that durable goods are often higher in price and more complex, thus consumers are most at risk of the perception of losing a bigger investment because they can actually lose a bigger investment. This suggests, that when it comes to consumer goods, loss aversion is subject to particular moderators as portrayed in the experiments by Kahneman and Tversky (1979) and Tversky and Kahneman (1991, 1992). Wilson et al. (2008) conducted a series of experiments to analyse loss aversion in individual decision-making. Their general results are in line with the concept of loss aversion when it comes to individuals evaluating their financial gains and losses. In addition, their findings indicate that the prospect theory might be of less explanatory value when it comes to decisions outside the financial domain. According to the authors, the value function in environmental and social domains bears a closer resemblance to a utility-based model, where the losses and gains are weighed equally. When it comes to social relations and goods or other things that cannot be measured in monetary value (such as the environment), loss aversion could be less prevalent.

2. *Loss framing is more effective than gain framing in altering behaviour (Level C).*

   In their systematic review of 47 articles, Homar and Cvelbar (2021) investigated the importance of loss aversion in environmental decisions. According to the authors, when it comes to environmental decisions, people are more likely to change to pro-environmental behaviour if an environmental problem such as climate change is framed as a loss that must be prevented. They argue that policymakers should, therefore, continuously stress the losses of not performing pro-environmental behaviour and not the gains of performing said behaviour.

3. *Loss aversion is considered to be a factor in causing unethical behaviour (Level B).*

   Belle and Cantarelli (2017) conducted a meta-analytic review of 137 experiments on the causes of unethical behaviour. Among the twelve causes identified, loss aversion is one possible cause of unethical behaviour according to their findings. However, no hard generalizable conclusions can be drawn from this meta-analysis, because only five studies have investigated the effect of loss aversion on unethical behaviour.

Conclusion

There is consistent evidence for the existence of the prospect theory. This means that people tend to experience loss aversion, consistent with Kahneman and Tversky's original "losses loom larger than gains" paradigm. There are some questions when it comes to measuring prospect theory and the different effects it predicts. Prospect theory does not merely include loss aversion, it also includes the cognitive weighing of gains. Nonetheless, loss aversion seems to be the effect that is most often measured and researched. Also, some questions pertaining to the workings of this bias have been raised regarding nonmonetary value. In real-life situations, an action is often not evaluated on the basis of exact monetary costs or gains with attached probabilities. On the contrary, decision-making is often highly complex with unknown outcomes, and it also often involves decisions that are not within the financial domain.

Practical implications

The prospect theory and in particular loss aversion can benefit and hamper change in organizations. Although loss aversion could be less prevalent in day-to-day decision-making when the effect of decisions is not expressed in concrete monetary value, it is still conceivable that the prospect theory can play a role in the organizational context. The findings of Homar and Cvelbar (2021) suggest loss-framing can be used to alter organizational behaviour. One could imagine that framing particular assignments as a failure that must be prevented might increase the pressure on employees/managers, and with that productivity. This might be done via nudging as these authors describe. However, considering consistently framing something as a loss increases the pressure, it is questionable whether it makes an organization more productive in the long run.

Furthermore, loss aversion can affect decision-making within organizations, which makes the decision-making process more error-prone. For instance, loss aversion might prevent organizations from making much-needed changes when confronted with the probabilities of losses. In addition, they might also display reckless behaviour when comparing sure and probable losses. A change project might not be cancelled even when there is a high probability of a large loss, because firms want to prevent sure losses at all times. This is in part related to the 'sunk-cost fallacy'. Even when decisions cannot clearly be defined in monetary value, it is important for board members and other employees not to cloud their judgement because of loss aversion.

Delay discounting

What is delay discounting?

People tend to prefer smaller immediate rewards over larger later rewards. This bias is called 'delay discounting' or 'hyperbolic discounting' because the extent of discounting often follows a hyperbolic curve (Logue, 1988). The subjective value of a reward is 'discounted' if the delay till the receipt of the reward increases. For example, people often prefer to receive € 100, today over € 110, in a week, but prefer € 110, in an hour instead of € 100, right now. It is remarkable that people cognitively devaluate future rewards but based on the 'money illusion' tend to mistakenly value money at face value (nominal value) instead of its purchasing power (real value). This means that people generally do not devaluate monetary value based on objective devaluation such as inflation. Delay discounting also applies to nonmonetary rewards, for instance, in health behaviour. People tend to choose short-term unhealthy behaviours, such as smoking, drinking, gambling, and overeating, instead of the long-term health benefits that follow from abstaining from these behaviours. Delay discounting was first introduced by behavioural economists as a theoretical model (Bleichrodt & Gafni, 1996). Later, delay discounting research became very popular in experimental psychology and clinical neuroscience (Noda et al., 2020). Scholars see delay discounting as a component of self-control and relate the concept to various maladaptive behavioural concepts such as impulsiveness, procrastination, addiction, and risk-taking. Regarding the social motive of control, the less people are affected by delay discounting the more control they have over their future.

Secondary (nonscientifically researched) biases related to delay discounting

Money illusion—the tendency to mistakenly value money at face value (nominal value) instead of its purchasing power (real value)

What is the relevance of delay discounting to organizations and change?

Delay discounting can be very relevant in an organizational context and for organizational change. Several notions can be made about the relevance of delay discounting. Firstly, organizations should care for and support their employees because healthy employees are more productive and cost less (Ford et al., 2011). They should prevent or decrease delay discounting among their employees to make them less susceptible to unhealthy and maladaptive behaviours associated with delay discounting. Reducing delay discounting among employees could also decrease procrastination and increase their efficiency. Thirdly, firms should try to reduce delay discounting specifically among employees responsible for negotiating deals with third parties or customers considering it reduces the subjective value of a reward but does not diminish the absolute value of rewards over time (inflation not included). Therefore, if dealmakers are susceptible to delay discounting, this could lead to suboptimal agreements for the organization. Fourthly, awareness of delay discounting among dealmakers could also be used the other way around. This bias could be exploited for marketing purposes to increase the value in the agreements made. Many organizations already use the effects of delay discounting; for instance, the 'buy now, pay later' principle is very common these days for consumer products. Furthermore, various organizations currently offer loans to consumers, which makes it possible for them to buy immediately without having to save up for the product. This construct often incorporates high interest rates, which makes consumers pay a lot more for the product over time.

Search strategy

Relevant databases were searched using the term 'hyperbolic discounting' and 'delay discounting' both separately and in combination with the terms 'organisation*,' 'work,' 'employ*,' 'leader*,' or 'chang*.' This search yielded 720 results. After removing the duplicates and thorough examination, 5 meta-analyses and 2 systematic reviews were included.

Main findings

1. *There is strong neuroscientific evidence for the cognitive processes of delay discounting (Level A).*

   In their systematic review of 31 neuroscientific MRI-studies Noda et al. (2020) found that delay discounting has a strong neurological basis. The MRI-studies display activation of the brain parts responsible for reward valuation, cognitive control and predictions, and affective networks during a delay-discounting task. In people with addiction or psychiatric disorders, the activation of these brain parts is even greater.

2. *Delay discounting is associated with impulsive, risk-taking, and procrastinating behaviour (Level C).*

   Story et al. (2014) found in their systematic review of 112 studies that the degree of delay discounting does not solely predict impulsive and risk-taking behaviour. The study focused primarily on impulsive and risky health behaviours regarding smoking, drug use, and overeating. They concluded that intention-incongruent actions are often triggered by environmental cues or motivational changes that make it impossible to predict impulsive or risky (health) behaviours based solely on delay discounting. In addition, Steel (2007) found in his meta-analysis of 691 independent correlations that delay discounting is a possible predictor of procrastination. However, other cognitive processes also affect this behaviour, which makes it remarkably difficult to predict procrastination solely based on the tendency to discount delays. These studies show that delay discounting affects behaviour but that a substantial amount of other cognitive and environmental factors should be considered when attempting to predict behaviour.

3. *Delay discounting is slightly to moderately related to risky choices (Level B).*

   Johnson et al. (2020) found in their meta-analysis of 26 studies, a small to moderate correlation between delay discounting and risky choices. As the correlations across the studies are highly variable, it is hard to make solid conclusions about the relationship between delay discounting and risky behaviour. Johnson et al. (2020) suppose that the high variation of correlations results from possible moderator variables. Because of this presumed multitude of moderator variables, it is problematic to predict risky behaviour based solely on delay discounting. Therefore, possible moderators such as environmental cues or motivation changes, intelligence (see main findings 2 and 4) should be taken into account.

4. *Intelligent people are less prone to delay discounting (Level B).*

   In their meta-analysis of 24 studies, Shamosh and Gray (2008) showed that intelligent people are less susceptible to delay discounting. Intelligent people demonstrated less of a preference for immediate smaller rewards versus delayed larger rewards. They state that this finding has a broad social impact because people with a higher delay discount tend to have a higher credit card debt and insufficient retirement savings and are generally less able to accumulate financial assets over time.

5. *There is no difference in delay discounting for men and women (Level B).*

   Cross et al. (2011) hypothesized that because men are over-represented in socially problematic behaviours, they are more impulsive than women, which they linked to delay discounting. However, in their meta-analysis of 277 studies with 741 effect sizes, they found no difference between women and men regarding delay discounting.

6. *Delay discounting can be reduced by training and manipulations (Level A).*

   Scholten et al. (2019) revealed in their meta-analysis of 98 studies that manipulations and trainings can successfully reduce delay discounting.

Their study showed that delay discounting is a changeable cognitive construct. The scholars found it remarkable that simple manipulations showed a greater reduction of delay discounting than active trainings. However, they presuppose that this difference stems from the research method used in the reviewed studies. The manipulation studies often used a within-subject design and tested the effect right after the manipulation, which makes it easier to detect an effect. The studies based on the trainings were generally looking for the long-term effect of the training on delay discounting. Because the effects of manipulations can be short-lived in practice and training focuses on long-term change, the scholars favour trainings over simple manipulations. They found that acceptance/mindfulness-based and future-oriented trainings as most promising to investigate further in future research. It is yet unclear what causes the trainings to reduce delay discounting; however, the scholars suggest that training should focus on the perception of time and the magnitude of the reward.

Conclusion

The bias of delay discounting has substantial scientific backing in the available literature. Noda et al. (2020) found neuroscientific evidence of delay discounting and showed the brain parts most strongly associated with the existence of the bias. In scientific evidence, delay discounting is linked to impulsive, risk-taking, and procrastinating behaviour. The meta-analyses show that predicting behaviour solely based on delay discounting is difficult because of the numerous variables that affect behaviour and moderate the effect delay discounting has on behaviour, such as environmental cues or motivational changes. In addition, two important moderating variables have been thoroughly researched, intelligence and sex differences. Studies show that intelligent people are less likely to discount future rewards and are, therefore, less prone to the previously stated dysfunctional behaviours. Furthermore, there is no difference between men and women regarding delay discounting. Despite the inability to create isolated, causal understanding of the effect of delay discounting on behaviour, it is beneficial to reduce this bias within people, because, in coherence with other factors, it is associated with erroneous and unhealthy behaviours. Scholars have found trainings focused on the long-term based on acceptance/mindfulness and future-oriented trainings most promising to investigate and use in practice.

Practical reflections

Following aforementioned findings, we can conclude that delay discounting has an effect on behaviour and is associated with behaviours with negative outcomes. However, the findings also state that understanding and predicting behaviour is complex and cannot solely be done based on delay discounting. This means that reducing delay discounting can have beneficial effects on the behaviour of employees, however behaviour will also be affected by copious other variables. Delay discounting should be taken seriously, but reducing this bias is not a magic bullet. Reducing delay discounting within employees could benefit their health, efficiency and could be profitable for dealmakers in the organization. Therefore, organizations could include long-term based acceptance/mindfulness-based and future-oriented trainings to reduce delay discounting bias for their employees. Furthermore, the understanding of delay discounting could be used for marketing purposes; however, ethical considerations should be taken into account.

Bibliography

Arkes, H. R., & Ayton, P. (1999). The sunk cost and concorde effects: Are humans less rational than lower animals? *Psychological Bulletin*, *125*(5), 591–600. https://doi.org/10.1037/0033-2909.125.5.591

Baron, J., Beattie, J., & Hershey, J. C. (1988). Heuristics and biases in diagnostic reasoning: II. Congruence, information, and certainty. *Organizational Behavior and Human Decision Processes*, *42*(1), 88–110. https://doi.org/10.1016/0749-5978(88)90021-0

Belle, N., & Cantarelli, P. (2017). What causes unethical behavior? A meta-analysis to set an agenda for public administration research. *Public Administration Review*, 77(3), 327–339. https://doi.org/10.1111/puar.12714

Blank, H., Musch, J., & Pohl, R. F. (2007). Hindsight bias: On being wise after the event. *Social Cognition*, *25*(1), 1–9. https://doi.org/10.1521/soco.2007.25.1.1

Bleichrodt, H., & Gafni, A. (1996). Time preference, the discounted utility model and health. *Journal of Health Economics*, *15*(1), 49–66. https://doi.org/10.1016/0167-6296(95)00031-3

Christensen-Szalanski, J. J., & Willham, C. F. (1991). The hindsight bias: A meta-analysis. *Organizational Behavior and Human Decision Processes*, *48*(1), 147–168. https://doi.org/10.1016/0749-5978(91)90010-q

Cross, C. P., Copping, L. T., & Campbell, A. (2011). Sex differences in impulsivity: A meta-analysis. *Psychological Bulletin*, *137*(1), 97–130. https://doi.org/10.1037/a0021591

Durand, R. (2003). Predicting a firm's forecasting ability: The roles of organizational illusion of control and organizational attention. *Strategic Management Journal*, *24*(9), 821–838. https://doi.org/10.1002/smj.339

Esmaeilikia, M., Radun, I., Grzebieta, R., & Olivier, J. (2019). Bicycle helmets and risky behaviour: A systematic review. *Transportation Research Part F: Traffic Psychology and Behaviour*, *60*, 299–310. https://doi.org/10.1016/j.trf.2018.10.026

Fenton-O'Creevy, M., Nicholson, N., Soane, E., & Willman, P. (2003). Trading on illusions: Unrealistic perceptions of control and trading performance. *Journal of Occupational and Organizational Psychology*, *76*(1), 53–68. https://doi.org/10.1348/096317903321208880

Ford, M. T., Cerasoli, C. P., Higgins, J. A., & Decesare, A. L. (2011). Relationships between psychological, physical, and behavioural health and work performance: A review and meta-analysis. *Work & Stress*, *25*(3), 185–204. https://doi.org/10.1080/02678373.2011.609035

Giroux, M. E., Coburn, P. I., Harley, E. M., Connolly, D. A., & Bernstein, D. M. (2016). Hindsight bias and law. *Zeitschrift Für Psychologie*, *224*(3), 190–203. https://doi.org/10.1027/2151-2604/a000253

Groß, J., & Pachur, T. (2019). Age differences in hindsight bias: A meta-analysis. *Psychology and Aging*, *34*(2), 294–310. https://doi.org/10.1037/pag0000329

Guilbault, R. L., Bryant, F. B., Brockway, J. H., & Posavac, E. J. (2004). A meta-analysis of research on hindsight bias. *Basic and Applied Social Psychology*, *26*(2–3), 103–117. https://doi.org/10.1080/01973533.2004.9646399

Hawkins, S. A., & Hastie, R. (1990). Hindsight: Biased judgments of past events after the outcomes are known. *Psychological Bulletin*, *107*(3), 311–327. https://doi.org/10.1037/0033-2909.107.3.311

Homar, A. R., & Cvelbar, L. K. (2021). The effects of framing on environmental decisions: A systematic literature review. *Ecological Economics*, *183*, 1–18. https://doi.org/10.1016/j.ecolecon.2021.106950

Hoye, A. (2018). Recommend or mandate? A systematic review and meta-analysis of the effects of mandatory bicycle helmet legislation. *Accident Analysis & Prevention*, *120*, 239–249. https://doi.org/10.1016/j.aap.2018.08.001

Janssen, W. (1994). Seat-belt wearing and driving behavior: An instrumented-vehicle study. *Accident Analysis & Prevention*, *26*(2), 249–261. https://doi.org/10.1016/0001-4575(94)90095-7

Johnson, K. L., Bixter, M. T., & Luhmann, C. C. (2020). Delay discounting and risky choice: Meta-analytic evidence regarding single-process theories. *Judgment and Decision Making*, *15*(3), 381–400. http://journal.sjdm.org/18/18308/jdm18308.pdf

Kahneman, D. (2011). *Thinking, fast and slow*. Farrar, Straus & Giroux Inc.

Kahneman, D., & Tversky, A. (1979). Prospect theory: An analysis of decision under risk. *Econometrica*, *47*(2), 263–291. https://doi.org/10.2307/1914185

Keil, M., Depledge, G., & Rai, A. (2007). Escalation: The role of problem recognition and cognitive bias. *Decision Sciences*, *38*(3), 391–421. https://doi.org/10.1111/j.1540-5915.2007.00164.x

Kruger, J., Chan, S., & Roese, N. (2009). (Not so) positive illusions. *Behavioral and Brain Sciences*, *32*(6), 526–527. https://doi.org/10.1017/s0140525x09991270

Langer, E. J. (1975). The illusion of control. *Journal of Personality and Social Psychology*, *32*(2), 311–328. https://doi.org/10.1037/0022-3514.32.2.311

Liu, A. Y., Vittinghoff, E., Chillag, K., Mayer, K., Thompson, M., Grohskopf, L., Colfax, G., Pathak, S., Gvetadze, R., O'Hara, B., Collins, B., Ackers, M., Paxton, L., & Buchbinder, S. P. (2013). Sexual risk behavior among HIV-uninfected men who have sex with men participating in a tenofovir preexposure prophylaxis randomized trial in the United States. *JAIDS Journal of Acquired Immune Deficiency Syndromes*, *64*(1), 87–94. https://doi.org/10.1097/qai.0b013e31828f097a

Logue, A. W. (1988). Research on self-control: An integrating framework. *Behavioral and Brain Sciences*, *11*(4), 665–679. https://doi.org/10.1017/s0140525x00053978

Muhm, J. R., Miller, W. E., Fontana, R. S., Sanderson, D. R., & Uhlenhopp, M. A. (1983). Lung cancer detected during a screening program using four-month chest radiographs. *Radiology*, *148*(3), 609–615. https://doi.org/10.1148/radiology.148.3.6308709

Neumann, N., & Böckenholt, U. (2014). A meta-analysis of loss aversion in product choice. *Journal of Retailing*, *90*(2), 182–197. https://doi.org/10.1016/j.jretai.2014.02.002

Noda, Y., Barr, M. S., ElSalhy, M., Masuda, F., Tarumi, R., Ogyu, K., Wada, M., Tsugawa, S., Miyazaki, T., Nakajima, S., & Mimura, M. (2020). Neural correlates of delay discount alterations in addiction and psychiatric disorders: A systematic review of magnetic resonance imaging studies. *Progress in Neuro-Psychopharmacology and Biological Psychiatry*, *99*, 1–15. https://doi.org/10.1016/j.pnpbp.2019.109822

Ortblad, K. F., Stalter, R. M., Bukusi, E. A., Ngure, K., Mujugura, A., Celum, C., Baeten, J. M., & Heffron, R. (2019). No evidence of sexual risk compensation following PrEP initiation among heterosexual HIV serodiscordant couples in Kenya and Uganda. *AIDS and Behavior*, *24*(5), 1365–1375. https://doi.org/10.1007/s10461-019-02720-4

Presson, P. K., & Benassi, V. A. (1996). Illusion of control: A meta-analytic review. *Journal of Social Behavior & Personality*, *11*(3), 493–510.

Pronin, E., Lin, D. Y., & Ross, L. (2002). The bias blind spot: Perceptions of bias in self versus others. *Personality and Social Psychology Bulletin*, *28*(3), 369–381. https://doi.org/10.1177/0146167202286008

Reinmueller, K., Kiesel, A., & Steinhauser, M. (2020). Adverse behavioral adaptation to adaptive forward collision warning systems: An investigation of primary and secondary task performance. *Accident Analysis & Prevention*, *146*, 1–12. https://doi.org/10.1016/j.aap.2020.105718

Scholten, H., Scheres, A., de Water, E., Graf, U., Granic, I., & Luijten, M. (2019). Behavioral trainings and manipulations to reduce delay discounting: A systematic review. *Psychonomic Bulletin & Review*, *26*(6), 1803–1849. https://doi.org/10.3758/s13423-019-01629-2

Shamosh, N. A., & Gray, J. R. (2008). Delay discounting and intelligence: A meta-ana lysis. *Intelligence*, *36*(4), 289–305. https://doi.org/10.1016/j.intell.2007.09.004

Steel, P. (2007). The nature of procrastination: A meta-analytic and theoretical review of quintessential self-regulatory failure. *Psychological Bulletin*, *133*(1), 65–94. https://doi.org/10.1037/0033-2909.133.1.65

Stefan, S., & David, D. (2013). Recent developments in the experimental investigation of the illusion of control: A meta-analytic review. *Journal of Applied Social Psychology*, *43*(2), 377–386. https://doi.org/10.1111/j.1559-1816.2013.01007.x

Story, G. W., Vlaev, I., Seymour, B., Darzi, A., & Dolan, R. J. (2014). Does temporal discounting explain unhealthy behavior? A systematic review and reinforcement learning perspective. *Frontiers in Behavioral Neuroscience*, *8*(76), 1–20. https://doi.org/10.3389/fnbeh.2014.00076

Tversky, A., & Kahneman, D. (1991). Loss aversion in riskless choice: A reference-dependent model. *The Quarterly Journal of Economics*, *106*(4), 1039–1061. https://doi.org/10.2307/2937956

Tversky, A., & Kahneman, D. (1992). Advances in prospect theory: Cumulative representation of uncertainty. *Journal of Risk and Uncertainty*, *5*(4), 297–323. https://doi.org/10.1007/bf00122574

Vaughan, M. (2013). *The thinking effect: Rethinking thinking to create great leaders and the new value worker* (Illustrated ed.). Nicholas Brealey.

Ward, N. J., & Wilde, G. J. (1996). Driver approach behaviour at an unprotected railway crossing before and after enhancement of lateral sight distances: An experimental investigation of a risk perception and behavioural compensation hypothesis. *Safety Science*, *22*(1–3), 63–75. https://doi.org/10.1016/0925-7535(96)00006-9

Wilson, R. S., Arvai, J. L., & Arkes, H. R. (2008). My loss is your loss . . . sometimes: Loss aversion and the effect of motivational biases. *Risk Analysis*, *28*(4), 929–938. https://doi.org/10.1111/j.1539-6924.2008.01065.x

Yan, Y., Bayham, J., Richter, A., & Fenichel, E. P. (2021). Risk compensation and face mask mandates during the COVID-19 pandemic. *Scientific Reports, 11*(1), 1–11. https://doi.org/10.1038/s41598-021-82574-w

Zhang, H., Basadur, T. M., & Schmidt, J. B. (2014). Information distribution, utilization, and decisions by new product development teams. *Journal of Product Innovation Management, 31*, 189–204. https://doi.org/10.1111/jpim.12200

5 Trusting, biases, organizational behaviour and change

Judith Stuijt, Cornell Vernooij, and Flore Louwers

A First Short Story of Trusting, Biases, and Change

Trusting is the need to view others as basically benign and to see the world as a benevolent place. Trust in leadership and trust in the organization have beneficial effects on commitment, job satisfaction, and performance. Conversely, a lack of trust in the organization's leaders may hinder change by causing or aggravating resistance to change. To be able to have confidence or faith in the people and the world around us, people rely on several mental shortcuts. People have the tendency to prefer information because of repeated exposure to that information (mere exposure effect). Thus, to create trust, organizational leaders should increase visibility of the change and themselves as leaders of the change in the organization. People have the tendency to judge the trustworthiness of information by relying on the - either positive or negative - valence of information. They put greater weight on negative events or stimuli compared to positive instances (negativity bias). As people perceive themselves to be more likely to experience positive events compared to others (optimism bias), they are likely to become overly optimistic about the time they need to complete a certain task. People make (inaccurate) decisions based on assigning causes to behaviour of themselves and others (attributional bias). Better understanding attributions can help to design and develop well-thought-out and contextual, sensitive and sensible 'paths to change' and to being more able to deal with resistance to change.

Introduction

Trusting, the need to view others as basically benign and to see the world as a benevolent place, is the fourth core social motive and one of the two affective motives (the other one is self-enhancing). Trust involves "confidence or faith that some other, upon whom we must depend, will not act in ways that occasion us painful consequences" (Boon, 1995). People are naturally inclined to trust others. This can make them vulnerable, but also facilitates interactions with others. People differ and some people are relatively paranoid instead of trusting, although most people are biased towards seeing the best in other people and do expect fairly good outcomes from the interaction with other people (Fiske, 2004). From an evolutionary perspective, trusting is advantageous since it facilitates group cohesion and provides a relatively efficient mechanism for group functioning (Fiske, 2004).

DOI: 10.4324/9781003288237-5

In the organizational context, trust is 'materialized' in bonds or relational ties between organizational members that reduce stress and provide security, safety and comfort. Trusting is present or visible in, for example, organizational citizenship behaviour, cooperation, commitment, organizational values and acceptance of change. Trust in general, also among employees, is a vital component of effective working relations. Leaders, managers and change agents must be aware of the potential effects of trust or a lack of trust in their organizations, especially during change processes. Trusting is related to change and management topics such as leadership, organizational culture, communication, resistance and capacity to change. Trust in leadership as well as organizational trust have beneficial effects on a wide variety of organizational outcomes such as organizational commitment, job satisfaction and performance (Dirks & Ferrin, 2002; Colquitt et al., 2007). Trust in leadership or management represents the belief that managers will act in their people's best interests (Fugate, 2013). Research shows that supervisory trust relates positively to affective commitment to a change initiative (Neves & Caetano, 2006). Reversely, a lack of trust in an organization 's leader may hinder change by causing or aggravating resistance to change (Kriegel & Brandt, 1996).

We have identified four primary biases related to the social motive of trusting:

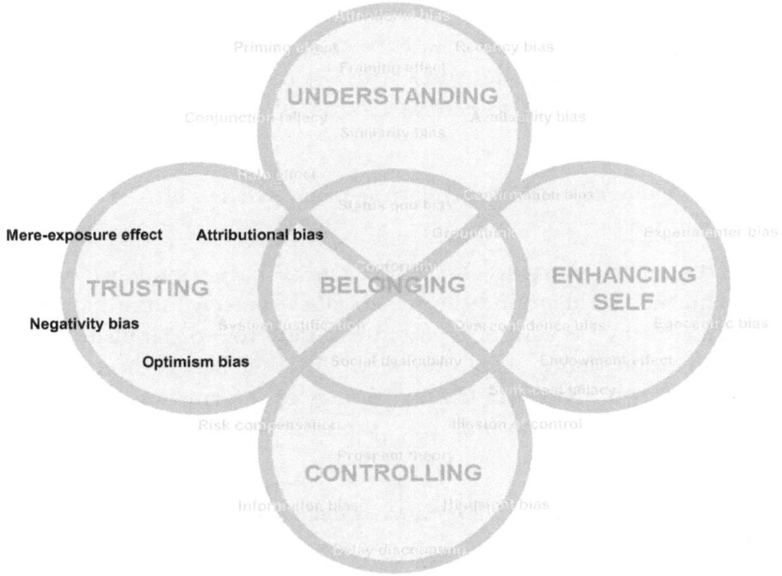

Figure 5.1 Primary Biases Related to the Core Social Motive of Trusting

Primary biases

Mere exposure effect
Negativity bias
Optimism bias
Attributional bias

Additionally, the following secondary biases are identified to be related to the social motive of trusting. These secondary biases are (when relevant) incorporated in the sections concerning the primary biases.

Secondary biases

Automation bias
Normalcy bias
Pro-innovation bias
Truthiness
Rhyme-as-reason effect
Illusory truth effect
Subjective validation
Declinism
Pessimism bias
Actor–observer bias
Empathy gap
Third person bias

In this chapter, the primary biases are categorized into (1) biases related to judgements regarding the trustworthiness of information and (2) biases related to judgements in prospective and causal reasoning.

Biases relating to judgements regarding the trustworthiness of information

One of the mental shortcuts that people take to have confidence or faith in others and the world around them is to falsely perceive information to be more trustworthy because of repeated exposure to—or familiarity with—that information (mere exposure effect). Another bias is the tendency to make judgements about the trustworthiness of information by relying on the valence of information (negative vs. positive) (negativity bias).

Biases relating to judgements in prospective and causal reasoning

People's inherent need to trust also leads to systematic errors in prospective and causal reasoning. One of these errors is their tendency to falsely assume that they are more likely than others to experience positive events, while perceiving they are less at risk than others to experience negative events (optimism bias). The second bias is all about the errors people make when assigning causes to their own behaviour and that of others (attributional bias).

Mere exposure effect

What is the mere exposure effect?

The mere exposure effect describes the human tendency to develop preferences for stimuli that are familiar. For this reason, it is also known as the 'familiarity principle.' A frequently used example is that when you hear a song on the radio for the first time, you hate it, but having heard it many times, you begin to like it. And after a while, you might even prefer the song over all other songs you know. The earliest recordings of the mere exposure effect date back to the end of the nineteenth century, when German psychologist Gustav Fechner wrote of a 'glow of warmth' felt in the presence of something familiar. But American social psychologist Robert Zajonc was the first to empirically test the mere exposure effect in 1968. In his experiments, Zajonc found that subjects who were shown Chinese characters several times responded more favourably to these characters. After Zajonc's study, the mere exposure effect has been documented by countless empirical studies and has had its influence and pervasiveness trumpeted by numerous psychology textbooks (e.g., Kalat, 2010; Myers & Dewall, 2016; Schacter et al., 2015) and reviews of the literature about human attraction (e.g., Berscheid & Walster, 1978; Berscheid & Reis, 1998; Montoya & Horton, 2014; Montoya et al., 2017).

Over the years, scientists and researchers have developed a multitude of theories about why the mere exposure effect occurs. The four most influential models so far are (1) Zajonc's affective model, (2) the original two-factor model, (3) the modified two-factor model, and (4) the processing fluency model. Zajonc's affective model states that people have evolved to experience an instinctive fear response when exposed to a novel stimulus. This fear response declines on repeated exposure of the stimulus and in the absence of negative consequences of the stimulus. This is called 'stimulus habituation.' Berlyne's two-factor model is consistent with Zajonc's approach. However, it goes one step further and proposes a second process besides habituation called 'stimulus satiation.' Satiation increases the amount of boredom after repeated exposure to the same stimulus, resulting in less positive affection towards the stimulus after having been exposed to it numerous times. As a third model, Bornstein, in 1989, introduced the modified version of the two-factor model, in which he added an evolutionary explanation for the mere exposure effect:

> It is adaptive for adults to prefer the familiar over the novel. Although there are sometimes advantages to exploring the new and unfamiliar

> in certain situations (e.g., one may be more likely to come upon an unnoticed but potentially useful object when unfamiliar stimuli are explored), some risk is inherent in any venture into the unknown.
>
> (p. 282)

The fourth model, the 'processing fluency model' was introduced by Jacoby and colleagues. The model proposed that previously perceived stimuli are encoded and processed more quickly and more easily than novel stimuli. However, people tend to 'misattribute' this fluency to liking, resulting in a more positive attitude towards the stimulus. These four models have been influential in thinking about and explaining the mere exposure effect. Although the scientific evidence about these theories is not conclusive (for more explanation, see main finding 2).

One concept related to the mere exposure effect is the 'illusory truth effect,' which describes the human tendency to believe information more easily when it has been repeated numerous times. One recent example of the illusory truth effect was displayed in the early stages of the global COVID-19 pandemic when the belief among American citizens arose that the drug 'hydroxychloroquine' would be a promising cure. The frequently made claims by Donald Trump and other politicians regarding the supposed effectiveness of the drug were repeated so often that many people started to believe them, even though there was little or no scientific evidence to back these claims.

Secondary biases related to the mere exposure effect

Illusory truth effect—the tendency to judge information as more valid after being exposed to it numerous times

Rhyme-as-reason effect—the tendency to judge a saying or aphorism as more accurate or valid when written in rhyme

Automation bias—the tendency to prefer suggestions from automated systems and to falsely ignore contradictory information made without automation (i.e., by humans)

A second related concept is the 'rhyme-as-reason effect', which posits that people are more likely to remember and believe statements when it contains a rhyme. This is why many popular statements, general sayings, or aphorisms use rhymes, for example, the following traditional aphorisms: "An apple a day keeps the doctor away," "What sobriety conceals, alcohol reveals," and "Woes unite foes." The mere exposure effect is suggested to be a factor explaining why people perceive rhyming statements as more truthful. Following the reasoning of the mere exposure effect, when people become more familiar with a statement due to repeated exposure to it, they tend to find it more convincing over time. So, if people repeat a certain statement more frequently because it contains a catchy rhyme, the repetition of the statement could cause them to find it more and more convincing.

Another bias considered to be related to the mere exposure effect is the 'automation bias' or the tendency to favour suggestions from automated decision-making systems and to ignore contradictory information made without automation, even if this information is correct (Cummings, 2004). Over the last few decades, the popularity and relevance of this bias have grown significantly, presumably because of our increasing usage of computerized decision-making systems based on artificial intelligence. The repeated exposure to automated decision-making systems is suggested to increase our familiarity with these systems and, eventually, cause an overreliance on them.

What is the relevance of the mere exposure effect to organizations and change?

The tendency to prefer the familiar over the unknown is also highly relevant to organizations, since it could have implications for decision-making, formation, and perseveration of norms and values and organizational behaviour. The appeal of the familiar is nearly ubiquitous in all organizations and can serve important functions—mostly as a way to increase predictability. For example, organizations often create norms and routines to reduce uncertainty and, presumably, increase the efficiency and productivity of the organization. Companies may pursue activities that feel familiar, including prospecting around familiar networks of individuals and organizations, hiring people with familiar backgrounds and skills, and rejecting novel—unfamiliar—approaches and initiatives (see similarity bias, chapter 3, Understanding). However, a company that favours its current business model simply because the management has grown familiar with it may miss out on necessary organizational changes that require novel behaviours. One example of such a company was Pan American World Airways, or Pan Am, America's former largest international air carrier for most part of the twentieth century. Pan Am was the first airline to offer jet aircrafts and computerized reservation systems, which gave them the status of industry innovator. However, Pan Am was unable to let go of its familiar, existing business model and did not invest in alternatives. This over-investment in its current business model led to the company's downfall in 1991, when Pan Am filed for bankruptcy protection, with competitor Delta Air Lines purchasing the remaining profitable assets for $416 million. Today, Pan Am's independent training organization called Pan Am's International Flight Academy is the only surviving division of Pan American World Airways.

Search strategy

Relevant databases were searched using the terms 'mere exposure effect' and 'familiarity principle' both separately and in combination with the terms 'organisation*,' 'work,' 'employ*,' 'leader*,' or 'chang*.' This search yielded 303 results. After removing the duplicates and thorough examination, 2 meta-analyses, 0 systematic reviews, and 3 studies were included.

Main findings

1. *People tend to prefer the familiar over the unknown (Level A).*

   There is empirical evidence for the mere exposure effect with consistent results for different stimuli, measurement instruments, modes of presentation, and exposure durations. In 1989, Bornstein performed a meta-analysis of 134 studies on the mere exposure effect. In this analysis, Bornstein identified a reliable effect of exposure on liking, concluding that "The first 20 years of research on Zajonc's (1968) mere exposure effect leaves little doubt the mere exposure-affect relationship is a robust and reliable phenomenon." Bornstein also studied methodological and subject variables influencing the exposure–affect relationship and found that the mere exposure effect was present using several types of incentives or stimuli (photographs, objects, words, etc.). Results also showed that the mere exposure effect was strongest within participants (1) when incentives were complex (vs. simple), (2) when participants were exposed to the incentive between one and ten times, (3) when the duration of exposure was relatively short, and (4) when there was a delay between exposure to the stimulus and the affect rating. Lastly, participants who clearly recognized the incentives showed less positive affect towards these incentives. So, according to the meta-analysis, recognition of an incentive is not a prerequisite for the mere exposure effect but could actually inhibit the effect. Around 28 years later, Montoya et al. (2017) confirmed Bornsteins' conclusions. Like Bornstein, they found several variables or moderators influencing the mere exposure effect, such as type of incentive, duration of exposure, and delay between presentation and affect rating. Montoya et al. concluded that the study found "tremendous consistency among mere exposure effects for different stimuli, measurement instruments, modes of presentation, and exposure durations."

2. *Several models explain the mere exposure effect but none has found full scientific support (Level A).*

   As pointed out in the introduction, the four most popular models for the mere exposure effect are Zajonc's approach, the original- and modified two-factor model and the processing fluency model. These models diverge somewhat in their predictions: In general, Zajonc's model stands apart from the other theories because it states that repeated exposure always leads to liking (rather than it having a negative effect on liking after numerous exposures, as presumed by the other models).

The two-factor models put weight on satiation, or 'boredom,' in the face of repeated exposures. Processing fluency models are different from the other models in the way they emphasize how individuals experience and then make sense of fluency (= misattribute fluency to liking). Despite these clear theoretical differences between the models, they all share two elements: Firstly, the models agree that an initial exposure produces a mental representation and subsequent exposures strengthen that representation. Secondly, they agree that exposure to previously viewed stimuli produces habituation or a decline in the initial fear response (Montoya et al., 2017). According to Montoya et al. (2017), a fifth model could explain the mere exposure effect—the 'representation matching model.' According to this model, the more a person is exposed to a stimulus, the more a person regards that stimulus as correct or how it should be, resulting in liking for that stimulus. However, this theory is not yet supported by empirical evidence. All in all, no single model of exposure effects has clearly emerged as one that is best supported by the range of empirical findings (Bornstein, 1989). The mere exposure effect raises a simple question: "Why do we like a stimulus the more frequently we have seen it?" The answer, however, seems to require a relatively complicated response, involving an understanding of memory systems, habituation, inhibition, neural responsiveness, cognitive representation formation, and recognition and preference systems (Montoya et al., 2017).

3. *People who are highly motivated to connect with others seem to be more susceptible to fall prey to the mere exposure effect (Level B).*

   In two randomized controlled studies among Singaporean university students, Kwan et al. (2015) found that when subjects had a relatively high motivation for social connectedness, more exposure to a certain object caused them to assume more familiarity with others and to prefer the object more. In contrast, when there was a strong motivation for personal distinctiveness, more exposure did not affect personal preference. So, the need for social connectedness seems to be positively related to the mere exposure effect. Importantly, results also showed that frequent exposure to an object enhanced affect-based trust.

4. *Exposure from in-group to out-group attributes leads to greater liking of the out-group by the in-group. However, if the in-group experiences a threat to identity the effect is reversed (Level B).*

   Two randomized controlled studies by Crisp et al. (2009) investigated the mere exposure effect in intergroup contexts. The researchers explored whether repeated exposure to out-group-relevant attitude objects would lead to less liking following a threat to identity. Results indeed showed that while exposure to out-groups led to greater liking under baseline conditions, this relationship was reversed following identity threat. These findings illustrate the possible negative effects of the mere exposure effect in the social context when people face a threat to their social identity.

5. *Preferring the familiar over the unknown could result in more compliant behaviour (Level B).*

   Another randomized controlled study of the mere exposure effect in social settings was done by Burger et al. (2001). The study investigated the impact of the mere exposure effect on compliance. Results showed that simply sitting across the table from a confederate (=mere exposure) momentarily increased liking enough to significantly increase compliance, as participants were more likely to comply with requests. These findings indicate that the mere exposure effect could result in more compliance.

Conclusion

There is strong empirical evidence for the existence of the mere exposure effect. People do tend to prefer the familiar over the unknown. Several models have been found to explain the mere exposure effect. However, none has found full scientific support. The answer to why we like something we experienced more frequently is rather complex and subject for further scientific research. Some interesting moderators and effects in intergroup context have been highlighted. People who are strongly motivated to connect with others seem to be more susceptible to prefer the familiar over the unknown. Exposing people to attributes of the out-group results in greater liking. However, when there is a threat to the identity of the in-group, the effect is reversed. Lastly, the mere exposure effect could prompt more compliant behaviour, as simply sitting close to someone we've met before increases our likelihood to comply with requests.

Practical reflections

Firstly, we point to the importance of trust and the need for leaders and managers to acknowledge this core social motive within their organization. This is highlighted by attachment theory, a theory of social and interpersonal behaviour of individuals developed by the British psychiatrist Bowlby (1907–1990). The theory proposes that trust is 'materialized' in attachments—enduring emotional bonds between people in family, group, and organizational settings that reduce stress and provide security, safety, and comfort. These attachments have implications for both the physical and psychological well-being of the individual.

Findings from scientific research point to the direction that mere exposure could increase trust (Kwan et al., 2015). This has implications for organizational leaders when managing a change process, especially since research has shown that trust positively relates to affective commitment to a change (Neves & Caetano, 2006). To create trust, organizational leaders are advised to increase their visibility in the organization, for example, by scheduling regular visits to divisions or teams. This can be enhanced by stimulating the need for connectedness within the organization and promoting the desire to connect with organizational members, for example by organizing team-building activities (Kwan et al., 2015). Combining exposure with strengthening the need for connectedness can thus be a powerful approach to effectuating the desired change.

Secondly, leaders and managers should be aware of the negative consequences that the mere exposure effect could have on their business. As pointed out in the introduction, a main focus on the familiar could hamper innovation and change within organizations. So, by proactively looking for unfamiliar experiences and letting go of risk-aversive behaviour instead, organizations have a good chance of strengthening their competitive advantage. Managers and organizational leaders must be aware of the value of diversity and new experience. One way to encourage diversity is by increasing the percentage of female managers and directors at the top of the organization. Following the reasoning of the mere exposure effect, being exposed to more female business leaders could result in employees becoming more accepting of them, thereby paving the way for more diversity at the top in the future (Kwan et al., 2015).

Some other practical suggestions derived from the main findings, such as frequent exposures to narratives or metaphors that embody certain organizational properties could foster the development of positive affective feelings and shared perceptions of organizational culture (Kwan et al., 2015). Managers and organizational leaders are thus advised to enhance the visibility of narratives or metaphors in the organization, such as a mission statement, a corporate vision, corporate values, or a corporate strategy. These social objects "influence organisations' members' ways of understanding and behaving in organisations" (Laroche, 1995, p. 62). They are essentially aimed at constructing a social meaning, which is an important process in organizations. Leaders can and must facilitate taking care of the 'management of meaning' (Smircich & Morgan, 1982) (Ten Have et al., 2019, p. 72).

Negativity bias

What is negativity bias?

The negativity bias (also named 'negativity effect' or 'negative bias') is the general tendency to attend to, - put greater weight on and to more easily believe negative information, events, or stimuli than positive instances (Joseph et al., 2020; Hilbig, 2009). The negativity bias is a crucial bias regarding the social motive trusting. As said earlier, trust takes years to build and only seconds to shatter. This entails the larger influence of negative behaviour on trust than positive behaviour. The negativity bias is a well-studied concept. Various reviews of the existing literature concerning this bias conclude that the belief "bad is stronger than good" is common across a wide range of social cognitive domains such as impression formation, memory, decision-making, and many others (Hilbig, 2009). The negativity bias is proposed to be evolutionarily adaptive because it predisposes our attentional processes to pay extensive attention to negative stimuli, allowing people to evade dangerous, life-threatening stimuli (Vaish et al., 2008). Paul Rozin and Edward Royzman were the first to coin the term negativity bias in their 2001 paper "Negativity Bias, Negativity Dominance, and Contagion." Since then, the bias has been investigated within various social psychological and cognitive domains, such as social impression formation, attention, learning, and decision-making.

In another 2001 book, *The Power of Bad: How the Negativity Effect Rules Us and How We Can Rule*, research psychologist Roy F. Baumeister and journalist John Tierney posit that there is plenty of real-world evidence for the negativity bias. For example, the notion that negative information usually has a stronger pull on our attention than positive information could explain why bad news sells more papers or why successful films, plays, and books are usually packed with negative events. The phenomenon 'truthiness' might help explain the link between the negativity bias and the excessive coverage of negative events by media. Truthiness refers to the belief that a particular statement or claim is true not because of supporting facts or evidence but because of a feeling that it is true or a desire for it to be true. The term was coined by American television comedian Stephen Colbert in his political satire programme *The Colbert Report* in 2005 to refer to the misuse of appeal to emotion and 'gut feeling' as a rhetorical device in American political discourse. The term has gained much public popularity and was even named Word of the Year for 2005 by the American Dialect Society.

When Colbert originally coined the term, he was referring only to politics; however, the accusation of misuse of appeal to emotion as a rhetorical device is also not uncommon in media. By framing information negatively, television makers, public figures, writers, and journalists are suggested to appeal to the public's emotion, thereby influencing the perceived plausibility of their messages regardless of actual evidence supporting this information.

Secondary biases related to the negativity bias

Truthiness—the tendency to judge a claim or statement as valid because of a personal feeling or desire for it to be true regardless of the absence of supporting facts or evidence

Subjective validation—the tendency to judge a statement or another piece of information to be correct if it has any personal meaning or significance

Declinism—the belief that a society is tending towards decline

Pessimism bias—the tendency to overestimate the likelihood of negative events while underestimating positive events

A phenomenon related to this is 'subjective validation' or people's tendency to consider a statement or another piece of information to be correct if it has any personal meaning or significance to them. Because negative information holds more significance for people, they could be prone to judge this information as more valid. A third related phenomenon related to the negativity bias is 'declinism' or the belief that the society is tending towards decline. This belief supposedly stems from the predisposition to view the past more favourably and the future more negatively. The term 'declinism' was coined by German historian Oswald Spengler in his book, *The Decline of the West*, which was released after the World War I and speculated that each civilization was destined to fail (Gopnik, 2011). The negativity bias could be one of the factors causing people to experience declinism. Since the negativity bias leads people to be more affected by emotionally negative events than similar, but positive, events, this could cause them to falsely perceive a general trend towards decline. The term 'negativity bias' is sometimes also referred to as the 'pessimism bias.' However, the two concepts are somewhat distinctive. While the negativity bias refers to the natural human tendency to attend to and put greater weight on negative information, pessimism bias refers to the proneness to overestimate the likelihood of negative events while underestimating the likelihood of positive events. This concerns beliefs about personal events and societal events. It is proposed to be the opposite of the optimism bias (also see the next section). However, empirical research suggests that people are generally optimistic about themselves, but pessimistic about society (Roser & Nagdy, 2014).

The negativity bias could have various effects on a daily basis by influencing social perceptions and impression formations. Firstly, when people are given both positive and negative adjectives to describe someone's personality, they place greater weight on the negative descriptions when forming a first impression (Hilbig, 2009). Secondly, memory and learning are likely to be affected by the negativity bias. Some research suggests that punishments for incorrect responses could be more effective in enhancing learning than rewards for correct responses since punishments are more likely to leave an imprint on our memory than rewards (Costantini & Hoving, 1973). Another domain in which the bias can have an influence is decision-making. Kahneman and Tversky (1984) found that when making decisions, people continuously place greater weight on negative aspects of an event in comparison to positive ones. In their prospect theory, Kahneman and Tversky (1979) state that potential costs are more heavily considered than potential gains (chapter 4, Controlling).

What is the relevance of the negativity bias to organizations and change?

The negativity bias could certainly be relevant to organizations and change. As stated in the introduction, the bias can have an impact on various processes such as impression formation, memory, and decision-making. As such, how employees convey certain information, cues, or issues and respond to this is highly likely to be influenced by this bias, thereby possibly impacting organizational and change-related outcomes. The negativity bias could also be an explanation as to why many big, established companies remain cautious and conservative, even in the face of profound technology advances and disruptions in the marketplace. As stated by the prospect theory, potential costs are more heavily weighted than potential gains. This could result in risk-aversive behaviour, thereby preventing organizations from innovating and taking the necessary risks to adjust to changing environments. An example of this is the international film photography company Kodak. When the photography market began shifting towards digital photography during the end of the twentieth century, Kodak was too risk-averse to innovate and instead remained focused on its core strength, film photography. However, film photography eventually became outdated, and its business decision made Kodak lose its competitive advantage to rival companies, such as Sony and Canon, that adjusted to the changing environment. This resulted in the company eventually filing for bankruptcy in 2002. Organizations, especially those involved in highly competitive and fast-changing markets, should be aware of the negativity bias since it can significantly affect competitive advantages and capacity to change. It would be advisable for organizational leaders, managers, and employees to deepen their knowledge about the processes that underlie the bias, the consequences, and possible interventions.

Search strategy

Relevant databases were searched using the term 'negativity bias' and 'negativity effect' both separately and in combination with the terms 'organisation*,' 'work,' 'employ*,' 'leader*,' or 'chang*.' This search yielded about 42 results. After removing the duplicates and thorough examination, 1 meta-analysis, 0 systematic reviews, and 2 studies were included.

Main findings

1. *People put greater weight on negative events or stimuli compared with positive instances (Level A).*

   In 2020, Joseph et al. conducted a meta-analysis on the occurrence of the negativity bias in which nearly 55,000 men and women of various cultural backgrounds were studied. The included studies used various methods to elicit negative and positive emotions in participants, such as watching a movie clip, looking at photographs, or reading a story. Across these studies, findings revealed a strong human tendency to be negatively biased. The impact of negative stimuli (e.g., sad, scary, or aggressive movie clips, photos, or stories) on participants' affective state was about twice as strong as the impact of positive stimuli.

2. *People might perceive information as more valid when it is more negative (Level D).*

   In a 2009 experimental study, Hilbig (2009) investigated the relationship between the negativity bias and judgements of truth. The premise of this study was that people are more likely to accept negative information as being the truth. This claim was derived from findings of previous research, indicating that negative instances tend to demand more attentional resources and that more elaborate processing can render messages more persuasive. In three experiments, Hilbig assessed participants' judgements of truth concerning statistical statements framed in either a positive or negative way. For example "85 percent of attempted instances of rape are successful" (negative frame) versus "15 percent of attempted instances of rape are unsuccessful" (positive frame). Although the information was the same in both conditions, framing the provided information in a negative way led the participants to judge them as more valid. This effect was robust across different judgement domains, using different assessment methods and different samples of participants. Interestingly, research has given very little attention to the cognitive mechanisms underlying these reported effects. Hilbig suggests that negative information can lead to more thorough processing, which may then produce the negativity bias since more elaboration can increase the persuasiveness of messages. He also points to social processes as a possible explanation. For example, we might have learned to trust negative information more, simply because others are much more unlikely to lie to us when bringing us bad news, whereas they may well exaggerate when informing us about something good. Likewise, people might propose that negative messages are more likely to be conveyed by sources they tend to trust, especially the media, given the strong focus on negative events in the news (Hilbig, 2009).

3. *It seems that since people have stronger reactions to the occurrence of future negative events compared to positive events, people tend to overestimate the probability of future negative events happening (Level D).*

   Bilgin (2012) conducted research on the relation between the negativity bias and subjective probability, which is referred to as the individual's personal judgement about whether a specific outcome is likely to occur (pessimism bias). Bilgin hypothesized that, through its impact on attention and information processing, a negativity bias would manifest in an increase in subjective probability. To test this hypothesis, Bilgin told his participants to assume that they were considering playing a gamble that offered a fifty-fifty chance of winning or losing $25. Participants were then asked to imagine playing the gamble and losing it. Results showed that the more unpleasant someone anticipated losing the $25 to be, the less confident that person was to win the gamble. Thus, the perceived unpleasantness of the loss was associated with ratings of the likelihood of winning the gamble. This has the potential downside of people usually being more pessimistic about their chances than objective probabilities justify. One positive note by Bilgin considering this finding is that increased subjective probability of potential losses may help people act sooner to reverse these losses, or if they are not reversible, to better cope with their outcomes (Bilgin, 2012).

Conclusion

Empirical evidence points to the existence of negativity bias, as scientific research has consistently shown that individuals display stronger reactions to negative than positive stimuli. There are also indications that people tend to perceive negative information as more valid and trustworthy and because they have stronger reactions to the occurrence of future negative events than positive ones, they tend to overestimate the probability of future negative events happening. However, some caution is warranted in generalizing these findings because of the low evidence level of these studies.

Practical reflections

Although most research has not (yet) focused on the negativity bias in the organizational context and its practical relevance to organizational leaders and managers, several practical reflections can be derived from the preceding findings. First and foremost, organizational leaders and managers would do well to acknowledge that organizational members are more likely to be affected by negative information than positive information. This knowledge could be particularly useful when communicating about change processes. As Hilbig's study (2009) indicated, people might perceive negative information as more valid and trustworthy. Managers or leaders could thus use stories and story structures that communicate *a sense of urgency* in communicating organizational change. That is to say, instead of solely focusing on the gains following the change, managers are advised to communicate what's at stake or what will be missed if the organization fails to act. A sense of urgency is often seen as a prerequisite for effective change. To illustrate this, Kotter (2012) states: "By far the biggest mistake people make when trying to change organizations is to plunge ahead without establishing a high enough sense of urgency in fellow managers and employees" (Ten Have et al., 2019). However, notwithstanding the stimulating effects of fear appeals or a sense of urgency, some caution is warranted. Negative stimuli such as threats and urgency can be effective in change. However, positive ambitions mirroring positive emotions and feelings create more self-efficacy (e.g., confidence one has to achieve the desired result) or action control when dealing with changes and challenges because they provide people with a broader scope of attention, more openness, and behavioural variety (Ten Have et al., 2019),

> On a more general note, the negativity bias can significantly affect organizations' competitive advantages and capacity to change. Since potential costs are more heavily weighted than potential gains, organizational members are prone to engage in risk-aversive behaviour, which prevents organizations from innovating and adjusting to their environments. In order to prevent this, organizational leaders should create a climate of innovation by encouraging their employees to engage in new behaviours necessary to drive the company to achieve new heights and provide them with the tools necessary to carry out these behaviours. However, to avoid excessive risk-taking that might jeopardize the organization, it would be prudent to clearly communicate the limits to risk-taking and to install procedures for review of any proposed risk that would breach these limits. In this way, organizational leaders cultivate a culture of curiosity and innovation, thereby ultimately strengthening their company's competitive advantage.

Optimism bias

What is the optimism bias?

The optimism bias (also called the 'optimistic bias') refers to people's tendency to perceive that they are likelier than others to experience positive events (such as being financially successful) and less at risk for negative events (such as getting cancer, injured, or divorced). Researchers have investigated this phenomenon extensively, and it appears to be remarkably resilient. Both men and women of all ages, ethnicities, and educational levels seem prone to fall prey to this bias (Weinstein & Klein, 1996). Psychologist Neil Weinstein first encountered the optimism bias in a 1980 experiment, in which over 200 college students participated. Weinstein asked the students to rate how much their chances of experiencing a certain event (positive or negative) differed from that of their classmates. It appeared that more than half of the students rated themselves either below average for a negative event or above average for a positive event. Weinstein concluded that people generally overestimate their chances of experiencing positive events and underestimate their chances of experiencing misfortune (Weinstein, 1980).

Various motivational and cognitive factors have been suggested to be the root cause of the optimism bias. On a cognitive level, people have more information available about themselves than they do about others. When people evaluate their own risks, they tend to focus on themselves instead of realistically looking at how they compare to others. As a result, when making judgements and comparisons about their risk compared to that of others, people generally ignore the average person and primarily focus on their own feelings and experiences (Shepperd et al., 2002). People are highly motivated to be optimistic because positive predictions are satisfying and make them feel good about themselves and their lives. As a result, people tend to focus on finding information that supports what they want to see happen rather than what will happen to them (Shepperd et al., 2002). From an evolutionary perspective, the tendency to see the glass half-full could have been advantageous for human survival. By believing that they are unlikely to fail and more likely to succeed, people increase their self-esteem, lower their stress levels, and eventually improve their overall well-being.

One bias proposed to be related to the optimism bias is the 'normalcy bias,' which is a psychological state of denial people enter in the event of a disaster, as a result of which they underestimate both the possibility of the disaster happening and its effects on their lifes. Experts attribute this denial to people's tendency to interpret warnings optimistically, often resorting to ambiguities to justify their neglect (Omer & Alon, 1994). This bias might explain why people are plagued by inaction during natural disasters or global crises. One example is the public response to the outbreak of COVID-19 in 2020. To slow the spread of the virus, many governments implemented social distancing policies, which urged civilians to stay home as much as possible. While most people complied with these regulations, others underestimated their personal risk of contracting the disease and therefore engaged less in protective behaviours by deciding to ignore these rules. The proposed influence of the optimism bias on adherence to social distancing policies was confirmed by a 2021 study. Findings indicated that individuals with high optimism bias engaged in less behavioural changes during the COVID-19 pandemic (Fragkaki et al., 2021).

Secondary biases related to the optimism bias

Normalcy bias—the tendency to respond to threat warnings with disbelief or minimization and to underestimate a disaster's potential adverse effects

Pro-innovation bias—the belief that all members of a social system should adopt and diffuse an innovation rapidly, without considering or allowing for an alteration to that innovation

Planning fallacy—the tendency to be overly optimistic regarding task completion times, leading to an underestimation of the time needed to complete a future task

A specific type of optimism bias is the 'pro-innovation bias' or a proneness to be highly optimistic regarding innovations. An example is the nuclear optimism that emerged the 1950s, which was characterized by a general feeling that all power generators in the future would be atomic in nature and that everything would use a nuclear power source in a positive and productive way (Sovacool, 2011). So far, however, this great evolution has not taken place.

The optimism bias can have serious repercussions, both at an individual level and at a systematic level. At an individual level, the bias could lead to feelings of well-being and self-esteem. According to research by Baumeister et al. (2003), self-esteem seems to be a valuable resource. People with high self-esteem are more active, happier, and in many ways better able to deal or cope with their environment. Baumeister (1993) also sees self-esteem as 'the likeliest candidate for a social vaccine' that protects people against susceptibility to a wide range of social vulnerabilities. However, the optimism bias could also cause people to ignore relevant information, thereby influencing decision-making. Furthermore, the bias could encourage more risky behaviours by causing people to ignore the potential unwanted outcomes (Shepperd et al., 2002) or stop them from taking preventative measures, such as buying insurance. At a systematic level, the optimism bias could even (partly) explain the global response to climate change (Pahl et al., 2014). The assumption that global warming doesn't affect us personally is proposed to prevent people from taking preventive measures. The optimism bias is also suggested to impact financial markets. Several economists have named the bias one of the core causes of the financial downfall in 2008. Unrealistic expectations of financial analysts and government officials that the market would continue growing, despite evidence to the contrary, and banks continuously engaging in high-risk decision-making, likely contributed to the eventual collapse (Sharot, 2011). Furthermore, the optimism bias is presumed to influence decisions in planning and (time) management. According to the bias, the costs and completion times of big projects tend to be underestimated and the benefits overestimated, possibly leading to an overspend on large-scale investment projects (Flyvbjerg, 2011). This relates to another bias, the 'planning fallacy,' or a specific form of optimism bias whereby people make highly favourable estimates of the time it will take to complete an upcoming task (even though they are aware that similar tasks have taken longer in the past). The main findings concerning the optimism bias below might thus also be applicable to the planning fallacy.

What is the relevance of the optimism bias to organizations and change?

The optimism bias could be highly relevant to organizations and change leaders, considering its presumed impact on corporate financial and investment decisions. By having unrealistic expectations of financial growth and success, organizations are prone to engage in high-risk decision-making and invest in loss-making activities. For instance, Barros and Silveira (2007) found that organizations with optimistic managers tend to choose a more aggressive financing policy, which causes the company to have more liabilities than assets, thereby putting the company in a high financial-risk category. Also, a 2011 study by Campbell et al. found that CEO turnover was related to the level of CEO optimism. Organizational boards discharged high-optimism CEOs more frequently than moderately optimistic CEOs (Wang et al., 2014). The optimism bias could also have detrimental effects on the planning and execution phase of organizational projects by causing employees to overestimate the benefits or financial gains, while underestimating costs, completion time, or other negative effects. This could eventually result in excessive costs or even project abandonment. One example of this is the famous Sydney Opera House, which was expected to be completed in 1963. However, unforeseen obstacles caused the project to drag on for 10 years longer than planned. The original cost was estimated at $7 million, its delayed completion, however, led to a cost of $102 million. One major reason for this was the government's insistence on starting construction early, even though construction plans were not yet finished. According to premier Joseph Cahill, it was crucial to start with the construction when public opinion about the Opera House was still favourable and funding was still in place. In his enthusiasm to complete the project, however, the premier disregarded criticisms and relied on intuitive estimations for its costs, ultimately leading to its massive delay and extra costs (Murray, 2003). All in all, organizations falling prey to the optimism bias are at risk of engaging in high-risk decision-making, venturing into loss-making activities, and poor execution planning. Therefore, it would be useful for organizational leaders to be aware of this bias and its possible impact on their business. This way, they can prematurely recognize this tendency before exerting its influence on the organization.

Search strategy

Relevant databases were searched using the term 'optimism bias' and 'optimistic bias' both separately and in combination with the terms 'organisation*,' 'work,' 'employ*,' 'leader*,' or 'chang*.' This search yielded about 23 results. After removing the duplicates and thorough examination, 1 meta-analysis, 0 systematic reviews, and 2 studies were included.

Main findings

1. *People tend to perceive they are more likely than others to experience positive events (Level A).*

   Klein and Helweg-Larsen (2002) conducted a meta-analysis on the optimism bias, studying more than 5,000 participants from different nationalities, ages, and educational levels. Findings showed that people fall prey to the optimism bias irrespective of gender, age, or educational level.

2. *When people engage in group discussions, they are more likely to be overly optimistic about the predicted time needed to complete a certain task (Level B).*

Scientific evidence for a certain kind of optimism bias in the prediction of task completion time, e.g., the planning fallacy (as stated in the introduction), comes from research by Buehler et al. (2005) and Koole and van't Spijker (2000), who conducted experiments to investigate this bias among university students. Essentially, results indicated, people usually predict they will finish a task sooner than they actually do. According to Buehler et al. (2005), people commit this fallacy even though they have experienced needing more time for similar tasks in the past. Apparently, then, this bias exerts stronger effects on people than their past experience or knowledge.

Also, Buehler et al. (2005) used an experimental study to explore the effects of group discussion on the planning fallacy. In this study, participants firstly predicted—individually and together—when they would complete several upcoming group projects. Then their actual completion times were measured. Results showed that participants generated more optimistic predictions through group discussion than they did individually. So, through group discussion, participants' tendency to focus primarily on factors promoting successful task completion was heightened. This selective focus on 'planning for success' enhanced the planning fallacy.

3. *The optimism bias is related to greater perceived control over future events (Level B).*

   In the beforementioned meta-analysis performed by Klein and Helweg-Larsen (2002), researchers also explored the relationship between perceived control and the optimism bias. Perceived control is described as the amount of control people perceive they have over future events. Klein and Helweg-Larsen found that greater perceived control showed a strong association with greater optimism bias. However, it is not clear in which causal direction the relationship between perceived control and optimism bias flows. One possibility is that beliefs in control over an outcome lead to more optimistic beliefs about the probability of that outcome. However, an alternative explanation is that an increase in optimism bias results in the feeling of being in control.

4. *Concrete action plans can be an effective aid in countering the optimism bias (Level B).*

   In an experimental study performed in 2000, Koole and van 't Spijker examined whether the optimism bias could be reduced through the formation of implementation intentions or concrete action plans that specify when, where, and how to act to reach particular goals. Results showed that the formation of implementation intentions led to an increase in optimistic completion predictions. This is in line with previous findings that contemplating the implementation of one's goals fosters an optimistic mindset (Armor & Taylor, 1998; Taylor & Gollwitzer, 1995). However, this increase in optimism bias was exceeded by an increase in actual rates of goal completion. The net result of the implementation intentions was thus a reduction in unfounded optimism in task-completion predictions. Therefore, the researchers concluded, the formation of implementation plans can be an effective aid in attacking optimistic bias in task-completion predictions.

Conclusion

In conclusion, scientific evidence consistently shows that the optimism bias influences human perceptions, attitudes, and behaviour and transcends gender, age, and other personal factors. The planning fallacy, which can be described as optimism during the planning phase of a project, is a frequently studied type of optimism bias. When participating in group discussions, people are more likely to be overly optimistic in time predictions, since the individual tendency to focus primarily on factors promoting successful task completion is heightened through group discussions. Furthermore, perceived control (e.g., perceived control over future events) is positively related to the optimism bias, although the causal direction of this relationship remains unclear. Lastly, a promising intervention for countering the effects of the optimism bias seems to be the formation of concrete action plans.

Practical reflections

If anything, these findings concerning the optimism bias confirm the relevance of the bias to organizations and change and can be applied in organizational and change contexts. There are several suggestions for organizational leaders. While planning for a certain (change) project, managers or project leaders should be aware of the effects of the optimism bias on time judgements (e.g., planning fallacy), since employees tend to be overly optimistic regarding their estimates of the time it will take to complete the project (phase). One suggestion to combat this is by forming implementation intentions or concrete action plans that specify when, where, and how to act to reach particular goals. The importance of goal setting is emphasized by Kouzes and Posner (2012) who state: "People need to know if they're making progress toward the goal or simply marking time. Their motivation to perform a task increases only when they have a challenging goal and receive feedback on their progress." Also, Heller (1998) addresses the concept of 'goal setting' as a way to influence or change employee behaviour. He advises: "Set personal objectives for people so they focus their minds on performance; reaching the goals will reinforce their enhanced drive." Implementation intentions are suggested to be effective because it requires vivid imagination of an intended action. The individual has to really visualize the situation in which a particular behaviour will be enacted. Moreover, the formation of implementation intentions explicitly recruits the individuals will power by asking them to commit themselves to the intended behaviour. Research has shown that such wilful commitment greatly enhances the effectiveness of implementation intentions (Koole & van't Spijker, 2000, p. 883). It might thus be useful for leaders and managers to invest in trainings, seminars, or workshops aimed at applying implementation intentions for all employees, including the top management. However, Koole and van 't Spijker mention some considerations for the usage of implementation intentions. Firstly, implementation planning only helps when people have chosen reasonable goals. Secondly, forming implementation intentions is only expected to be effective when people are committed to their goals. Thirdly, forming implementation intentions to execute a specific behaviour might reduce a person's flexibility to perform alternative behaviours, which may be harmful under rapidly changing conditions where flexibility is essential. Fourthly, people's limited energy resources to engage in wilful planning should be taken into account.

Companies could also note the detrimental effects of group discussions. Presumably, people engage in consultation or discussion because they believe it will improve the accuracy of their predictions. However, group discussion can exacerbate the tendency towards unrealistic predictions through an even greater tendency to 'plan for success' (Buehler et al., 2005). This is an important finding for organizations, since planners or project managers in organizations often develop their predictions during team meetings. Even when these employees make predictions individually, they usually interact with others to collect information, opinions, and advice (Heath & Gonzalez, 1995). It may be beneficial for planners and (project) managers to collect individual predictions or information instead of engaging in group discussion. Another suggestion would be to consult external, neutral observers rather than relying solely on predictions from members within the organization (Buehler et al., 2005).

Attributional bias

What is attributional bias?

In social psychology, the attributional bias is a group of biases that refers to the systematic errors that people make when assigning causes to behaviour of themselves and others. Research on attributional biases is founded in attribution theory, which explains how and why people create meaning about others' and their own behaviour (also mentioned in attentional bias, chapter 2, Understanding). It's a form of sense-making and linking the cause and effect of behaviour. Two questions are central to attribution theory: (1) Why do I do what I do? (2) Why do others do what they do?

The starting point of the attribution theory was in 1958, when well-known psychologist Fritz Heider published his book *The Psychology of Interpersonal Relations*. Heider classified the attribution theory into two types:

1. *Internal attributions*—attributing "the locus of causality to factors within the individual such as personality traits, skill, and effort" (Gok et al., 2012)
2. *External attributions*—attributing "the locus of causality to situational factors beyond the control of the individual such as task difficulty and luck" (Gok et al., 2012)

Heider stated that "our perceptions of causality are often distorted by our needs and certain cognitive biases" (Forsyth, 1987). In other words, because people are motivated to find explanations for behaviours, they fall prey to attributional biases. Over the years, researchers have identified various types of attributional biases, all of which propose ways in which people display biased interpretations of information. One of these biases is the 'fundamental attribution error,' which is the tendency to explain others' behaviour as being caused by a given person's personality (i.e., internal attribution), while ignoring the surrounding situational demands. For example, when an employee is late for a meeting, colleagues are more likely to assume it's because of laziness rather than, for example, a traffic jam.

Very closely related to the fundamental attribution error is the 'actor–observer bias.' Social psychologists Jones and Nisbett, who introduced this bias in 1971, state that when we observe other people, we tend to focus on the person, whereas when we are actors, our attention is focused on situational factors. For example, when another person receives a low score on a general knowledge quiz, people are inclined to ascribe this score to their low intelligence. However, when they receive the same low score, they are more likely to assign this to the difficulty or inappropriateness of the questions.

Another related bias is the 'third-person bias,' which is when that people tend to overestimate the effects of mass media communication on others compared to themselves. According to Perloff (1999), the vast majority of research on the third-person bias attributes the psychological underpinnings of this bias to attribution theory. A last attributional bias related to this is the 'empathy gap,' or the presumed tendency to underestimate the influence of varying mental states on our own behaviours and that of others. Following this reasoning, the human inability to consider how others may be affected by their emotions causes people to make errors when assigning causes to the behaviours of others.

Secondary biases related to the attributional bias

Fundamental attribution error—the tendency to overvalue dispositional explanations of others' behaviours (i.e., make internal attributions) while undervaluing dispositional explanations

Actor–observer bias—the tendency to assign causes of behaviour differently depending on whether one is an actor or an observer

Third-person bias—the proneness to overestimate the effects of mass media communication on others compared to oneself

Empathy gap—the tendency to underestimate the influence of varying mental states on self behaviour and make decisions that only satisfy one's current emotion, feeling, or state of being

Hostile attribution bias—the tendency to interpret others' ambiguous behaviours as hostile rather than benign

One type of attributional bias that receives some specific attention, specifically considering its possible impact on organizations and change, is the 'hostile attribution bias' or the tendency to interpret others' ambiguous behaviours as hostile rather than benign. For example, when people observe two other people whispering, they may assume that those people are talking negatively about them. In this case, they made an attribution of hostile intent, even though the other people's behaviour was potentially benign. The term 'hostile attribution bias' was first coined in the 1980s by Nasby, Hayden, and DePaulo. In an experimental study, the researchers showed a group of aggressive adolescent boys (aged 10–16 years) several photographs of people. It was found that a subgroup of them (particularly aggressive and/or rejected children) exhibited a consistent tendency to attribute hostile intent to the photographs, even when the cues were ambiguous or benign. This finding led to a considerable amount of scientific research exploring the link between the hostile attribution bias and aggression. So far, the available scientific research on this hypothesized relationship has shown mixed results. hostile attribution bias can be linked to moral disengagement, a term first coined by Albert Bandura in 1999, referring to the justification of immoral behaviour when it is not consistent with dominant norms and values. It is a process of cognitive reframing to prevent people from feeling bad when doing bad things (Ten Have et al., 2019). Both cognitive mechanisms are proposed to relate to aggressive behaviour. While the hostile attribution bias is assumed to be a precursor to aggression, moral disengagement can be seen as a justification of it, applied by people to rationalize and justify their past aggressive behaviour.

Attributional biases are presumed to have significant consequences at the individual as well as societal level. The attributional bias could, for example, be an explanation for the noncompliance with the health recommendations installed to combat COVID-19, such as social distancing and self-isolation. A 2020 study showed that people attributing their risk of getting infected to internal factors, such as age or personal hygiene, rated their COVID-19 risk being significantly lower, whereas people who made more situational attributions, such as attributing their risk to government decision-making and other people's cleanliness, rated their risk significantly higher (Dunning et al., 2020). The authors of the study suggest that noncompliance may be justified by these risk perceptions.

What is the relevance of attributional biases to organizations and change?

From the perspective of organizations and change, the human tendency to focus mainly on personal factors (skills, competencies, characteristics, etc.) when evaluating the other is illustrated in the way organizational success (or failure) is attributed to leaders and entrepreneurs, but not to circumstances. Famous CEOs like Steve Jobs, Jeffrey Bezos, and Elon Musk have been praised for the enormous success of Apple, Amazon, and Tesla, respectively, and countless of managers, authors, and consultants have tried to draw leadership lessons from them. However, people are not inclined to ask themselves: "Could it be that the success of Apple's stores had not so much to do with Steve Jobs himself but rather with Apple's product introductions?" Instead, the public, media, and stock-market don't seem to doubt that Jobs had played a decisive role.

Attributional biases within organizations affect relationships and performance, and are specifically relevant to change management, as different attributions can be given to the reason for change, which in turn may affect the outcome of the change. This stresses the need for a proper change diagnosis before any change initiative. Attribution theory helps leaders understand their followers and the need for change. For example, leaders' "attributions about the causes of subordinate performance can affect the way in which a leader subsequently interacts with subordinates" (Offermann et al., 1998, p. 1135). Hostile attribution specifically could be relevant to organizations and change, since employees who are prone to attribute hostile intent to ambiguous behaviour of colleagues might be more likely to engage in antisocial or aggressive behaviour, thereby possibly creating a hostile work environment. It is thus self-explanatory that these behaviours are to be avoided at all costs. Considering the possible relevance of hostile attributions to organizations and change, we have chosen to include this bias in our search (see search strategy below).

Search strategy

Relevant databases were searched using the term 'attribution theory,' 'attribution bias,' and 'hostile attribution' both separately and in combination with the terms 'organisation*,' 'work,' 'employ*,' 'leader*,' or 'chang*.' The searched yielded more than 600 articles. After removing the duplicates and thorough examination, 1 meta-analysis and 6 studies were included.

Main findings

1. *When making economic decisions, people make use of causal attributions (Level B).*

   In their 2012 experimental study, Gurevich et al. explored the relationship between causal attributions and economic decisions. The researchers proposed that the well-known rational choice theory, a mathematical approach to decision-making in strategic environments, was not sufficient to explain the irrational economic decisions made by people in real-life situations. Instead, when making an economic decision, the researchers hypothesized people are influenced by the process of causal thinking. Results indeed indicated a positive relationship between causal attributions and economic decisions: ". . . what this research shows is that when people make economic decisions they may 'violate' expectations based on rational considerations such as these predicted by rational choice theory. However, their decisions are not arbitrary but rather crafted according to predictable rules complying with social motivation considerations such as these reflected by attribution theory" (Gurevich et al., 2012).

2. *When groups perform poorly due to low effort, leaders make more negative comments than when they perform poorly because of inability or bad luck (Level A).*

   An experimental study by Offermann et al. (1998) investigated the relationship between leaders' attributions to employee performance and future leader-member interactions and performance. Results showed that when leaders perceive that group performance is poor because of low effort, they tend to make more negative comments than when they perceive the performance to be low because of inability or bad luck. Furthermore, the researchers found that leaders also were most verbally active when their groups succeeded because of good luck (Offermann et al., 1998).

3. *Individually focused attributions for past success cause groups to consider more divergent alternatives before making a shared decision, facilitate the sharing of unique information, and improve decision-making (Level A).*

   In two experiments, Goncalo and Duguid (2008) studied the relationship between causal attributions and the quality of group decision-making. Results indicated that causal attributions may have important consequences for group performance. Individually focused attributions for past success led to various positive outcomes such as the consideration of more divergent alternatives, improved sharing of unique information, and improved decision-making. This implies that focusing on individual achievement is important for group performance. Reversely, increasing emphasis on teamwork and the attribution of success to team effort may have negative effects on creativity and can ultimately lower the quality of group decision-making (Goncalo & Duguid, 2008).

4. *Internal attributions to favourable events have a positive effect on performance, while external attributions to favourable events have a negative effect on performance (Level C).*

   A meta-analysis by Harvey et al. (2014) examined the predictive power of attributions in organizational contexts. Findings indicated that employees' internal attributions to favourable events were associated with better performance, while the opposite was the case for external attributions. This finding implies that internal attributions could be important for organizational success (Harvey et al., 2014).

5. *Individuals learn more from their successes than from their failures, but they learn more from the failures of others than from others' successes (Level D).*

   Drawing on attribution theory, a study by KC et al. (2013) investigated how people learn from their own past experiences with both failure and success and from the experiences of others. Findings of their study suggested that people learn more from their success than from their failure. KC et al. also found that the failure of others has a greater positive effect on individual performance than others' success. According to this study, focusing on one's successes and others' failures would thus be the best way for individuals to enhance learning (KC et al., 2013).

Conclusion

Based on scientific evidence, it is likely that attributional bias is important for (change) management. Evidence indicates that attributions can influence performance, decision-making, economic decisions, and learning in organizations and are thus likely to be a valuable factor during organizational change (Ten Have et al., 2019). High-quality research shows that attributions are of importance when making economic decisions, causing people to make irrational economic decisions governed by faulty causal reasoning. Research in the organizational field specifically points to the role of attributions in leader-member interactions and group-performance. Research also points to the direction that internal attributions could be important for organizational success and that focusing on one's successes and others' failures could be beneficial for individual performance. Having said that, some caution in generalizing these last findings is required considering the fairly low quality of these studies.

Practical reflections

On a more general note, attributions help understand employees in their processes of interpreting, comprehending, and decision-making in organizational contexts. They help leaders understand followers and followers understand their leaders. They shed light on how information, for example, about a new strategic direction or a culture change, is processed. As such, attributions help to design and develop well-thought-out and contextual, sensitive, and sensible 'paths to change.' For example, different attributions can be assigned as the reasons for change, which in turn may affect the outcome of the change. Also, when confronted with possible change, people will start thinking about causes and effects. It is helpful to understand these and the underlying processes to be better able to deal with factual or possible resistance (Ten Have et al., 2019). Bridges (1991) emphasizes the importance of understanding resistance and its causes:

> It's the process of letting go that people resist, not the change itself. Their resistance can take the form of foot-dragging or sabotage, and you have to understand the pattern of loss to be ready to deal with the resistance and keep it from getting out of hand.

Heifetz et al. (2009) points out the value of resistance to change and pleas for the protection of the voices of dissent. He states:

> The voices of dissent are the naysayers, the sceptics, who not only question this initiative but question whatever is on the agenda of today. They are princes of darkness, often resting on the negative. But they are valuable for implementing adaptive change because they are canaries in the coal mine, early-warning systems, and because in addition to being unproductive and annoying much of the time, they have the uncanny capacity for asking the really tough key question that you have been unwilling to face up to yourself or that others have been unwilling to raise. In many organizations, dissenters get marginalized, silenced, or even fired, which deprives the organisation of their valuable, if unpopular service.
>
> (Ten Have et al., 2019)

The main findings related to attributional bias can also be instrumental in guiding cooperation and, eventually, enhancing performance. The main findings suggest that a focus on internal attributions, the individual in a team, the success of self, and the failure of others all seem to contribute to better cooperation and a better 'return' on collective, social efforts. This is illustrated by Goncalo and Duguid (2008):

> When attributions for group success focused on the contributions made by each individual, groups subsequently considered more alternatives prior to reaching consensus and the alternatives considered were also more divergent than those considered by groups who attributed their success to the group as a whole. In addition, individually focused attributions for success also increased the sharing of unique information and raised the likelihood of reaching the correct solution.
>
> (p. 40)

Organizational leaders and managers are thus advised to stimulate their subordinates to focus on their own, individual contribution to group or team performance.

Furthermore, the lack of evidence regarding the hostile attribution bias should be noted. However, this bias does address some issues that hold relevance in organizations and change. Importantly, the hostile attribution bias is most likely to creep up when information is ambiguous, since this leaves room for negative interpretations of that information. With regard to change processes, leaders and managers should provide open and clear communication, as this reduces ambiguity. As a result, they could reduce hostile interpretations of employees while stimulating trust and commitment. This relates to the justice theory, which divides organizational justice into three elements—distributive justice (outcomes), interactional justice (interaction), and procedural justice (process). Distributive justice can be described as perceived fairness of how rewards and costs are distributed across group members (e.g., employees). Interactional justice concerns the way in which group members (e.g., employees) are treated when decisions are made; employees feel they are being treated fairly when they are provided with explanations for decisions and are being treated with dignity, respect, and sensitivity. Lastly, procedural justice reflects the perceived fairness of decision-making processes and the degree to which they are consistent, accurate, unbiased, and open to voice and input. With regard to change processes, Michel and González-Morales (2013) state that

> change managers should monitor the event characteristics and manage the change process by informing employees frequently and comprehensively, providing participation and voice opportunities and enacting effective leadership behaviours. Such actions positively influence employees' perception of fairness and organisational support, trust in management, commitment and increased employee-organisation value congruence.

The importance of clear and unambiguous communication to enhance trust is also emphasized by equity theory. This social psychological theory, introduced in 1965 by workplace and behavioural psychologist John Adams, posits that people compare remuneration for their work against that of their peers to conclude whether they are being treated fairly or not. Getting rewarded too little compared with one's peers may result in frustration or anger. Getting rewarded too much, on the other hand, may result in feelings of guilt. When employees raise concerns about fairness, managers should be open to alleviating those concerns. Managers should always ensure that employees perceive fair treatment when they compare themselves with colleagues (Ten Have et al., 2019). And managers should focus on internal equity by "achieving and communicating internal salaries equity, internal fringe benefits equity, internal promotion opportunities equity and internal status equity" (Khalifa, 2011).

Bibliography

Armor, D. A., & Taylor, S. E. (1998). Situated optimism: Specific outcome expectancies and self-regulation. In M. P. Zanna (Ed.), *Advances in experimental social psychology* (pp. 309–379). Academic Press.

Barros, L., & Silveira, A. (2007). Overconfidence, managerial optimism and the determinants of capital structure. *Brazilian Review of Finance,* 6(3). Available at SSRN 953273.

Baumeister, R. F. (1993). *Self-esteem: The puzzle of low self-regard* (1st ed.). Plenum Press.
Baumeister, R. F., Campbell, J. D., Krueger, J. I., & Vohs, K. D. (2003). Does high self-esteem cause better performance, interpersonal success, happiness, or healthier lifestyles? *Psychological Science in the Public Interest*, *4*(1), 1–44. https://doi.org/10.1111/1529-1006.01431
Baumeister, R. F., & Tierney, J. (2001). *The power of bad: How the negativity effect rules us and how we can rule it*. Penguin Press.
Berscheid, E., & Reis, H. T. (1998). Attraction and close relationships. In D. T. Gilbert, S. T. Fiske, & G. Lindzey (Eds.), *The handbook of social psychology* (4th ed., pp. 193–281). McGraw-Hill.
Berscheid, E., & Walster, E. H. (1978). *Interpersonal attraction* (2nd ed.). Addison-Wesley.
Boon, S. D. (1995). Trust. In A. S. R. Manstead & M. Hewstone (Eds.), *Blackwell encyclopedia of social psychology* (pp. 656–657). Blackwell.
Bornstein, R. F. (1989). Exposure and affect: Overview and meta-analysis of research, 1968–19 87. *Psychological Bulletin*, *106*(2), 265–289. https://doi.org/10.1037//0033-2909.106.2.265
Buehler, R., Messervey, D., & Griffin, D. (2005). Collaborative planning and prediction: Does group discussion affect optimistic biases in time estimation? *Organizational Behavior and Human Decision Processes*, *97*(1), 47–63. https://doi.org/10.1016/j.obhdp.2005.02.004
Burger, J. M., Soroka, S., Gonzago, K., Murphy, E., & Somervell, E. (2001). The effect of fleeting attraction on compliance to requests. *Personality and Social Psychology Bulletin*, *27*(12), 1578–1586. https://doi.org/10.1177/01461672012712002
Bilgin, B. (2012). Losses loom more likely than gains: Propensity to imagine losses increases their subjective probability. *Organizational Behavior and Human Decision Processes*, *118*(2), 203–215. https://doi.org/10.1016/j.obhdp.2012.03.008
Bridges, W. (1991). *Managing transitions: Making the most of change*. Addison-Wesley.
Campbell, T. C., Gallmeyer, M., Johnson, S. A., Rutherford, J., & Stanley, B. W. (2011). CEO optimism and forced turnover. *Journal of Financial Economics*, *101*(3), 695–712. https://doi.org/10.1016/j.jfineco.2011.03.004
Colquitt, J. A., Scott, B. A., & LePine, J. A. (2007). Trust, trustworthiness, and trust propensity: A meta-analytic test of their unique relationships with risk taking and job performance. *Journal of Applied Psychology*, *92*(4), 909–927. https://doi.org/10.1037/0021-9010.92.4.909
Costantini, A. F., & Hoving, K. L. (1973). The effectiveness of reward and punishment contingencies on response inhibition. *Journal of Experimental Child Psychology*, *16*(3), 484–494. https://doi.org/10.1016/0022-0965(73)90009-x
Crisp, R. J., Hutter, R. R. C., & Young, B. (2009). When mere exposure leads to less liking: The incremental threat effect in intergroup contexts. *British Journal of Psychology*, *100*(1), 133–149. https://doi.org/10.1348/000712608x318635
Cummings, J. N. (2004). Work groups, structural diversity, and knowledge sharing in a global organization. *Management Science*, *50*(3), 352–364. https://doi.org/10.1287/mnsc.1030.0134
Dirks, K. T., & Ferrin, D. L. (2002). Trust in leadership: Meta-analytic findings and implications for research and practice. *Journal of Applied Psychology*, *87*(4), 611–628. https://doi.org/10.1037/0021-9010.87.4.611
Dunning, A., Travis, E., & Pownall, M. (2020). *Dispositional and situational attribution of COVID-19 risk: A content analysis of response typology (Version: 1)* (pp. 1–28). https://psyarxiv.com/czskd/; https://doi.org/10.31234/osf.io/czskd
Fiske, S. T. (2004). *Social beings: Core motives in social psychology*. John Wiley & Sons.

Flyvbjerg, B. (2011). Over budget, over time, over and over again: Managing major projects. In K. Pinto (Ed.), *The Oxford handbook of project manage ment* (pp. 321–344). Oxford University Press. https://doi.org/10.1093/oxfordhb/9780199563142.003.0014

Forsyth, D. R. (1987). *Social psychology*. Brooks/Cole.

Fragkaki, I., Maciejewski, D. F., Weijman, E. L., Feltes, J., & Cima, M. (2021). Human responses to Covid-19: The role of optimism bias, perceived severity, and anxiety. *Personality and Individual Differences, 176*, 1–7. https://doi.org/10.1016/j.paid.2021.110781

Fugate, M. (2013). Capturing the positive experience of change: Antecedents, processes, and consequences. In S. Oreg, A. Michel, & R. T. By (Eds.), *The psychology of organizational change: Viewing change from the employee's perspective*. Cambridge University Press.

Gok, K., Deshpande, S., Deshpande, A. P., & Hunter, G. (2012). Comparing promoter and employee attributions for the causes of firm failure: The case of an Indian petrochemical company. *The International Journal of Human Resource Management, 23*(12), 2576–2596. https://doi.org/10.1080/09585192.2011.610514

Goncalo, J. A., & Duguid, M. M. (2008). Hidden consequences of the group-serving bias: Causal attributions and the quality of group decision making. *Organizational Behavior and Human Decision Processes, 107*(2), 219–233. https://doi.org/10.1016/j.obhdp.2008.02.011

Gopnik, A. (2011, September 5). Decline, fall, rinse, repeat. *The New Yorker*. Retrieved February 7, 2022, from https://www.newyorker.com/magazine/2011/09/12/decline-fall-rinse-repeat

Gurevich, G., Kliger, D., & Weiner, B. (2012). The role of attribution of causality in economic decision making. *The Journal of Socio-Economics, 41*(4), 439–444. https://doi.org/10.1016/j.socec.2011.07.005

Harvey, P., Madison, K., Martinko, M., Crook, T. R., & Crook, T. A. (2014). Attribution theory in the organizational sciences: The road traveled and the path ahead. *Academy of Management Perspectives, 28*(2), 128–146. https://doi.org/10.5465/amp.2012.0175

Heath, C., & Gonzalez, R. (1995). Interaction with others increases decision confidence but not decision quality: Evidence against information collection views of interactive decision making. *Organizational Behavior and Human Decision Processes, 61*(3), 305–326. https://doi.org/10.1006/obhd.1995.1024

Heifetz, R. A., Grashow, A., & Linsky, M. (2009). *The practice of adaptive leadership: Tools and tactics for changing your organization and the world*. Harvard Business Review Press.

Heller, J. (1998). *Essential managers: Managing change*. D. K. Publishing.

Hilbig, B. E. (2009). Sad, thus true: Negativity bias in judgments of truth. *Journal of Experimental Social Psychology, 45*(4), 983–986. https://doi.org/10.1016/j.jesp.2009.04.012

Joseph, D. L., Chan, M. Y., Heintzelman, S. J., Tay, L., Diener, E., & Scotney, V. S. (2020). The manipulation of affect: A meta-analysis of affect induction procedures. *Psychological Bulletin, 146*(4), 355–375. https://doi.org/10.1037/bul0000224

Kahneman, D., & Tversky, A. (1979). Prospect theory: An analysis of decision under risk. *Econometrica, 47*(2), 263–291. https://doi.org/10.2307/1914185

Kahneman, D., & Tversky, A. (1984). Choices, values, and frames. *American Psychologist, 39*(4), 341–350. https://doi.org/10.1037/0003-066x.39.4.341

Kalat, J. W. (2010). *Introduction to psychology* (9th ed.). Wadsworth Publishing.

KC, D., Staats, B. R., & Gino, F. (2013). Learning from my success and from others' failure: Evidence from minimally invasive cardiac surgery. *Management Science, 59*(11), 2435–2449. https://doi.org/10.1287/mnsc.2013.1720

Khalifa, M. H. E. (2011). Perceptions of equity and job satisfaction: A study of university employees in Egypt. *International Journal of Management, 28*(4), 130–143.

Klein, C. T., & Helweg-Larsen, M. (2002). Perceived control and the optimistic bias: A meta-analytic review. *Psychology & Health, 17*(4), 437–446. https://doi.org/10.1080/0887044022000004920

Koole, S., & Van't Spijker, M. (2000). Overcoming the planning fallacy through willpower: Effects of implementation intentions on actual and predicted task-completion times. *European Journal of Social Psychology, 30*(6), 873–888. https://doi.org/10.1002/1099-0992(200011/12)30:6<873::AID-EJSP22>3.0.CO;2-U

Kotter, J. P. (2012). *Leading change*. Harvard Business Review Press.

Kouzes, J., & Posner, B. (2012). *The leadership challenge: How to make extraordinary things happen*. Better World Books.

Kriegel, R. J., & Brandt, D. (1996). *Sacred cows make the best burgers*. Warner Books, Inc.

Kwan, L. Y. Y., Yap, S., & Chiu, C. Y. (2015). Mere exposure affects perceived descriptive norms: Implications for personal preferences and trust. *Organizational Behavior and Human Decision Processes, 129*, 48–58. https://doi.org/10.1016/j.obhdp.2014.12.002

Laroche, H. (1995). From decision to action in organizations: Decision-making as a social representation. *Organizational Science, 6*(1), 62–75. https://doi.org/10.1287/orsc.6.1.62

Michel, A., & González-Morales, M. (2013). Reactions to organizational change: An integrated model of health predictors, intervening variables, and outcomes. In S. Oreg, A. Michel, & R. By (Eds.), *The psychology of organizational change: Viewing change from the employee's perspective* (pp. 65–92). Cambridge University Press.

Montoya, R. M., & Horton, R. S. (2014). A two-dimensional model for the study of interpersonal attraction. *Personality and Social Psychology Review, 18*(1), 59–86. https://doi.org/10.1177/1088868313501887

Montoya, R. M., Horton, R. S., Vevea, J. L., Citkowicz, M., & Lauber, E. A. (2017). A re-examination of the mere exposure effect: The influence of repeated exposure on recognition, familiarity, and liking. *Psychological Bulletin, 143*(5), 459–498. https://doi.org/10.1037/bul0000085

Murray, P. (2003). *The saga of Sydney Opera house: The dramatic story of the design and construction of the icon of modern Australia*. Routledge.

Myers, D. G., & DeWall, C. N. (2016). *Exploring psychology*. Worth Publishers.

Neves, P., & Caetano, A. (2006). Social exchange processes in organizational change: The roles of trust and control. *Journal of Change Management, 6*(4), 351–364. https://doi.org/10.1080/14697010601054008

Offermann, L. R., Schroyer, C. J., & Green, S. K. (1998). Leader attributions for subordinate performance: Consequences for subsequent leader interactive behaviors and ratings. *Journal of Applied Social Psychology, 28*(13), 1125–1139. https://doi.org/10.1111/j.1559-1816.1998.tb01671.x

Omer, H., & Alon, N. (1994). The continuity principle: A unified approach to disaster and trauma. *American Journal of Community Psychology, 22*(2), 273–287. https://doi.org/10.1007/bf02506866

Pahl, S., Sheppard, S., Boomsma, C., & Groves, C. (2014). Perceptions of time in relation to climate change. *WIREs Climate Change, 6*(3), 375–388. https://doi.org/10.1002/wcc.340

Perloff, R. M. (1999). The third person effect: A critical review and synthesis. *Media Psychology, 1*(4), 353–378. https://doi.org/10.1207/s1532785xmep0104_4

Roser, M., & Nagdy, M. (2014, November 8). Optimism and pessimism. *Our World in Data*. Retrieved January 31, 2022, from https://ourworldindata.org/optimism-pessimism

Rozin, P., & Royzman, E. B. (2001). Negativity bias, negativity dominance, and contagion. *Personality and Social Psychology Review*, *5*(4), 296–320. https://doi.org/10.1207/s15327957pspr0504_2

Schacter, D. L., Gilbert, D. T., Wegner, D. M., & Nock, M. K. (2015). *Introducing psychology* (3rd ed.). Worth Publishers.

Sharot, T. (2011). The optimism bias. *Current Biology*, *21*(23), 941–945. https://doi.org/10.1016/j.cub.2011.10.030

Shepperd, J. A., Carroll, P., Grace, J., & Terry, M. (2002). Exploring the causes of comparative optimism. *Psychologica Belgica*, *42*(1–2), 65–98. https://doi.org/10.5334/pb.986

Smircich, L., & Morgan, G. (1982). Leadership: The management of meaning. *The Journal of Applied Behavioural Science*, *18*(3), 257–273. https://doi.org/10.1177/002188638201800303

Sovacool, B. K. (2011). *Contesting the future of nuclear power*. World Scientific.

Taylor, S. E., & Gollwitzer, P. M. (1995). Effects of mindset on positive illusions. *Journal of Personality and Social Psychology*, *69*(2), 213–226. https://doi.org/10.1037/0022-3514.69.2.213

Ten Have, S., Rijsman, J., Ten Have, W., & Westhof, J. (2019). *The social psychology of change management: Theories and an evidence-based perspective on social and organizational beings*. Routledge.

Vaish, A., Grossmann, T., & Woodward, A. (2008). Not all emotions are created equal: The negativity bias in social-emotional development. *Psychological Bulletin*, *134*(3), 383–403. https://doi.org/10.1037/0033-2909.134.3.383

Wang, J., Zhuang, X., Yang, J., & Sheng, J. (2014). The effects of optimism bias in teams. *Applied Economics*, *46*(32), 3980–3994. https://doi.org/10.1080/00036846.2014.948678

Weinstein, N. D. (1980). Unrealistic optimism about future life events. *Journal of Personality and Social Psychology*, *39*(5), 806–820. https://doi.org/10.1037/0022-3514.39.5.806

Weinstein, N. D., & Klein, W. M. (1996). Unrealistic optimism: Present and future. *Journal of Social and Clinical Psychology*, *15*(1), 1–8. https://doi.org/10.1521/jscp.1996.15.1.1

Zajonc, R. B. (1968). Attitudinal effects of mere exposure. *Journal of Personality and Social Psychology*, *9*(2), 1–27. https://doi.org/10.1037/h0025848

6 Self-enhancing, biases, organizational behaviour and change

Maarten Hendriks, Cornell Vernooij, and Flore Louwers

A First Short Story of Self-Enhancing, Biases, and Change

Self-enhancing is the need to view the self as basically worthy or improvable. In an organizational context, self-enhancement is related to change vision, change capacity, commitment, and resistance to change, cooperation, leadership, and culture. People have the desire to feel good about themselves and to see themselves in a positive light. To be able to do so, humans rely on several mental shortcuts. People seem to tend to rely on their own perspective over those of others when making judgements (egocentric bias). This can be lessened by providing feedback, treating people fairly, and training/remembering (e.g., nudging or exemplary behaviour) to perceive certain situations from other vantage points. It is also indicated that we are overly confident in ourselves and the social group we identify with (overconfidence effect). Forming diverse teams and organizing activities enhancing organizational identity, such as team-building exercises or informational campaigns could help reduce this tendency. Furthermore, people seem to have the tendency to seek out, interpret, favour, and recall information that is consistent with their own expectations (confirmation bias). To minimize its influence, changes should be communicated in a vivid, in-depth way concerning the purpose of the change. For group discussions, it could be wise to appoint a devil's advocate. While testing or analysing change initiatives people influence the research outcomes through their own convictions and expectations (experimenter bias). Double-blind research techniques can be helpful to reduce this. People prefer to retain an object they possess than acquire the same object if they do not own it (endowment effect). This leads to the tendency to attach a higher value to objects when owned. Being aware of these dynamics and the role of both selling and buying parties is likely to minimize the effect. While making decisions, people tend to continue an already initiated endeavour because of the time, effort, or money that they have invested in it (sunk-cost fallacy). Barriers can be implemented to overcome this, such as activating a decision-maker's need to externally justify the project-related decisions, distributing responsibility to various decision-makers, or stimulating to focus on alternatives and consider opportunity costs.

DOI: 10.4324/9781003288237-6

Introduction

Self-enhancing, the need for viewing the self as basically worthy or improvable is the fifth core social motive and one of the two affective motives (the other one is trusting). Self-enhancement "involves either maintaining self-esteem or being motivated by the possibility of self-improvement . . ., people like to feel good about themselves. People feel instantly good when they receive positive feedback about themselves" (Fiske, 2004). Self-enhancement is related to the human urge for constant (personal) growth. Also, self-enhancement helps maintain the position in the group, and the group has the potential to enhance the self. Social exclusion makes people feel bad and can lead to social and self-destructive behaviours. Social inclusion, on the other hand, stimulates the opposite (see chapter 7, Belonging). Self-enhancement can be impactful in organizational and change contexts for example in increasing the effectiveness of individuals on their own, but also in teams and organizations. Therefore, leaders, managers, and change agents have to be aware of the need and potential for self-enhancement and the mental shortcuts people rely on. We have identified six primary biases related to the social motive of self-enhancing:

Primary biases

Egocentric bias
Overconfidence effect
Confirmation bias

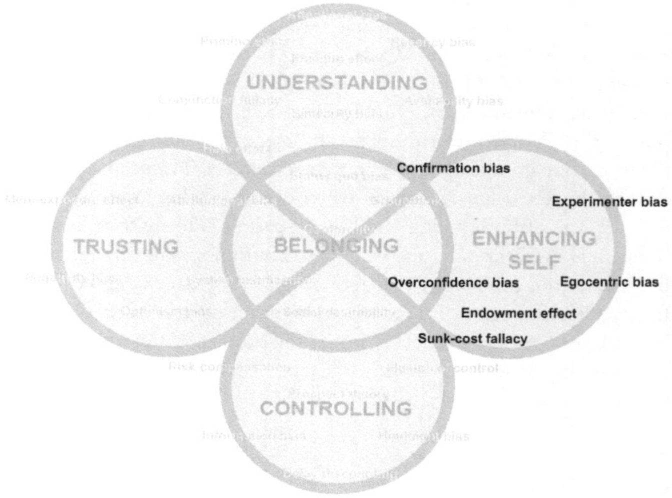

Figure 6.1 Primary Biases Related to the Core Social Motive of Self-Enhancing

Experimenter bias
Endowment effect
Sunk-cost fallacy

Additionally, the following secondary biases are identified to be related to the social motive of self-enhancing. These secondary biases are (when relevant) incorporated in the sections concerning the primary biases.

Secondary biases

Bias blind spot
Forer effect
Restraint bias
Social comparison bias
Ostrich effect
Continued influence effect
Moral credential effect
Illusion of validity
Backfire bias
Congruence bias
Zero-sum bias
Reactive devaluation
Curse of knowledge
Choice-supportive bias
Not-invented-here syndrome

In this chapter, we have categorized the six biases as follows: (1) biases concerning beliefs about oneself and one's abilities (egocentric bias and overconfidence bias), (2) biases concerning beliefs and expectations about the world in general (confirmation bias and experimenter bias), and (3) biases concerning beliefs about earlier investments (endowment effect and sunk-cost fallacy).

Egocentric bias

What is the egocentric bias?

The egocentric bias is the tendency of people to rely on their own perspective when making judgements about others and to have a better opinion of oneself than reality reflects. Information in the human brain is more easily triggered when it involves information relating to the self. Memories, ideas, and beliefs are more easily recalled when it matches someone's own beliefs. As a consequence, people assume that other people share their perspectives, when often, in reality, others have different and opposing perspectives. This usually translates into over/underestimating the frequency of other people's engagement in certain behaviours. This bias results in a decreased ability to clearly see and judge daily events. One common example of the egocentric bias is the amount of credit people give themselves for collaborative endeavours. When people work together on a group project and are asked how much they contribute relative to their coworkers, it is highly likely the sum of the percentages the group members give will add up to more than 100 percent. This overestimation of one's input stems from an egocentric bias in recalling one's contributions. People have an easier time remembering their own inputs (in terms of time, ideas, etc.) than those of others. As a result of this, their views about their own contributions become inflated.

The term 'egocentric bias' was first coined in 1980 by American psychologist Anthony Greenwald, who stated that people tend to recall information better when it relates to themselves in some way, causing them to exaggerate their role in a situation. Greenwald also argued that people encode information better when they have a direct role in the outcome of a situation, causing them to fall prey to the egocentric bias (Goleman, 1985). Over the years, the egocentric bias has received considerable public attention, especially in politics and the mental health sector (Delavande & Manski, 2012; Goleman, 1985). For example, findings on voting behaviour have indicated that the more strongly people favour a certain candidate, the higher they estimate that candidate's likelihood of winning the election. For example, research concerning the 2008 American Election found out that voters who showed a strong preference for Barack Obama predicted that he had a 65 percent chance of becoming president, while voters preferring John McCain predicted that Obama only had a 40 percent chance of winning the elections (Delavande & Manski, 2012). The recent COVID-19 pandemic has also yielded several studies that relate to the egocentric bias. For example, when being reminded of self-protective behaviour (e.g., mask-wearing), people tend to focus much more on their own actions and too little on the actions of others, even though those others may be just as relevant to self-protection (Vieites et al., 2021).The egocentric bias is also suggested to amplify the perceived importance of one's own contributions and devaluate the perceived importance of peer contributions in collaborative settings and social relationships. In an organizational context, firms, teams, or colleagues diving into collaborative endeavours may be influenced by the egocentric bias. When this happens, the devaluation of others' work and overvaluation of one's own work could have detrimental effects on the organizational culture, team spirit, and coworker-relationship, respectively.

Secondary biases related to the egocentric bias

Self-serving bias—the tendency to take undue credit for positive events or outcomes, while blaming external factors for negative events

Spotlight effect—the proneness to overestimate the amount of attention others pay to oneself

Forer effect—the tendency to believe that generic personality descriptions apply specifically to oneself

Zero-sum bias—the tendency to intuitively judge that one person's gain would be another's loss (e.g., a zero-sum situation) even when this is not the case

Reactive devaluation—the proneness to disparage proposals made by another (antagonistic) party

Not-invented-here syndrome—the tendency to avoid using knowledge or buying products from an external party

Curse of knowledge—the susceptibility to assume others share the same background knowledge on a certain topic that one has expertise in

Information about the self can exert a disproportionate influence on various kinds of judgements. The egocentric bias is therefore linked to several secondary biases. The self-serving bias, or the tendency to take undue credit for positive events or outcomes while blaming external factors for negative events, partly overlaps with the egocentric bias. The biases are sometimes even used interchangeably in the literature. However, the key difference is that the egocentric bias is rooted in false assumptions regarding other people's reality, whereas the self-serving bias constitutes a skewed perception of one's own reality. For example, when a student receives a low-test score, the egocentric bias would make the student overestimate the number of other students who also receive a low grade to normalize their bad performance. A student showcasing the self-serving bias would attribute their low grade to poor teaching or bad exam questions. The spotlight effect is described as the tendency in people to overestimate the degree of attention others pay to them, or, in other words, to always feel like they are 'in the spotlight.' For example, when giving a presentation, people falsely assume that the audience notices that they are nervous. The spotlight effect can be seen as an extension of the egocentric bias. However, it solely focuses on the amount of perceived attention from others concerning one's behaviour (including all of their mistakes and lesser qualities) or aspects of one's appearance. The literature points out that the spotlight effect is specific to social-evaluative concerns, suggesting that people are more likely to experience the spotlight effect in situations in which they perceive they are being evaluated (Brown & Stopa, 2007). A theory extending to this finding is the theory of social facilitation. This theory states that the presence of others causes 'evaluation apprehension,' which is uneasiness or worry about being judged by others. When people focus on what other people may think of them, arousal is created (Rosenberg et al., 1969). According to social psychologist Robert Zajonc (1968), arousal consequently positively influences the performance of simple tasks and negatively influences that of difficult tasks.

The tendency to attend to information relating to the self is also present in the Forer effect (also called the Barnum effect). This effect is a psychological phenomenon whereby individuals perceive that general characterizations apply specifically to them, even when the statements are so generalized that they could apply to the vast majority of people. This effect could explain the popularity of paranormal beliefs and practices such as fortune-telling (Carroll, 1994) and suggests that humans naturally tend to attend more to personally relevant information. The zero-sum bias is another bias related to the egocentric bias. This bias is the tendency to believe that one person's gain automatically entails another's loss. Zero-sum thinking is proposed to stimulate competitive (or less cooperative) behaviour since others are seen as a competitive threat. It is also presumed to be caused by egocentric thinking (e.g., believing that one is entitled to a certain share of a resource at the possible expense of others) (Burleigh et al., 2016). Another phenomenon related to competition is 'reactive devaluation' or the tendency to devalue and reject proposals made by another party, especially when this other party is perceived negatively or as antagonistic. This reactionary response is supposedly caused by zero-sum thinking because any gain of the opposing side is believed to be to detrimental to self. A bias closely linked to reactive devaluation is the 'not-invented-here syndrome,' which is the tendency to avoid using knowledge or buying products from an external party. It is proposed that people have an aversion to ideas or products from the outside, supposedly because people have reduced trust in things, they didn't have personal involvement in creating. Another phenomenon called 'curse of knowledge' is also presumed to be connected to egocentric thinking. The curse of knowledge is described as the tendency to falsely assume others share the same background knowledge on a certain topic that one has expertise in or has extended knowledge about (Kennedy, 1995). This is suggested to be caused by egocentric thinking. Since people generally have difficulty understanding others' perspectives, they find it hard to imagine what it would be like not knowing something that they do.

What is the relevance of the egocentric bias to organizations and change?

People in a company need to work together to achieve a common goal. To do that collaboration, negotiation, and finding common ground are everyday practices in the continuous social interaction employees and managers experience. Organizations and change projects continuously face problems concerning collaboration, negotiation, and finding common ground. The egocentric bias exposes a blind spot in human reasoning. The overuse of one's own perspective as a reference point and thus decreasing the ability to clearly make decisions in daily situations could very well act as a barrier to effective collaboration and social interaction. Focusing on the needs, responsibilities, and aspects that are closely related to oneself can create a blind spot for the needs, responsibilities, achievements, or concerns of others. It could therefore be beneficial for managers and change agents to understand how people tend to reason from their own perspective, project their own perspective on other people, and what you can do to lessen or overcome this.

Search strategy

Relevant databases were searched using the term 'egocentric' and 'self-serving bias' and 'social exchange' both separately and in combination with the terms 'organisation*,' 'work,' 'employ*,' 'leader*,' and 'chang*.' The search yielded more than 473 articles. After removing the duplicates and thorough examination, 0 meta-analyses, 0 systematic reviews, and 10 studies were included.

Main findings

1. *People have a better opinion of self (or the in-group) than others (or the out-group) when compared to reality (Level C).*

   The egocentric bias was found across multiple experiments (Farrar & Ostojić, 2018). Employee's descriptions of their own communication behaviour are related poorly to descriptions contributed by peers, subordinates, and superiors. In addition, the urge was found to rate themselves better than others rated them (Sypher & Sypher, 1984). In addition, egocentric bias was found to be present in the context of military leadership, where leaders significantly overestimated their own leadership qualities in relation to others (Foster et al., 2018). The overestimation of oneself not only seems to put strain on the people directly involved, but also on the ones closely surrounding these people, such as their partners (Hyman et al., 2014).

2. *People generally overestimate the amount of attention other people are paying them (Level D).*

   In addition, evidence was found to support the existence of the 'spotlight effect' (as a form of egocentric bias). Gilovich et al. (2000) found in a number of studies that people who were asked to put on a T-shirt depicting either a flattering or potentially embarrassing image overestimated the number of observers who would be able to recall what was pictured on the shirt. In addition, they found that people also overestimated how easily their fellow participants recalled the positive or negative things they said during a discussion.

3. *The older people get, the more they tend to consider events stronger from their own perspective (Level D).*

   Bradford et al. (2020) performed an event-related brain potential study, where participants had to answer questions about false-belief tasks. The egocentric bias was related to age. While older adults continued to consider the story events from their knowledge of reality, younger participants acknowledged the character's perspective.

4. *Providing narrative feedback strongly reduces egocentric bias (Level B).*

   Providing personal narrative feedback to people influences the degree to which they adjust their perspective-judgement and strongly reduces the level of egocentric bias they exhibit (Damen et al., 2021).

5. *Egocentric bias effects can be lessened by framing, interactional justice, or mindfulness training (Level D).*

   Scholars are also focused on overcoming the egocentric bias and in line with this, potential factors that could lessen egocentric thinking. Evidence shows that the spotlight effect was reduced through simple visual and mental framing. When asking people to imagine an event in the far future compared to the near future, a significant reduction in egocentric bias was perceived. Also, by letting people perceive a situation through a 'third-person' (vs. first person) vantage point or looking at themselves in a mirror, the egocentric bias was significantly reduced (Macrae et al., 2016; Greenberg, 1984). In addition, perceived interactional justice (the degree to which the people affected by the decision are feeling treated in terms of dignity and respect) was found to lessen egocentric bias (Leung et al., 2004). Also, mindfulness training could lessen egocentric bias, because it strengthens utilizing other perspectives (Pandey et al., 2018).

Conclusion

Evidence from previously mentioned studies supports the existence and effects of the egocentric bias. Memories, ideas, and beliefs are more easily recalled when it matches one's own belief and involves oneself in some way, resulting in the overuse of one's own perspective as a reference point at the expense of that of the others. People show consistent egocentric bias when estimating their own contributions to a group and they consistently overestimate their own communicative skills in relation to others. Framing, perceived interactional justice, giving narrative personal feedback, and mindfulness training offer possibilities to lessen or overcome the effects of the egocentric bias. By helping (forcing) people perceive situations from different vantage points, multi-perspective reasoning is encouraged, and egocentric bias can be lessened.

Practical reflections

As the egocentric bias illustrates, information is more salient when it involves the self, because people perceive the world through their own mental framework. Considering the possible adverse effects of egocentric thinking on organizational behaviour and social interactions, organizations and managers need to be aware that people consistently reason from their own perspectives and assume that others share that perspective. This leads to overestimations of one's own actions and contributions, gaps, and barriers in social interactions. This could occur at various levels within organizations as leaders could tend to overestimate their contributions and qualities just as much as employees (Foster et al., 2018).

Regarding change, egocentric thinking and the importance of individual perspectives help understand how and why people react to or, possibly, resist change. The way that a change is received is highly dependent on individual perspectives. This is stipulated by Lazarus and Folkman (1984), who state that 'visions' and a 'sense of urgency' are not 'givens' from the perspective of the people involved. Depending on the person and the situation, a vision, or sense of urgency can be associated with a threat, harm, loss, or a challenge (Ten Have et al., 2019, p. 115). It is very hard to account for all other possible perspectives. Nevertheless, there are some things to keep in mind to lessen the effects of egocentric bias. Egocentric bias can quiet easily be lessened by reminding people (nudging) to perceive certain situations from other vantage points by literally changing their vantage point. Treating people fairly, providing narrative feedback, and mindfulness training (letting people practice in assuming different perspectives) all seem to contribute to people shedding their own personal perspective of a situation. By implementing decision-making processes that are consistent, accurate, unbiased and open to voice and input, managers and leaders could account for a more just the change process (Ten Have et al., 2019). But most importantly, managers need to be aware that they themselves are susceptible to the bias and have an important role in showing their awareness (in terms of exemplary behaviour) with their teams to strengthen perspective changes.

Overconfidence effect

What is overconfidence effect?

The overconfidence effect (or 'overconfidence bias') describes people's tendency to be overbearing regarding the accuracy of their judgements or their abilities (Brookins et al., 2014; Cristofaro et al., 2020). People that fall prey to the overconfidence effect feel less inhibition regarding their own capabilities or judgements and can, as a consequence, make inaccurate or wrong decisions.

Of all social cognitive biases and heuristics, the overconfidence effect can be seen as one of the most pronounced when it comes to maintaining a positive self-concept. Ever since its introduction, this bias has gained increasing popularity. In his 2011 book, *Thinking Fast and Slow*, Daniel Kahneman referred to overconfidence as "the most significant of the cognitive biases." This statement was confirmed by Bazerman and Moore, who in 2013 called the overconfidence the 'mother of all biases' (Cristofaro et al., 2020). According to some scientific researchers, the overconfidence effect is "the most pervasive and potentially catastrophic" of all the cognitive biases human beings fall prey to (Plous, 1993). Overconfidence has been blamed for, among other things, the subprime mortgage crisis of 2008, the nuclear accident at Chernobyl, and the sinking of the Titanic (Labib & Read, 2013; Moore & Swift, 2011). More generically, it is often linked to legal disputes, stock crashes, political partisanship, and even wars (Barber & Odean, 2000; Johnson, 2005).

One well-known disaster of which the overconfidence effect is proposed to be one of the main causes is the Deepwater Horizon oil spill, which is regarded as one of the largest environmental disasters in American history. On April 20, 2010, a floating drilling rig on the Deepwater Horizon, located in the Gulf of Mexico, was destroyed by an eruption of oil and gas. The explosion set off the worst oil spill in the petroleum industry and killed 11 crew members. According to the investigations exploring the possible causes of the explosion, overconfidence on the part of BP, the company leasing the rig, the rig operator, and the rig contractor, was one of the root causes as all parties were pushing too close to the edge and overestimated their risk-management decisions in order to prevent such catastrophic situations. In light of the presumed causal role of the overconfidence effect in these catastrophes, researchers and practitioners remain interested in the assessment and development of techniques that could reduce this bias (Brookins et al., 2014).

The overconfidence effect is linked with several secondary biases. Firstly, the overconfidence bias strongly relates to the 'bias blind spot' mentioned in chapter 1, which is described as people's tendency to believe they are less biased in their judgements than others. The term, named after the visual blind spot, was introduced by social psychologist Emily Pronin and her colleagues Daniel Lin and Lee David Rovis in 2002. It proposes that most people exhibit the bias blind spot. Students believe that they are less biased than their classmates, airline passengers believe they are less biased than other passengers, and Americans believe they are less biased than their fellow citizens (Pronin et al., 2002). Or, as Kahneman puts it, "we can be blind to the obvious, and we are also blind to our blindness." It is suggested that this bias is strongly linked to the core motive of self-enhancing and proneness to be overly confident, as the desire to see oneself as above average on desirable attributes could lead people to believe they are less subject than others to the influence of mental shortcuts that might flaw their judgements (Ehrlinger et al., 2005). A specific type of overconfidence regards to self-control. Usually, people tend to overestimate their ability to control impulsive behaviour, a phenomenon referred to as the 'restraint bias.' This inflated self-control belief may lead to greater exposure to temptation and increased impulsiveness. A bias that is strongly related to restraint bias and the overconfidence effect is the moral credential effect. This entails the increased likelihood of someone with an established status of an egalitarian to show less egalitarian behaviour later. It is proposed to be caused by overconfidence in one's own self-concept or self-image, leading the person to worry less about the consequences of subsequent immoral behaviour later on.

Secondary biases related to the overconfidence bias

Restraint bias—the tendency to overestimate one's ability to control impulsive behaviour

Moral credential effect—when a status or reputation of being egalitarian establishes an unconscious license in someone that increases the likelihood of them showing less egalitarian behaviour later on

Ostrich effect—the tendency to avoid negative information that threatens to confirm negative self-beliefs

Choice-supportive bias—the tendency to retroactively exaggerate the positive attributes of an option one has chosen and to downgrade the renounced alternatives

Bias blind spot—the tendency of people to believe they are less biased in their judgements than others

Dunning-Kruger effect—people with limited knowledge or competence in a given domain greatly overestimate their own knowledge or competence in that domain; for people with high knowledge or competence the opposite is true

Our natural proneness to protect our ego and to maintain our self-image is also proposed to be one of the root causes of the ostrich effect, which is the tendency to avoid negative information that threatens to confirm the negative beliefs we have about ourselves. Instead of facing this information, people 'put their heads in the sand' to shield themselves from further psychological harm (Karlsson et al., 2005). However, by avoiding this information, they miss out on feedback that could help them monitor their goal progress. The motivation to maintain the ego is also suggested to be one of the causes of the 'choice-supportive bias' or the tendency to retroactively exaggerate the positive attributes of an option one has chosen and to downgrade the renounced alternatives. Since one's self-concept can be shaped partly by the choices made, memories of chosen as well as forgone options can affect one's sense of well-being. The choice-supportive bias usually results in memories that depict the self in a highly favourable light by making the positive results of our choices seem even better.

The overconfidence effect and related secondary biases are linked with several psychological theories and constructs about the self and self-esteem. Self-esteem is a social psychological construct that can be defined as "an individual's positive or negative evaluation of himself or herself" (Jones, 1990, in: Smith et al., 2015). Humans are intrinsically motivated to feel good about themselves and to enhance their self-esteem. Self-enhancing biases like the overconfidence effect are instrumental in the process that helps 'produce' certain self-esteem for an individual. Another coping strategy to sustain self-esteem, especially when faced with setbacks and disappointments of daily life that are threatening to the self-image, is the process of self-affirmation or reflecting on important aspects of one's life irrelevant to the threat or engaging in an activity that disconnects salient important values from the threatening event. In this way, when faced with situations threatening their self-esteem, people can be affirmed by engaging in activities that remind them of 'who they are' (Ten Have et al., 2019).

An alternative way in which people enhance themselves is by social comparison. According to the social comparison theory, people may interpret, distort, or ignore information coming from social comparison in order to see themselves more positively. Many great philosophers, including Aristotle, Rousseau, and Kant were already aware of the power of social comparisons. Karl Marx stated:

> A house may be large or small. As long as the surrounding houses are equally small, it satisfies all social demands for a dwelling. But let a palace reside beside the little house, and it shrinks from a little house to a hut.
>
> (Useem, 1975)

As can be implied from Marx' quote, comparing yourself with someone seen as physically or mentally better than oneself could lead to negative feelings and low self-esteem. People also tend to have feelings of dislike and competitiveness with someone seen as physically or mentally better than oneself, which is referred to as the 'social comparison bias.' Moreover, people use self-reinforcement to enhance their sense of self. This involves giving yourself positive approval of certain behaviour. Although self-reinforcement can help people to a certain level, in the end almost everybody needs reinforcement from others, or social reinforcement, to fulfil social needs. Social reinforcement involves positive stimuli from others such as praise, a compliment, a smile, touch, or even attention. For the human being as a social animal, social reinforcement is essential and vital. To function in a healthy and productive way, social beings need recognition of some form. Social reinforcement is crucial for mental and physical health, functioning, and performance. Without social reinforcement, people can become depressed or unhealthy, which is detrimental to our everyday functioning and (job) performance (Ten Have et al., 2019).

So, several social psychological concepts and theories are related to our need to maintain a positive self-concept, such as self-esteem, self-affirmations, social comparison theory, and social reinforcement theory. However, people are not solely motivated to maintain a positive view of themselves, but also an accurate self-view. According to the 'theory of self-verification,' people tend to seek confirmation of their self-concept, whether positive or negative (Swann & Ely, 1984). People use several self-verification strategies to create self-verifying worlds (Swann, 2012), such as systematic communication of self-views to others. People display identity cues, for example by the clothes they wear, or through performing certain actions that they believe confirm their identity. Some theorists contend that the desire for self-enhancement is more prepotent than rival motives such as self-verification. The literature however suggests that motives related to self-verification and motives related to self-enhancement are both influential in human thinking and behaviour, but in different ways (Ten Have et al., 2019).

What is the relevance of the overconfidence effect to organizations and change?

The intrinsic need to uphold our self-esteem could lead us to fall prey to the overconfidence effect. For people to function in an effective and healthy way, self-esteem is important. This could particularly be the case in times of uncertainty. Change, but also daily challenges, may put pressure on people's self-esteem. Baumeister (1993) described self-esteem as a social vaccine that plays a significant role in people's ability to cope with their environments. Notwithstanding the fact that self-esteem is necessary to function, biases like the overconfidence effect could negatively influence decision-making in various areas of professional live such as investment banking, medicine, and others. Concrete examples include over-entry by entrepreneurs, excessive trading and overexposure to risk by investors, and mistakes by medical-lab personnel (Brookins et al., 2014). For this reason, it can be beneficial to understand more about how this bias works and in what ways it might be diminished.

Search strategy

Relevant databases were searched using the term 'overconfidence effect' and 'overconfidence bias' both separately and in combination with the terms 'organisation⋆,' 'work,' 'employ⋆,' 'leader⋆,' and 'chang⋆.' This search yielded about 140 results. After removing the duplicates and thorough examination, 0 meta-analyses, 0 systematic reviews and 2 studies were included.

Main findings

1. *People seem to be prone to making overly confident judgements regarding themselves and the social group they belong to (level D).*

   Individuals belonging to a social group seem to be prone to making overly confident judgements about their relative standing within the group, which is called 'within-group overconfidence.' In addition, individuals also are susceptible to making overly confident judgements about the ability of the group to which they belong to, which is called 'between-group overconfidence.' In their experimental research, Brookins et al. (2014) explored these two types of judgements and their interaction with each other. Results showed that participants tended to make overly confident judgements at both levels, that is, concerning their own standing within the group as well as the group to which they belong (Brookins et al., 2014). Interestingly, results also showed that between-group confidence reduced within-group confidence. In other words, the presence of overly confident judgements about one's group mitigated within-group overconfidence. According to the researchers, this could be explained as follows. When an individual believes that its group's performance relative to other groups is high, this would also lead to an inflated belief about the performance of the peers relative to representative 'others.' For a given level of overconfidence in one's own performance relative to representative others, this will lead to a reduction in overconfidence relative to the peers.

2. *Strong group identity seems to reduce the degree of individual within-group overconfidence (Level D).*

   In their study, Brookins et al. (2014) also explored the relation between group identity and the overconfidence effect. They hypothesized that having a strong group identity would reduce within-group overconfidence. Results indeed showed that a strong group identity reduced the tendency to make overly confident judgements about one's relative standing within the group. The researchers reasoned that since strong group identity is linked to redefining the self in collective terms, such a redefinition of the self should lead to a reduction in within-group relative overconfidence with collective goals and interests merging with individual goals and interests.

3. *People with high self-esteem, self-efficacy, and emotional stability might be more susceptible to overconfidence regarding the accuracy of their judgements and their abilities (Level D).*

   In their 2020 experimental study, Cristofaro et al. explored the relationship between the overconfidence effect and personal traits. To capture personal traits, they measured core self-evaluations (CSEs) (e.g., evaluations that individuals make about themselves), due to their ability to predict job performance and to explain some facets of decision-making processes. High CSE's would indicate a high level of self-esteem, self-efficacy, and emotional stability. The researchers explored how high versus average levels of CSE were related to the overconfidence bias. Results showed that high levels of CSE resulted in higher susceptibility of overconfidence bias. Thus, researchers concluded that an average level of core self-evaluations is preferable in avoiding overconfidence bias in managers (Cristofaro et al., 2020).

Conclusion

High-quality scientific evidence supporting the existence of the overconfidence effect seems to be limited. Thus, caution is warranted in interpreting and generalizing results. Nevertheless, the available research does point to the direction that the bias exists and that people are usually overconfident in their judgements concerning themselves and the social group they identify with. This doesn't necessarily have to be a bad thing. Overconfidence in competence encourages actions that people wouldn't undertake if they were less confident and may nevertheless be very successful. However, unwarranted confidence in one's own knowledge and competence can yield risky behaviour and lack of openness for disconfirming information, and thus lead to poor performance and severe mistakes.

Practical reflections

The scientific findings help to gain a greater understanding about the overconfidence effect. Being confident in the self is essential as a human being to function in an effective and healthy way. This is particularly essential when uncertainty arises, for instance in times of change. Being overly confident might induce inaccurate or risky decision-making. Thus, the overconfidence effect is certainly an important phenomenon to be aware of in the organizational or change context. Several suggestions arise for leaders and managers trying to mitigate the effects of potential excessive overconfidence. Firstly, focus on forming a strong organizational identity. According to Brookins et al. (2014), strong organizational identity is linked to higher job satisfaction, lower turnover, and better customer evaluations. Activities enhancing organizational identity, such as team building exercises, or informational campaigns highlighting between-organization comparisons, could help employees reduce the tendency to make overly confident judgements about one's relative standing within the group (Brookins et al., 2014). Secondly, the finding concerning the relationship between high self-evaluations and overconfidence is relevant to organizational leaders and managers. According to Cristofaro et al. (2020), self-esteem, self-efficacy and emotional stability are personality traits, and are considered impossible to influence in an absolute way. Nevertheless, practitioners can mitigate its influence on the organization by creating ad hoc teams. This means forming teams of employees with varying levels of self-esteem, self-efficacy, and emotional stability. By this, they can avoid overconfidence within their teams. According to the researchers, human resource managers could measure the level of self-evaluations of each employee within organizations. This way, they are able to appropriately suggest to department or unit heads the 'best team composition' to achieve better organizational performance (Cristofaro et al., 2020).

Confirmation bias

What is confirmation bias?

Following the findings on egocentric bias, we found out that people often have a better opinion of oneself than is reflected by reality. Translating this principle to one's own believes people also tend to think they are right and hold onto their beliefs strongly. Changing someone's opinion generally takes a considerable amount of time and effort. For people it is easier to disregard alternative perspectives than to adapt their existing beliefs. The preference for existing beliefs or values underlies the confirmation bias (also called the 'myside bias'). In short, the confirmation bias posits that people have the tendency to seek out, interpret, favour, and recall information that is consistent with their own expectations (Hernandez & Preston, 2013). The bias is ought to operate unconsciously. Arguments supporting our position simply spring to mind more easily (Mercier & Landemore, 2012).

Long before social psychological experiments on confirmation bias, the phenomenon had been observed and documented numerous times throughout history. Italian poet Dante Alighieri noted it in 1320 in his work *Divine Comedy*, in which Dante (the lead character) is cautioned with the following words: "opinion—hasty—often can incline to the wrong side, and then affection for one's own opinion binds, confines the mind." Three hundred years later, English philosopher and scientist Francis Bacon wrote in his philosophical work *Novum Organum* (1620):

> The human understanding when it has once adopted an opinion . . . draws all things else to support and agree with it. And though there be a greater number and weight of instances to be found on the other side, yet these it either neglects or despises, or else by some distinction sets aside or rejects.

English cognitive psychologist Peter Wason was the first to empirically test the confirmation bias. In the 1960s he conducted a number of experiments now known as the 'Wason's rule discovery task.' In these experiments, participants were asked to identify a rule applying to triples of numbers. The experimenter told participants that (2/4/6) conformed to the rule. Participants generated triples, after which the experimenter disclosed whether the triple obeyed the rule or not (Nickerson, 1998). While the actual rule was 'any ascending sequence,' participants often thought the rule was more specific, such as 'the middle number is the average of the first and last number.' Also, participants only tested examples that obeyed their hypothesized rule (see 'congruence bias'). So, if they thought the rule was "the middle number is the average of the first and last," they would offer a triple that fitted this rule, such as (10/20/40) rather than a triple that violated it, such as (10/30/35).

Wason concluded that people indeed tend to seek information that confirms their existing beliefs.

Since Wason's experiments, the bias has been studied across various domains, such as politics, the organizational field, and science. These studies have indicated several detrimental effects of the confirmation bias. For example, in the scientific field, confirmation bias could lead to inductive reasoning (the accumulation of supportive evidence), producing systematic errors in research. Indeed, various studies have shown that researchers rate studies that report findings consistent with their prior expectations more favourably than studies reporting findings inconsistent with their previous expectations (Hergovich et al., 2010). Similarly, in the medical field, doctors may prematurely focus on a particular disease they assume their patients have and then seek only confirming evidence, thereby running the risking of misdiagnosing their patients.

At the individual level, this type of bias could prevent people from looking at situations or others objectively, possibly leading to prejudiced thinking and even stereotyping. For example, research showed that when children in a video were given a label of high or low socioeconomic status, people used that label to make judgements about their future academic ability, solely focusing on their pre-existing beliefs (Darley & Gross, 1983). Also, confirmation bias might influence political opinions and voting behaviour, as one 2012 study found that people with strong prior beliefs on social issues such as the death penalty evaluate related information in a manner that is consistent with their prior beliefs (Hernandez & Preston, 2013). On an aggregate level, the confirmation bias might hinder socio-political cooperation by interfering with the ability to consider other viewpoints (which is needed to reach collaboration) and even cause or aggravate social political divides between citizens.

This is illustrated in many forms in the COVID-19 pandemic, for example, discussions between extreme groups of pro- and anti-vaxxers. Extreme pro-vaxxers consider vaccination as the Holy Grail out of the pandemic leading to potential tunnel vision and restraints for unvaccinated people and extreme views including vaccination compulsion. Anti-vaxxers on the other hand, focused on and emphasized the side effects of the vaccines for they were already distrusting of the pharmaceutical industry. This was perceived as salient evidence of the disorganized nature of the vaccine development and has intensified their negative beliefs concerning the vaccines (Saleska & Choi, 2021).

For both groups, it led to extreme views aggravating even further the social political divides. Thereby the bias can be disastrous, creating or extending conflicts, from emotionally charged debates to wars and each opposing party becoming overconfident that it is in the stronger position by interpreting the evidence in their favour. This is recently even being amplified by the use of social media, in which confirmation bias is increased by the use of algorithmic editing (creating filter bubbles). By doing so, information is only displayed to individuals they are likely to agree with, while excluding opposing views. All in all, considering the potential impact of the confirmation bias on an individual as well as on an aggregate level, it seems worthwhile to further explore this bias and its underlying mechanisms as well as the psychological theories and (secondary) biases that are related.

The tendency to firmly stick to our existing beliefs is linked with several social psychological theories and other biases. Specifically, adherence to beliefs regarding social systems lies at the foundation of the system-justification theory (chapter 7, Belonging), which suggests that people seek to maintain views of their social systems, and their attendant norms, rules and social structures, as relatively legitimate, even when confronted with information suggesting the opposite (Jost & Banaji, 1994). In addition, the confirmation bias is proposed to be one of the root causes for the 'continued influence effect,' which is the tendency to continue to rely on misinformation and false claims in reasoning, even long after this information has been proven false. One other special type of the confirmation bias is the 'congruence bias' or the tendency of people to over-rely on testing their initial hypothesis (the most congruent one) while neglecting to test alternative hypotheses. People seem to stick firmly to their initial beliefs and disregard information disproving these beliefs. This also holds relevance in the 'illusion of validity,' which is described as the tendency to overrate one's ability to make accurate predictions and interpret data objectively to strengthen one's assumptions and predictions. In the context of research, observers' or experimenters' adherence to their own expectations and predictions could lead them to (subconsciously) influence participants. This is strongly linked to the experimenter bias, which is also known as the 'expectancy observer bias.'. Interestingly, people are susceptible to rejecting given evidence against their beliefs and tend to even strengthen their initial beliefs, which is an effect referred to as the 'backfire bias.' Another specific type of confirmation bias is the 'selection bias,' which occurs when a flawed selection process in an experimental study causes systematic differences between the characteristics of the individuals or groups selected for the study and those who are not. This results in the sample obtained not being representative of the population intended to be analysed (Henderson & Page, 2007).

Secondary biases related to the confirmation bias

Continued influence effect—the tendency to continue to rely on misinformation and false claims in reasoning, even long after this information has been proven false

Congruence bias—the tendency to over-rely on testing one's initial hypothesis

Illusion of validity—the tendency to overrate one's ability to make accurate predictions and interpret data subjectively to strengthen one's assumptions and predictions

Backfire bias—the tendency to strengthen one's initial beliefs when encountering evidence that supports the opposite

Selection bias—the tendency to select individuals, groups, or data for analysis in such a way that proper randomization is not achieved, thereby failing to ensure that the sample obtained is representative of the population intended to be analysed

What is the relevance of the confirmation bias to organizations and change?

The confirmation bias seems highly relevant to science and politics but is also present in the context of organizations and change. As stated in the introduction, the bias could have a huge impact on our social perceptions, attitudes, decisions, and behaviour. In organizations, this could have a huge effect. Imagine the organizational leader of a big company having the idea of launching a new product and considering it to be "the one product to rule the world." The leader then directs a team to conduct market research to explore its desirability and feasibility. The team (keeping the opinion of the leader in mind and with the tendency to please the leader) conducts the research and reports back. The leader (having the image of the product "being the product to rule the world") does not let the data do the talking and interprets the data confirming the initial idea. While this is a hypothetical scenario, it could very well be part of common practice in everyday business. In addition, the bias could also exert its influence on recruitment and selection. For example, during the interview stage of the recruitment procedure, interviewers' confirmation bias could influence their hiring decisions. Research indicates that interviewers often select those candidates who confirm their own beliefs, even though others may be equally or better qualified, which eventually could prohibit a diverse and inclusive workplace (Agarwal, 2018). Therefore, it would be advisable for managers and organizational leaders to learn more about confirmation bias, as this could reveal relevant information about how organizational members perceive, reason, and behave. With an increased understanding and knowledge of the confirmation bias, active steps can be taken to combat its occurrence.

Search strategy

Relevant databases were searched using the term 'confirmation bias' both separately and in combination with the terms 'organisation*,' 'work,' 'employ*,' 'leader*,' and 'chang*.' This search yielded about 40 results. After removing the duplicates and thorough examination, 0 meta-analyses, 0 systematic reviews, and 2 studies were included.

Main findings

1. *People tend to prefer information that is consistent with their prior beliefs (Level C).*

   In two experimental studies, Hernandez and Preston (2013) explored the occurrence of the confirmation bias with regard to political beliefs. Hernandez and Preston hypothesized that participants with strong prior beliefs on social issues like the death penalty evaluate related information in a manner that is consistent with their prior beliefs. To test for this, the researchers asked the participants to report their political ideology (from strongly liberal to strongly conservative) and read a short article in favour of the death penalty. After reading, participants answered six questions on the article such as "How reliable is the message?" "How intelligent do you consider the argument?" and "How much do you believe the facts that were in the reading?" Results showed that conservatives and liberals were polarized in their judgements, consistent with their prior attitudes (e.g., conservatives, who show support for the death penalty in general, agreed with the pro-death penalty arguments in the article, while liberals did not). This suggests that people tend to prefer information consistent with their prior beliefs.

2. *Presenting information in a way that prompts deeper analytical processing seems to promote consideration of alternative information (Level C).*

The aforementioned research by Hernandez and Preston (2013) also investigated how a seemingly irrelevant feature of a message, in this case, disfluency, can lead people to re-evaluate information on previously formed attitudes and reduce confirmation bias effects. In their research, fluency was defined as the relative ease experienced during processing, which could be altered by features such as the visual clarity of text (Hernandez & Preston, p. 178). For example, a 12-point Times New Roman font can be considered fluent, whereas a Comic Sans italicized font can be regarded as disfluent. The researchers hypothesized that the effort associated with disfluency would prompt a deeper, more analytical, and critical processing of the information itself. This would allow for greater consideration of counter-attitudinal arguments, and more scepticism towards attitude-consistent information, thereby reducing confirmation bias. Results indeed showed that conservatives and liberals evaluated a death penalty article consistent with their political beliefs when it was presented fluently; however, the bias declined when the argument was presented disfluently. These findings were supported by a second experiment, in which they studied confirmation bias in assessments of guilt. It turned out that participants gave less biased judgements of guilt when the facts were presented disfluently. These findings suggest that disfluency may offer an opportunity for better judgement and discourse between opposing positions, ultimately giving what was once an overlooked message a chance to be seen (Hernandez & Preston, p. 181).

3. *When managers are depleted, they seem more likely to reject information that is inconsistent with their own beliefs (Level C).*

In a study, J. Li et al. (2019) investigated the role of the confirmation bias in managerial voice endorsement. They theorized that when individuals are more depleted, they tend to give more weight to information consistent with their initial preference or stance and reject inconsistent information. In the organizational context, managers would be more inclined to reject employees' upward voice. Results of their study confirmed that depleted managers tended to make fast decisions on voice endorsement and were more likely to reject the voice of their employees. Interestingly, the detrimental effect of ego depletion was reduced when the manager perceived that the voicing employee was an expert on the issue at hand.

Conclusion

Despite the popularity of the confirmation bias, the availability of scientific evidence for this phenomenon seems to be quite limited. It does point to the direction that the confirmation bias exists and that some factors are likely to affect our susceptibility to it, such as the style of an argument's presentation. Presentations that prompt a deeper, more analytical, and critical processing of the information could reduce the confirmation bias. Regarding the organizational context, the confirmation bias has been linked to managerial voice endorsement (J. Li et al., 2019). Paradoxically, while managers can particularly benefit more from employee upward voice when they are more depleted, it is this depleted state that makes them less likely to pay attention to or endorse that kind of voice. This can lead to a quick rejection of a voice. Note that this does not seem to occur when the manager sees the voicing employee as an expert on the matter at hand.

Practical reflections

In managing change, organizational leaders and change agents have to be aware of the human tendency to stick to our initial beliefs, considering its possible adverse impact on organizational decision-making and social treatment in the organizational context. On a more general note, managers are advised to observe certain situations in which the confirmation bias is most likely to exert its influence, for example, during group discussions where individuals tend to be highly motivated to voice their own point of view or defend their arguments. Such discussions are likely to create polarization and overconfidence (Mercier & Landemore, 2012). A suggestion for managers would be to appoint someone to play the devil's advocate during such discussions, who can ask the tough questions necessary to create some dissent and stimulate the formation of alternative ideas and opinions. This stimulates constructive conflict, improving group decision-making. "Giving authority to or appointing high-status individuals as change agents also sends strong cues to others that the organisation encourages and rewards speaking up" (Ng & Van Dyne, 2001, p. 221). This also counteracts the threat of groupthink (chapter 7, Belonging). As the research by J. Li et al. (2019) points out, managers should be aware of the detrimental effects of ego depletion when they receive information that is inconsistent with their own beliefs, and consequently, their response to employee voice. One suggestion for managers is to postpone responding to employees' voices when they notice signs of mental depletion or low willpower and ensure their employees get back to them later when they are in a better, rested state. In the organizational change context, change communicators are advised to present information in a way that prompts deeper analytical processing, so employees are stimulated to question their existing beliefs and attitudes and consider alternative information (Hernandez & Preston, 2013). One strategy is to ensure that the change message is presented in a vivid, appealing way and contains both inspiring and in-depth information concerning the rationale, or purpose of the change. Bridges (1991) emphasizes the importance of clarifying the purpose: What is the idea behind what you're doing? People need a picture of how the outcome will look; participation requires imagination. Watkins (2013) pleads for an inspiring vision, built on a foundation of intrinsic motivators, making people part of the story and containing evocative language to inspire and motivate people.

Experimenter bias

What is the experimenter bias?

The experimenter bias exerts itself when researchers unknowingly influence participants, data, or outcomes during experimental studies, which in turn can degrade the study's internal validity. This bias can creep up at different phases of the research process—from selecting the study sample to measuring the outcomes to interpreting the analysis (Sacket, 1979). The experimenter bias differs from plain cheating in that the experimenters do not intend scientific misconduct. Instead, they subtly and often unconsciously manipulate certain elements in their experiment that makes the expected result more likely than it otherwise should be (Strickland & Suben, 2012). This is an odd bias in this book because it is not a general cognitive or social bias and is mostly present in research. However, as said by American psychologist George Kelly, people act as naïve scientists. This holds true especially during organizational change processes: Prior to the change, an organizational diagnosis is conducted (pre-test); based on this diagnosis, a change process is suggested (manipulation); and during the change process, the progress is measured (post-test). The change managers and leaders of the organization are similar to scientists in a change process. In addition, when pre- or post-measures are done through interviews, the interviewers can either consciously or subconsciously direct the outcome of these conversations by asking suggestive questions. The experimenter bias is therefore highly important to consider in change processes. It is related to the confirmation bias. Because the experimenters tend to look for information that validates their hypothesis, they are prone to overlook information that contradicts their argument. The experimenter bias is also referred to as the 'observer expectancy effect,' the 'experimenter effect,' the 'observer bias,' or the 'expectancy bias.' These terms are used interchangeably as they all refer to the specific bias that influences the research direction of experimenters or observers.

One famous example of the experimenter bias is the case of Clever Hans, an Orlov Trotter horse claimed by its owner van Osten to be the first 'speaking' and thinking animal. In the first decade of the twentieth century, Hans drew worldwide attention to Berlin for solving calculations by tapping numbers or letters with the hoof in order to answer questions. However, it was found that claims were debunked because the horse was unable to answer correctly when it could not see the questioner or when the questioner himself didn't know the correct answer. It turned out that the questioner's behaviour was a crucial element in the horse giving the right answers. As the horse's taps approached the right answer, the questioner's facial micro-expressions showed increased tension, which was released when the horse made the correct final tap. The horse thus learned to give the correct answer by reading the microscopic signals on the face of the questioner (Samhita & Gross, 2013).

In the organizational context, one specific type of experimenter bias has been introduced—the 'funding bias' or 'sponsorship bias.' This bias describes the tendency of a scientific study to support the (business) interests of the study's financial sponsor. The sponsoring company, in the hope of advancing its business interests, might disregard results contradicting its interests while publicizing the results that support its interests. One 2016 study seems to support this bias. In an analysis of 60 experimental studies investigating the health effects of sugary beverages between 2001 and 2016, less than 3 percent of studies that found sugary beverages linked to higher rates of diabetes and obesity were underwritten by the sugar-sweetened beverage industry. Conversely, if a study found no link between sugary beverage consumption and poorer health, the probability of this study being funded by sugar-sweetened beverage companies was almost 100 percent (Schillinger et al., 2016).

Of the several methods introduced to overcome this bias, one of the most popular is the double-blind experiment, where the observer or experimenter is unaware of the identity or treatment group of their subjects while conducting research. However, this technique is not always possible, as the reality of doing research is not always in a controlled laboratory setting, especially not during organizational change. Therefore, researchers and practitioners remain interested in finding potential techniques to combat the experimenter bias and strengthen the quality of research.

Secondary biases related to the confirmation bias

Funding bias—the tendency of a scientific study to support the (business) interests of the study's financial sponsor

What is the relevance of the experimenter bias to organizations and change?

At first glance, the experimenter bias might not seem specifically relevant to organizations and change management due to its specific focus on researchers. However, as many organizations conduct one or more change programmes, have their R&D departments, base their interventions and programmes on scientific research, fund research, and are involved in research-related activities, they should be aware of this bias and its possible consequences on the quality of research. In organizational change, agents have to be aware of this bias because change interventions involve both observers (change agents) and subjects (organizational members), who can both unintentionally influence each other in subtle ways. According to the 'social reinforcement theory,' positive interpersonal stimuli like praise, a compliment, a smile, touch, or even attention can reinforce behaviour, as a positive reaction follows the behaviour. Within organizations, social reinforcement is probably one of the most important instruments of leaders and relevant others such as change agents (Manz & Sims, 1987). Adding to that, the social learning theory explains how most behaviours that people display are the result of social learning, either deliberately or inadvertently, through the influence of example. In organizations, people copy the behaviour of others (e.g., their leaders and relevant others such as change agents). These social psychological theories illustrate how change agents could subconsciously influence organizational members to behave in a certain way, either by subtly praising desired behaviour or displaying the desired behaviour themselves. While this bias can be beneficial to help organizational members display the desired behaviours needed for change, caution is warranted. For example, when evaluating whether a previously implemented change intervention has led to the desired behavioural changes within a team or department, an accurate, unbiased view of employee behaviours is crucial to reach a valid analysis. Change agents, however, could unintentionally steer employee behaviour in such a way that desired outcomes are obtained, thereby obstructing the validity of their analysis.

Search strategy

Relevant databases were searched using the terms 'experimenter bias' and 'observer bias' both separate and in combination with the terms 'organisation*,' 'work,' 'employ*,' 'leader*,' and 'chang*.' This search yielded 192 results. After removing the duplicates and thorough examination, 0 meta-analyses, 3 systematic reviews, and 2 study were included.

Main findings

1. *Experimenters tend to influence their research outcomes through their own convictions and expectations (Level A).*

   In their 2012 and 2013 systematic reviews, Hróbjartsson et al. explored the occurrence of the experimenter bias in experiments using randomized clinical trials. In their 2012 review, results of 16 trials involving 2854 participants showed that nonblinded assessors were more optimistic in their estimates of effect sizes compared to blinded assessors, indicating an experimenter bias. The 2013 review, involving 21 trials and 4391 participants, confirmed these results. In addition, Strickland and Suben (2012) found support for the experimenter bias in experimental philosophy studies. They found a positive relation between experimenter hypothesis and participant ratings indicating a general tendency among experimenters to obtain the results that they expected. This also suggests that experimenters can influence their participants by creating their own favourable stimuli to test their hypothesis. Additionally, Stubbs et al. (2014) found experimental support for the experimenter bias in the coding of property rights scores, that is, the degree to which the laws of countries protect private property rights. Using cross-national data of 156 countries during a ten-year period, the researchers assessed whether the subjective coding of property rights scores was influenced by experimenter bias. Results indeed showed that experimenters subjectively coding property rights scores consistently gave more favourable scores when their country was in economic health or prosperity in contrast to when it was in economic recess. These results indicate that experimenters are influenced by their own convictions (in this case, concerning their country's economy), thereby impacting their perspectives and decisions.

2. *Double-blind techniques help to reduce the experimenter bias (Level B).*

   In their systematic reviews, Hróbjartsson et al. (2012, 2013) showed that using double-blind techniques reduces the experimenter bias, as these techniques generated substantially less biased effect estimates. In their review, Holman et al. (2015) supported this finding by showing that nonblind studies tend to report higher effect sizes and more significant values. Additionally, the researchers found that double-blind techniques were uncommon in the field of life sciences, suggesting a better and more thorough approach is needed to combat the experimenter bias.

Conclusion

High-level scientific evidence for the experimenter bias has been found across various fields such as life sciences, philosophy, and clinical research. This experimenter bias occurs when researchers' expectations and convictions influence study outcomes, thereby negatively impacting the validity of their research. Double-blind techniques can be used to minimize the risk of experimenters influencing participants, but these techniques cannot be applied to all research types and practical situations, which is why alternative techniques need to be explored to combat this bias and strengthen the validity of scientific research.

Practical reflections

The experimenter bias addresses issues that are relevant to and useful for organizations, specifically for those involved in the research field or managing an organizational change. Organizations, teams, and managers involved in research need to be aware of the (unintended) impact of the experimenter bias on study outcomes. If anything, the available evidence shows that scientific research is susceptible to experimenter bias, which should be taken into consideration when interpreting study results and generalizing these to the organizational practice. When either conducting research or analysing research manuscripts, organizations are advised to keep in mind that double-blind techniques are preferable as these minimize the risk of experimenter bias. As illustrated by the social reinforcement and social learning theories, change agents and organizational members in change programmes can unintentionally influence each other in subtle ways, and it would be prudent for change agents to be aware of this. According to Strickland and Suben (2012), a useful approach to combat the experimenter bias involves making sure that the experimenters are unaware of the relevant hypothesis. One strategy is to use a 'blind' stimulus creation in which the person or people designing the actual survey stimuli would be blind to a hypothesis. According to Holman et al. (2015), it might also be worthwhile to use multiple observers and trust in the 'wisdom of crowds' to reduce experimenter bias. By implementing or insisting on double-blind checks and using multiple observants, research is likely to be more robust, reliable, replicable, and valid.

Endowment effect

What is the endowment effect?

The endowment effect refers to people's preference to retain an object they possess than acquiring the same object if they do not own it. In short, people tend to attach a higher value to objects when they own these objects (Achtypi et al., 2021). This bias is closely linked to the prospect theory (chapter 4, Controlling) and the related concept of loss aversion (losses loom larger than gains): An already owned object cannot easily be given up or sold because it evokes a sense of loss in the owner. This effect also conceptually links with the status quo bias (chapter 7, Belonging), which indicates that people tend to prefer the current, established situation over a new situation or change. The term 'endowment effect' was coined by Richard Thaler in the 1980s. According to the standard economic theory, which was prevailing at that time, the price a buyer was willing to pay for something should be equal to their willingness to accept the loss of that item. However, with the introduction of the endowment effect, Thaler challenged this belief. Soon after its introduction, researchers started to empirically test for this bias. For example, in an experimental study by Kahneman et al. (1991), participants' perceived value of products such as mugs and pens increased substantially once they came to own these products. This indicates that the mere possession of an item raises its value in the eyes of the individual in question (Kahneman et al., 1991), thus lending support to the existence of the endowment effect. This bias has also gained popularity in the commercial field, as many retailers try to leverage the endowment effect in their marketing strategies. Various retailers in different sectors offer a free return policy, knowing that when someone already owns the product, they will value the product more and will be less likely to return the product. The same principle is used by giving away a free trial or sample. This way the consumer owns a part of the product, after which they will value the product more than before they had it and will be more likely to buy the initial product. Initially, the endowment effect was attributed mostly to loss aversion. Over the years, however, researchers have proposed other drivers explaining why this effect occurs. This is where the core social motive of self-enhancement comes into play. Research suggests that the motivation to see ourselves in a positive light can spill over to our possessions, causing people to value objects more when they associate them with themselves (Beggan, 1992).

What is the relevance of the endowment effect to organizations and change?

When it comes to changing organizations, the endowment effect could explain why change is often hard to attain. In light of the endowment effect, an organizational change could be experienced as a change in the current established situation (endowment) and therefore be met with reluctance. This is to say, organizational members might be hesitant to embark on change because they overvalue their current situation. As people are naturally motivated to bolster and support the current situation or 'status quo' (also see status quo bias in chapter 8, Belonging), change might be difficult to reach. The underlying mechanisms behind the endowment effect thus not only help to further understand the reasons for resistance to change, but it is also insightful for the ones who have to lead the change. In addition, the endowment effect could complicate negotiations within or between firms, for example, when considering a merger or acquisition. Consider a firm that has been offered a sum of money by a rival company to be acquired. In negotiations, the board of the firm to be acquired might overvalue the company, thereby possibly delaying or impeding negotiations. This becomes even more problematic when considering the plethora of small details being discussed in such negotiations.

Search strategy

Relevant databases were searched using the terms 'endowment effect' both separately and in combination with the terms 'organisation*', 'work', 'employ*', 'leader*' and 'chang*'. This search yielded 663 results. After removing the duplicates and thorough examination, 2 meta-analyses and 9 studies were included.

Main findings

1. *Selling prices usually exceed buying prices, but this is likely to be the result of strategic trading by both buyers and sellers rather than endowed sellers experiencing loss-aversion (Level B).*

Yechiam et al. (2017) investigated the occurrence of the endowment effect in monetary lotteries. In their meta-analysis of 43 studies, they found that selling prices exceeded buying prices. Following the reasoning of the endowment effect, this discrepancy should be attributed to the seller who is suffering from loss aversion. Interestingly, however, results showed that sellers were, in fact, more accurate in pricing than buyers, indicating a possible cognitive bias on behalf of the buyers. In this vein, a recent meta-analysis by Achtypi et al. (2020) suggests that the discrepancy in product prices between sellers and buyers is partly caused by buyers because they seek a 'good deal' (under the market price), while sellers price their goods according to their beliefs about the quality of the good and the distribution of the market prices. The authors found that beliefs about the market price do not differ between buyers and sellers. This implies that the discrepancy in pricing might not be induced by ownership but by what suits their interests most, given their beliefs about the market. In addition, three experimental studies by Smitizsky et al. (2021), in which a total of 565 people participated, found that pricing discrepancy is, in part, caused by the strategic buying and selling of goods (i.e., 'sell high, buy low'), instead of endowed individuals experiencing a loss-aversion, as predicted by the endowment effect. According to this study, the discrepancy is partly caused by the seller consciously setting high prices in a strategic way to gain more funds. All in all, the discrepancy in product pricing between sellers and buyers cannot be entirely attributed to the endowment effect, as strategic trading by both sellers and buyers is likely to play a role.

2. *There are signs that in negotiations people (especially in groups) tend to demand a higher price for their own (intangible) goods (Level D).*

A 2013 study by Galin explored the endowment effect in negotiations over intangible assets, such as leisure time. It was also investigated if and how the endowment effect influences negotiations in groups and between individuals. In one case, students would sell leisure time (=endowment) by shifting from two to three seminars, while in the other case, they would buy leisure time by shifting from two to one seminar. Students in both an individual and collective setting demanded a higher price when adding a seminar (e.g., losing endowment or 'selling') than when they were willing to pay for dropping a seminar (e.g., gaining endowment of 'buying') So, students were fairly unwilling to give up their endowment. Additionally, this was stronger for groups than individuals, as according to the author, groups are inclined to polarize and strengthen their stance. However, Galin also notes that the endowment effect present in the study might also be explained by negotiation strategies falling within rational economic theory (sell high, buy low). Also, given the fact that the evidence level of this study is fairly low, more research is needed on the endowment effect and its relation to group versus individual effects.

3. *In cultures that emphasize the collective versus the self, people might be less inclined to overvalue their own goods (Level D).*

   Maddux et al. (2010) researched the differences in Western and Eastern cultures related to the endowment effect. According to their predictions, the endowment effect should be less influential for individuals from Eastern cultures, given their emphasis on the collective and self-criticism, as compared to Western cultures, which stress the individual and self-enhancement. Comparing European Canadians and Asian Canadians, Maddux et al. (2010) found that people were less prone to overvalue their own goods in Eastern cultures, whereas they were more inclined to overvalue their own goods through enlarged emphasis on the self in Western cultures.

Conclusion

In conclusion, there seems to be little doubt that there is a general discrepancy between the selling and buying price for the same good (Yechiam et al., 2017; Achtypi et al., 2020; Smitizsky et al., 2021). However, the causes of this discrepancy remain unclear, with various findings questioning whether it is the mere possession of a good or rather strategic positioning of the price by both the buyer and the seller. In negotiations concerning intangible goods such as leisure time, people tend to demand a higher price for their own goods. This might complicate negotiations, especially in groups negotiating, given their tendency for polarization. Lastly, research suggests that different cultures that emphasize different values, such as independence of the individual versus interdependence of the individual, might influence the amount of overvaluation of one's own goods. While this research did not have a very high level of evidence, the intuition and the rationale of this finding could be of great importance in the current, globalized economy where different cultures engage in doing business.

Practical reflections

For organizational and change management, the endowment effect addresses some underlying mechanisms that help explain resistance to change: as people are naturally motivated to bolster and support the current situation or status quo, they might be hesitant to embark on an organizational change that constitutes a loss of this status quo. It is helpful to understand these mechanisms to be better able to deal with factual or possible resistance. Bridges (1991) also emphasizes the importance of understanding resistance and its causes:

> It's the process of letting go that people resist, not the change itself. Their resistance can take the form of foot-dragging or sabotage, and you have to understand the pattern of loss to be ready to deal with the resistance and keep it from getting out of hand.
>
> (p. 15)

The endowment effect can cause stalemates in negotiations. As scientific research suggests, people, especially groups, are likely to demand unreasonably high prices or returns for their goods in negotiations. However, as evidence implies, buyers use the strategy of 'low-balling' to make a good deal. The stalemate is thus more likely to be a combination of sellers protecting their endowment and buyers wanting to get a 'good-deal' than a pure case of loss aversion on behalf of the seller. Being aware of these dynamics and the role of both parties is likely to minimize such stalemates.

One last insight concerns the potential role of cultural characteristics in engaging in new organizational endeavours and changes. Maddux et al. (2010) provide an example in their article of how Japanese individuals were quicker to buy or adopt new technology than Americans, even when there were stronger incentives for the Americans to do so. Japanese consumers where thus more willing to forego their current endowment in favour of a new one. This finding could have broader implications for organizational change as Western firms might be more reluctant to make organizational changes, given their proneness to overvalue their own goods and attached loss aversion. In some cases, this could seriously hamper the future prospects and competitiveness of Western organizations. Eastern organizations on the other hand might be less inclined to maintain their status quo endowment and be able to reap the benefits of changing. Although more nuance in terms of what constitutes *Western* and *Eastern* culture is needed and more extensive research asked for as well, the basic intuition is becoming increasingly relevant, especially in a globalized world, where organizations and multinationals are conducting their business across the globe.

Sunk-cost fallacy

What is the sunk-cost fallacy?

The sunk-cost fallacy describes people's tendency to continue an endeavour because they have already invested time, effort, or money in it. Investments previously made thereby overshadow other factors to be taken into account when making decisions (such as present and future costs and benefits). This leads to suboptimal choices and committing oneself to decisions that are no longer in one's best interests. Richard Thaler, the economist who also coined the term 'endowment effect' first introduced the 'sunk-cost fallacy,' suggesting that "paying for the right to use a good or service will increase the rate at which the good will be utilized" (1980, p. 47). Psychologists Arkes and Ayton later expanded this definition by describing the sunk-cost fallacy as "a greater tendency to continue an endeavour once an investment in money, effort, or time has been made" (1999, p. 124).

Initially, the sunk-cost fallacy was used in the economic context since the size of financial investments was proposed to be an important predictor of the influence of the fallacy on economic decision-making. However, its use has been expanded to other domains as well, from long-term decisions regarding education continuation (Coleman, 2010) to our day-to-day decisions regarding activities and social interactions. The following example shows how the sunk-cost fallacy influences day-to-day decisions. Say, for example, you purchased a ticket for a play, but your friend invites you to have dinner together in a restaurant the same night. You would actually prefer to go to the restaurant, but because you already bought the ticket, you decide to go to the theatre instead (Roth et al., 2015). The sunk-cost fallacy does not only affect small day-to-day decisions, but also impact decisions by governments and companies. A famous example of the sunk-cost fallacy impacting large-scale decisions was the Concorde supersonic airplane project. Already in early development stages, the plane was significantly more expensive than expected and the financial success of the project was unclear. However, British and French governments still continued funding the project, justifying that the large amount of money that had already been invested should not be wasted (Arkes & Ayton, 1999). After finishing the project, the British government judged it to be a commercial disaster that should never have been started. Following this event, researchers and writers started to call the sunk-cost fallacy the 'Concorde fallacy,' and to this day, the two are often used interchangeably.

One proposed cause of the sunk-cost fallacy relates to the loss aversion phenomenon (see prospect theory chapter 4, Controlling). Abandoning an endeavour after investing resources is likely to cause a feeling of loss, and as people usually tend to avoid losses, they are likely to follow through on a decision that they have invested in, even if it is not in their best interest. Supporting evidence of loss aversion as a potential explanation for the sunk-cost effect comes from research in which people reported that their sunk-cost decisions were motivated by loss avoidance (Strough et al., 2008).

What is the relevance of the sunk-cost fallacy to organizations and change?

The sunk-cost fallacy is relevant and helpful in the context of organizations and change, since it can help better understand the tendency of organizations to remain committed to failing change projects and initiatives.

A well-known example of an attempt to desperately save a failing initiative based on early investments is Saturn, a division created in the 1980s by General Motors. The rationale behind the creation of this new vehicle line was to create a different type of company that would not be subject to the rules and regulations of the large GM company. Despite its great plans, however, Saturn never proved profitable. The contrary became true when 20 years after its launch, Saturn had cost the GM Company over $15 billion, without making any profit. Instead of withdrawing and trying to recover their initial investments, management escalated even further and recommitted another $3 billion to transform the semi-independent company into a general GM division, which turned out to be just as loss-making. Saturn finally shut down in 2010, after 27 years of excessive cost-making. Apparently, despite the new division never making a single cent of profit, the pull of the board of General Motors towards 'protecting' their earlier investments in Saturn was simply too strong (Sibony, 2019). As this example illustrates, the sunk-cost fallacy could have detrimental effects on corporate decision-making, resulting in continued investment in loss-making activities and excessive costs. Therefore, it would be prudent for organizational leaders and change agents to be aware of this bias and its influence on their decision-making processes.

Search strategy

Relevant databases were searched using the term 'sunk cost fallacy' and 'sunk cost effect' both separate and in combination with the terms 'organisation*,' 'work,' 'employ*,' 'leader*,' and 'chang*.' This search yielded about 150 results. After removing the duplicates and thorough examination, 2 meta-analyses, 0 systematic reviews, and 0 studies were included.

Main findings

1. *People are influenced in their decision-making by earlier investments made (Level A).*

   In 2015, Roth et al. conducted a meta-analysis on the sunk-cost fallacy in which 100 individual studies were included. The researchers found that when deciding between two equally attractive options, people were influenced by their earlier investments, thus indicating a sunk-cost fallacy. According to the researchers, their results gave "little doubt on the sunk cost fallacy's general existence." Additionally, outcomes of this meta-analysis revealed that the decision-maker's familiarity with economic decision-making (e.g., having a business background or being explicitly trained in economic decision-making) does not seem to play an important role in economic-decision-making. Apparently, knowing about basic microeconomic principles does not prevent individuals from falling prey to the sunk-cost fallacy, the researchers concluded.

These results were confirmed by Wang and Keil in 2007. In their meta-analysis, in which the results of 20 sunk-cost experiments were analysed, a profound overall sunk-cost effect was found.

2. *Sunk-cost effects are particularly present in experiments involving information technology (IT) (Level A).*

   In the aforementioned meta-analysis by Wang and Keil (2007), strong sunk-cost effects were particularly found in experiments involving IT projects as opposed to non-IT projects. This finding is supported by earlier survey data suggesting that 30–40 percent of all IT projects involve some degree of project escalation and experimental research demonstrating the sunk-cost fallacy to be significant in IT project escalation (Wang & Keil). According to the researchers, reasons why IT projects are particularly susceptible to sunk-cost effects remain unclear and need to be further investigated.

3. *Older adults are less likely to be influenced by the sunk-cost fallacy than younger adults (Level B).*

   The meta-analysis by Roth et al. (2015), found that participants' age influenced the sunk-cost fallacy, as older adults were less likely to fall prey to the fallacy than younger adults. This supports findings from earlier experimental research and can be theoretically explained by the finding that younger adults generally weigh negative information more heavily than positive information, whilst older adults' decisions reflect a more balanced view of gains and losses.

Conclusion

The scientific evidence is clear: People are likely to be influenced by their previous investments when making decisions. Decision-making regarding IT projects is considerably susceptible to sunk-cost effects. While younger adults are particularly likely to fall prey to this bias, even people familiar with the general principles of economic decision-making are not immune to it.

Practical reflections

From a managerial perspective, research on the sunk-cost effect can provide important insights into corporate decision-making behaviour. Firstly, managers who are responsible for projects should be aware that they and their employees might continue with a certain project even though other aspects point to the contrary. According to Roth et al. (2015), barriers can be implemented to overcome this, such as activating a decision-maker's need to externally justify the project-related decisions or distributing responsibility to various decision-makers. Another strategy is to educate employees to enhance decision quality. As Wang and Keil (2007) suggest in their article, it would also be prudent to encourage employees to focus on alternatives and consider opportunity costs and to make negative feedback unambiguous. These tactics might reduce the risk of the negative impact of the sunk-cost fallacy on corporate decision-making.

Bibliography

Achtypi, E., Ashby, N. J. S., Brown, G. D. A., Walasek, L., & Yechiam, E. (2021). The endowment effect and beliefs about the market. *Decision, 8*(1), 16–35. https://doi.org/10.1037/dec0000143

Agarwal, P. (2018, December 10). Here is how bias can affect recruitment in your organization. *Forbes*. Retrieved February 8, 2022, from https://www.forbes.com/sites/pragyaagarwaleurope/2018/10/19/how-can-bias-during-interviews-affect-recruitment-in-your-organisation/?sh=53e9e9e71951

Arkes, H. R., & Ayton, P. (1999). The sunk cost and concorde effects: Are humans less rational than lower animals? *Psychological Bulletin, 125*(5), 591–600. https://doi.org/10.1037/0033-2909.125.5.591

Bacon, F. (1620). *Novum organum*. Reprinted in Burtt, E. A. (Ed.). (1939). *The English philosophers from Bacon to Mill* (p. 36). Random House,

Barber, B. M., & Odean, T. (2000). Trading is hazardous to your wealth: The common stock investment performance of individual investors. *The Journal of Finance, 55*(2), 773–806. https://doi.org/10.2139/ssrn.219228

Baumeister, R. F. (1993). *Self-esteem: The puzzle of low self-regard* (1st ed.). Plenum Press.

Bradford, E. E., Brunsdon, V. E., & Ferguson, H. J. (2020). The neural basis of belief-attribution across the lifespan: False-belief reasoning and the N400 effect. *Cortex, 126*, 265–280. https://doi.org/10.1016/j.cortex.2020.01.016

Beggan, J. K. (1992). On the social nature of nonsocial perception: The mere ownership effect. *Journal of Personality and Social Psychology, 62*(2), 229–237. https://doi.org/10.1037/0022-3514.62.2.229

Bridges, W. (1991). *Managing transitions: Making the most of change*. Addison-Wesley.

Brookins, P., Lucas, A., & Ryvkin, D. (2014). Reducing within-group overconfidence through group identity and between-group confidence judgments. *Journal of Economic Psychology, 44*, 1–12. https://doi.org/10.1016/j.joep.2014.05.003

Brown, M. A., & Stopa, L. (2007). The spotlight effect and the illusion of transparency in social anxiety. *Journal of Anxiety Disorders, 21*(6), 804–819. https://doi.org/10.1016/j.janxdis.2006.11.006

Burleigh, T. J., Rubel, A. N., & Meegan, D. V. (2016). Wanting "the whole loaf": Zero-sum thinking about love is associated with prejudice against consensual non-monogamists. *Psychology & Sexuality, 8*(1–2), 24–40. https://doi.org/10.1080/19419899.2016.1269020

Carroll, R. T. (1994). Forer effect—the skeptic's dictionary—Skepdic.com. *Skeptic's Dictionary*. Retrieved February 8, 2022, from http://skepdic.com/forer.html

Coleman, M. D. (2010). Sunk cost, emotion, and commitment to education. *Current Psychology, 29*(4), 346–356. https://doi.org/10.1007/s12144-010-9094-6

Cristofaro, M., Giardino, P. L., & Leoni, L. (2020). The influence of core self-evaluations on group decision making processes: A laboratory experiment. *Administrative Sciences, 10*(2), 29, 1–16. https://doi.org/10.3390/admsci10020029

Damen, D., van Amelsvoort, M., van der Wijst, P., Pollmann M., & Krahmer, E. (2021). Lifting the curse of knowing: How feedback improves perspective-taking. *Quarterly Journal of Experimental Psychology*, *74*(6), 1054–1069. https://doi.org/10.1177/1747021820987080

Darley, J. M., & Gross, P. H. (1983). A hypothesis-confirming bias in labeling effects. *Journal of Personality and Social Psychology*, *44*(1), 20–33. https://doi.org/10.1037/0022-3514.44.1.20

Delavande, A., & Manski, C. F. (2012). Candidate preferences and expectations of election outcomes. *Proceedings of the National Academy of Sciences*, *109*(10), 3711–3715. https://doi.org/10.1073/pnas.1200861109

Ehrlinger, J., Gilovich, T., & Ross, L. (2005). Peering into the bias blind spot: People's assessments of bias in themselves and others. *Personality and Social Psychology Bulletin*, *31*(5), 680–692. https://doi.org/10.1177/0146167204271570

Farrar, B. G., & Ostojić, L. (2018). Does social distance modulate adults' egocentric biases when reasoning about false beliefs? *PLoS One*, *13*(6), e0198616, 1–17. https://doi.org/10.1371/journal.pone.0198616

Fiske, S. T. (2004). *Social beings: Core motives in social psychology*. John Wiley & Sons.

Foster, C. A., Clarke, J. A., & Packard, G. A. (2018). Can I see the real me? Leadership ability and the better-than-average effect. *Military Psychology*, *30*(5), 390–397. https://doi.org/10.1080/08995605.2018.1478545

Galin, A. (2013). Endowment Effect in negotiations: Group versus individual decision-making. *Theory and Decision*, *75*(3), 389–401. https://doi.org/10.1007/s11238-012-9350-3

Gilovich, T., Medvec, V. H., & Savitsky, K. (2000). The spotlight effect in social judgment: An egocentric bias in estimates of the salience of one's own actions and appearance. *Journal of Personality and Social Psychology*, *78*(2), 211–222. https://doi.org/10.1037/0022-3514.78.2.211

Goleman, D. (1985). *Vital lies, simple truths: The psychology of self-deception*. Simon & Schuster.

Greenberg, J. (1984). The art of compromise in a social psychology. *American Psychological Association*, *29*(6), 495–496.

Henderson, M., & Page, L. (2007). Appraising the evidence: What is selection bias? *Evidence-Based Mental Health*, *10*(3), 67–68. https://doi.org/10.1136/ebmh.10.3.67

Hergovich, A., Schott, R., & Burger, C. (2010). Biased evaluation of abstracts depending on topic and conclusion: Further evidence of a confirmation bias within scientific psychology. *Current Psychology*, *29*(3), 188–209. https://doi.org/10.1007/s12144-010-9087-5

Hernandez, I., & Preston, J. L. (2013). Disfluency disrupts the confirmation bias. *Journal of Experimental Social Psychology*, *49*(1), 178–182. https://doi.org/10.1016/j.jesp.2012.08.010

Holman, L., Head, M. L., Lanfear, R., & Jennions, M. D. (2015). Evidence of experimental bias in the life sciences: Why we need blind data recording. *PLoS Biology*, *13*(7), e1002190, 1–12. https://doi.org/10.1371/journal.pbio.1002190

Hróbjartsson, A., Thomsen, A. S. S., Emanuelsson, F., Tendal, B., Hilden, J., Boutron, I., Ravaud, P., & Brorson, S. (2012, February 2). Observer bias in randomised clinical trials with binary outcomes: Systematic review of trials with both blinded and non-blinded outcome assessors. *BMJ*, *344*(2), e1119. https://doi.org/10.1136/bmj.e1119

Hróbjartsson, A., Thomsen, A. S. S., Emanuelsson, F., Tendal, B., Hilden, J., Boutron, I., Ravaud, P., & Brorson, S. (2013). Observer bias in randomized clinical trials with

measurement scale outcomes: A systematic review of trials with both blinded and nonblinded assessors. *Canadian Medical Association Journal, 185*(4), 201–211. https://doi.org/10.1503/cmaj.120744
Hyman, I. E., Roundhill, R. F., Werner, K. M., & Rabiroff, C. A. (2014). Collaboration inflation: Egocentric source monitoring errors following collaborative remembering. *Journal of Applied Research in Memory and Cognition, 3*(4), 293–299. https://doi.org/10.1016/j.jarmac.2014.04.004
Johnson, D. D. P. (2005). Overconfidence and war: The havoc and glory of positive illusions. *Foreign Affairs, 84*(2), 154. https://doi.org/10.2307/20034298
Jones, E. E. (1990). *Interpersonal perception.* W. H. Freeman.
Jost, J. T., & Banaji, M. R. (1994). The role of stereotyping in system-justification and the production of false consciousness. *British Journal of Social Psychology, 33*(1), 1–27. https://doi.org/10.1111/j.2044-8309.1994.tb01008.x
Kahneman, D., Knetsch, J. L., & Thaler, R. H. (1991). Anomalies: The endowment effect, loss aversion, and status quobias. *Journal of Economic Perspectives, 5*(1), 193–206. https://doi.org/10.1257/jep.5.1.193
Karlsson, N., Seppi, D. J., & Loewenstein, G. F. (2005). The "Ostrich effect": Selective attention to information about investments. *Journal of Risk and Uncertainty, 38*(2), 95–115. https://doi.org/10.2139/ssrn.772125
Kennedy, J. (1995). Debiasing the curse of knowledge in audit judgment. *The Accounting Review, 70*(2), 249–273. http://www.jstor.org/stable/248305
Labib, A., & Read, M. (2013). Not just rearranging the deckchairs on the Titanic: Learning from failures through risk and reliability analysis. *Safety Science, 51*(1), 397–413. https://doi.org/10.1016/j.ssci.2012.08.014
Lazarus, R. S., & Folkman, S. (1984). *Stress, appraisal, and coping*. Springer Publishing.
Leung, K., Tong, K. K., & Ho, S. S. Y. (2004). Effects of interactional justice on egocentric bias in resource allocation decisions. *Journal of Applied Psychology, 89*(3), 405–415. https://doi.org/10.1037/0021-9010.89.3.405
Li, J. J., Barnes, C. M., Yam, K. C., Guarana, C. L., & Wang, L. (2019). Do not like it when you need it the most: Examining the effect of manager ego depletion on managerial voice endorsement. *Journal of Organizational Behavior, 40*(8), 869–882. https://doi.org/10.1002/job.2370
Macrae, C. N., Mitchell, J. P., McNamara, D. L., Golubickis, M., Andreou, K., Møller, S., Peytcheva, K., Falben, J. K., & Christian, B. M. (2016). Noticing future me. *Personality and Social Psychology Bulletin, 42*(7), 855–863. https://doi.org/10.1177/0146167216644961
Maddux, W., Yang, H., Falk, C., Adam, H., Adair, W. L., Endo, Y., Carmon, Z., & Heine, S. J. (2010). For whom is parting with possessions more painful? Cultural differences in the endowment effect. *Psychological Science, 21*(12), 1–25. https://doi.org/10.2139/ssrn.1670617
Manz, C. C., & Sims, H. P. (1987). Leading workers to lead themselves: The external leadership of self- managing work teams. *Administrative Science Quarterly, 32*(1), 106–129. https://doi.org/10.2307/2392745
Mercier, H., & Landemore, H. (2012). Reasoning is for arguing: Understanding the successes and failures of deliberation. *Political Psychology, 33*(2), 243–258. https://doi.org/10.1111/j.1467-9221.2012.00873.x
Moore, D. A., & Swift, S. A. (2011). The three faces of overconfidence in organizations. In D. Katz (Ed.), *Social psychology of organizations*. Routledge.

Ng, K., & van Dyne, L. (2001). Individualism-collectivism as a boundary condition for effectiveness of minority influence in decision making. *Organizational Behavior and Human Decision Processes*, *84*(2), 198–225. https://doi.org/10.1006/obhd.2000.2927

Nickerson, R. S. (1998). Confirmation bias: A ubiquitous phenomenon in many guises. *Review of General Psychology*, *2*(2), 175–220. https://doi.org/10.1037/1089-2680.2.2.175

Pandey, A., Chandwani, R., & Navare, A. (2018). How can mindfulness enhance moral reasoning? An examination using business school students. *Business Ethics: A European Review*, *27*(1), 56–71. https://doi.org/10.1111/beer.12171

Plous, S. (1993). *The psychology of judgment and decision making*. McGraw-Hill Education.

Pronin, E., Lin, D. Y., & Ross, L. (2002). The bias blind spot: Perceptions of bias in self versus others. *Personality and Social Psychology Bulletin*, *28*(3), 369–381. https://doi.org/10.1177/0146167202286008

Rosenberg, M. J., Rosenthal, R., & Rosnow, R. L. (1969). The conditions and consequences of evaluation apprehension. In *Artifacts in behavioral research* (pp. 211–263). New York, NY: Oxford University Press. https://doi.org/10.1093/acprof:oso/9780195385540.003.0007

Roth, S., Robbert, T., & Straus, L. (2015). On the sunk-cost effect in economic decision-making: A meta-analytic review. *Business Research*, *8*(1), 99–138. https://doi.org/10.1007/s40685-014-0014-8

Sackett, D. L. (1979). Bias in analytic research. *Journal of Chronic Diseases*, *32*(1–2), 51–63. https://doi.org/10.1016/0021-9681(79)90012-2

Saleska, J. L., & Choi, K. R. (2021). A behavioral economics perspective on the COVID-19 vaccine amid public mistrust. *Translational Behavioral Medicine*, *11*(3), 821–825. https://doi.org/10.1093/tbm/ibaa147

Samhita, L., & Gross, H. J. (2013). The "clever hans phenomenon" revisited. *Communicative & Integrative Biology*, *6*(6), e27122, 1–3. https://doi.org/10.4161/cib.27122

Schillinger, D., Tran, J., Mangurian, C., & Kearns, C. (2016). Do sugar-sweetened beverages cause obesity and diabetes? Industry and the manufacture of scientific controversy. *Annals of Internal Medicine*, *165*(12), 895–897. https://doi.org/10.7326/l16-0534

Sibony, O. (2019). *You're about to make a terrible mistake: How biases distort decision-making and what you can do to fight them*. Little, Brown Spark.

Smith, G. E., Thomas, E. F., & McGarty, C. (2015). "We must be the change we want to see in the world": Integrating norms and identities through social Interaction. *Political Psychology*, *36*(5), 543–557. https://doi.org/10.1111/pops.12180

Smitizsky, G., Liu, W., & Gneezy, U. (2021). The endowment effect: Loss aversion or a buy-sell discrepancy? *Journal of Experimental Psychology: General*, *150*(9), 1890–1900. https://doi.org/10.2139/ssrn.3588012

Strickland, B., & Suben, A. (2012). Experimenter philosophy: The problem of experimenter bias in experimental philosophy. *Review of Philosophy and Psychology*, *3*(3), 457–467. https://doi.org/10.1007/s13164-012-0100-9

Strough, J., Mehta, C. M., McFall, J. P., & Schuller, K. L. (2008). Are older adults less subject to the sunk-cost fallacy than younger adults? *Psychological Science*, *19*(7), 650–652. https://doi.org/10.1111/j.1467-9280.2008.02138.x

Stubbs, T., King, L., & Stuckler, D. (2014). Economic growth, financial crisis, and property rights: Observer bias in perception-based measures. *International Review of Applied Economics*, *28*(3), 401–418. https://doi.org/10.1080/02692171.2014.884549

Swann, W. B. J. (2012). Self-verification theory. In P. A. M. van Lange, A. W. Kruglanski, & E. T. Higgins (Eds.), *Handbook of theories of social psychology* (Vol. 2, pp. 23–42). Sage Publications.

Swann, W. B. J., & Ely, R. J. (1984). A battle of wills: Self-verification versus behavioral confirmation. *Journal of Personality and Social Psychology, 46*(6), 1287–1302. https://doi.org/10.1037/0022-3514.46.6.1287

Sypher, B. D., & Sypher, H. E. (1984). Seeing ourselves as others see us. *Communication Research, 11*(1), 97–115. https://doi.org/10.1177/009365084011001005

Ten Have, S., Rijsman, J., Ten Have, W., & Westhof, J. (2019). *The social psychology of change management: Theories and an evidence-based perspective on social and organizational beings*. Routledge.

Thaler, R. (1980). Toward a positive theory of consumer choice. *Journal of Economic Behavior & Organization, 1*(1), 39–60. https://doi.org/10.1016/0167-2681(80)90051-7

Vieites, Y., Ramos, G., Andrade, E. B., Pereira, C., & Medeiros, A. (2021). Can self-protective behaviors increase unrealistic optimism? Evidence from the COVID-19 pandemic. *SSRN Electronic Journal*, 2–39. https://doi.org/10.2139/ssrn.3852013

Wang, J., & Keil, M. (2007). A meta-analysis comparing the sunk cost effect for IT and non-IT projects. *Information Resources Management Journal, 20*(3), 1–18. https://doi.org/10.4018/irmj.2007070101

Wason, P. C. (1960). On the failure to eliminate hypotheses in a conceptual task. *Quarterly Journal of Experimental Psychology, 12*(3), 129–140. https://doi.org/10.1080/17470216008416717

Watkins, M. D. (2013). *The first 90 days: Proven strategies for getting up to speed faster and smarter, updated and expanded*. Harvard Business Review Press.

The Wharton School and Department of Sociology Michael Useem. (1975). *Protest movements in America*. Bobbs-Merrill.

Yechiam, E., Ashby, N. J. S., & Pachur, T. (2017). Who's biased? A meta-analysis of buyer—seller differences in the pricing of lotteries. *Psychological Bulletin, 143*(5), 543–563. https://doi.org/10.1037/bul0000095

Zajonc, R. B. (1968). Attitudinal effects of mere exposure. *Journal of Personality and Social Psychology, 9*(2), 1–27. https://doi.org/10.1037/h0025848

7 Belonging, biases, organizational behaviour, and change

Judith Stuijt, Cornell Vernooij, and Julius Winter

A First Short Story of Belonging, Biases, and Change

Belonging—the need for strong stable relationships—is the central and most fundamental core social motive and can be seen as the essence of human motivation. The formation and sustainability of social connections are among the most powerful, universal, and influential human drives that shape human emotion, cognition, and behaviour. Belongingness is related to change and management concepts such as mission, vision, leadership, organizational culture, resistance to change, commitment, compliance, and change capacity. As people have the urge to connect with and belong to a group, they tend to converge their thoughts, feelings, or behaviour towards a social or group norm (conformity). By having critical norms within a group, groups can increase the quality of decision-making. People also have the desire to maintain harmony and conformity in a group, which can lead to faulty decisions (groupthink). By having clarity on the reasons for forming the group and by setting clear group goals, the tendency to engage in groupthink can be minimized. Additionally, people tend to show socially desirable behaviour (social desirability bias), which may overshadow negative feelings when faced with organizational change. This can be overcome by stimulating alternative opinions and voices of dissent. People prefer the current state of affairs (status quo bias) and anything that deviates from this stable state can be met with fear or resistance. Actively challenging the status quo could help to reduce this bias. Lastly, people view their social systems as relatively legitimate even when confronted with information suggesting otherwise (system-justification bias).

Introduction

As social animals, people have a desire to form and maintain social bonds. This motive helps groups survive, and belonging to a group helps the social animal survive. The (perceived) presence or absence of belonging may influence loyalty, solidarity, and cooperation in organizations and communities and the well-being and health of people as well as the organizational climate. From the perspective of change and organization, the need to belong is relevant to the understanding of organizations, teams, individuals, and their commitments and cooperation. Belongingness is also relevant to key themes

DOI: 10.4324/9781003288237-7

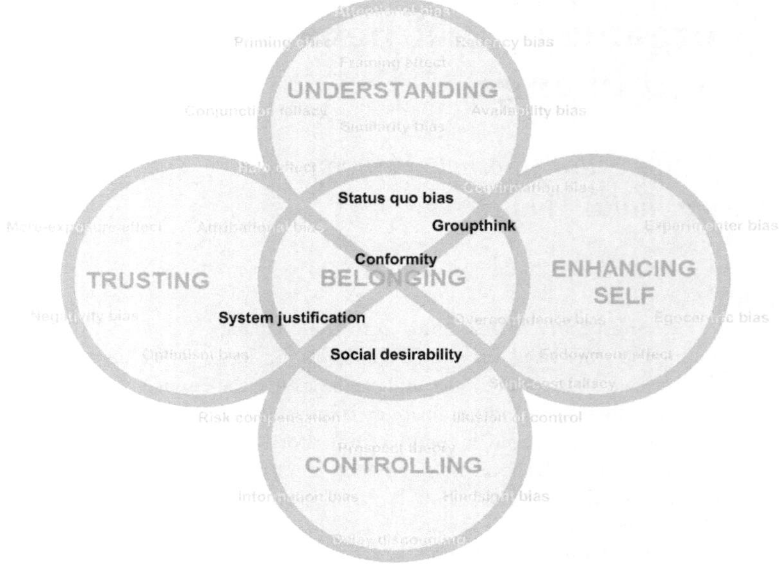

Figure 7.1 Primary Biases Related to the Core Social Motive of Belonging

in the field of organization and change, such as (a shared) vision and mission, organizational culture(s), and change capacity. In times of organizational change, the sense of belonging of certain individuals and groups may come under pressure, potentially leading to negative consequences. Change leading to scarcity, or the reallocation of resources may, for example, decrease cohesion and prosocial behaviour. Therefore, leaders, managers, and change agents have to be aware of the need to belong and its importance for organizations and change.

We have identified five primary biases related to the social motive of belonging:

Primary biases

Conformity
Groupthink
Social desirability bias
Status quo bias
System-justification bias

Additionally, the following secondary biases are identified to be related to the social motive of belonging. These secondary biases are (when relevant) incorporated in the sections concerning the primary biases.

Secondary biases

Bandwagon effect
Courtesy bias
Omission bias
Authority bias

Conformity

What is conformity?

Conformity is the convergence of individuals' thoughts, feelings, or behaviour towards a social or group norm (Allen, 1965). People have the urge to connect with and belong to a group, and consensus is instrumental in belonging. If there is dissent or disagreement, people become uncertain, uncomfortable, and vulnerable to social influence. Agreeing with others, on the other hand, provides certainty and comfort; it assures people that they are in contact by sharing a common reality. Conformity presents itself when our deep-seated need to belong causes us to adapt our behaviours to feel like we are part of the group.

Early studies in the 1950s by psychologist Solomon Asch famously showed how the social pressures from others could cause someone to conform. Using a line judgement task, Asch put a uninformed participant (the participant did not know the answer to the question beforehand) in a room with seven confederates, who had agreed with the experimenter in advance what their responses would be when presented with the line task. The uninformed participant thought that the other seven confederates were also uninformed (which was not true). Asch gathered the group in a classroom and showed a card with a line on it, followed by another card with 3 lines on it labelled A, B, and C. He then asked the participants to say which line matched the length of the line on the first card. The confederates purposefully gave the wrong answer on several trials. Asch was interested to see whether the real participant would change his answer and respond the same way as the confederates (which was an obvious incorrect answer) or stick with what his eyes plainly told him. The results showed that over various trials, about 75 percent of participants conformed at least once, even though they knew perfectly well that their answer conflicted with their perception. The power of conformity was enough to make them yield, even on a very simple question with a very clear answer. Asch's study has received tremendous attention over the years and has led to extensive investigations on conformity as a social psychological phenomenon. The concept of conformity has a strong link with groupthink (the bias that is discussed in the next section).

Early research of Kelman (1958) distinguished three kinds of conformity: compliance, internalization, and identification. Compliance occurs when people agree with the majority in order to get a specific reward or a favourable reaction from the group (as shown in the experiments of Asch) even though they do not have to agree with the group intrinsically. Internalization occurs when people agree with the group because the ideas and actions of the group are in line with their intrinsic values. This is the highest level of conformity, in which a permanent response to social influence is present. Identification is when a person conforms to the expectations of a specific role set by another person or group. For example, firemen put out fires because that's what is expected of them. With identification, there does not necessarily have to be a change in a person's own opinion.

The proposition that conformity is an essential social mechanism can be illustrated by heaps of day-to-day examples—from obeying rules and following fashion trends to consumption behaviours. Conformity is well demonstrated in films as well. One illustrative example is the famous 1985 film *The Breakfast Club*, which features five American high-school students who meet in detention on a Saturday morning and discover that they have a lot more in common then they previously thought. The film depicts all the struggles these teenagers face with acceptance by their parents and peers and their tendency to conform to their social groups. A more recent example of conformity considers the COVID-19 pandemic. Packer et al. (2021) found for instance that because of the pandemic, uncertainty, loss of agency, and social disconnection increased conformity. Adding to this, recent research on the effects of the COVID-19 pandemic on consumer behaviour indicates a positive relation between pandemic severity and conformity consumer behaviour (Li et al., 2021). Common examples of these conformity consumer behaviours are the vast array of people stockpiling goods such as hand sanitizer, canned foods, and toilet paper.

What is the relevance of conformity to organizations and change?

The basic assumption is that people want to belong to a group, and by 'conforming,' they change their behaviour to optimally fit in and stay in the group. More negatively, this can be seen as 'breaking under group pressure.' It strongly relates to the core social motive of belonging: People have the desire to fit in a group, as this can provide them with security and fulfil their social needs. In operating and changing, organizations must reckon with this and can make use of it. Leadership, a shared vision, and a mission are instrumental in stimulating the right amount of conformity, as are role models and relevant others in a group or team. The concept of conformity is related to subjects like change vision and change capacity and commitment and engagement. The question of whether there is sufficient conformity to state an ambition or change a goal or target is not a theoretical one and is highly relevant to practice. A lack of it may lead to disengagement or even harmful actions. Maurer (2010) considers the underestimation of the potential power of employee engagement as an important mistake in change processes. He points to the extensive research of the Gallup organization: "In average organizations the ratio of engaged to actively disengaged employees is near 8:1. Actively disengaged employees erode an organization's bottom line while breaking the spirits of colleagues in the process. Within the U.S. workforce, Gallup estimates this cost to be more than $300 billion in lost productivity alone." As shown, the commitment to change is not a given. "People will usually have some reaction to change. This reaction can range from total commitment to open hostility" (Ten Have et al., 2019).

Search strategy

Relevant databases were searched using the term 'conformity' and 'social norms' both separately and in combination with the terms 'organisation*,' 'work,' 'employ*,' 'leader*,' or 'chang*.' This search yielded more than 600 articles. After removing the duplicates and thorough examination, 0 meta-analyses, 0 systematic reviews, and 8 studies were included.

Main findings

1. *Norms about critical thinking within a group improve the quality of decisions, whereas norms of consensus do not (Level A).*

   Two randomized controlled before-and-after studies showed that norms of critical thinking about ideas within a group improved the overall quality of decision-making, whereas consensus norms within a group did not improve the quality. Thus, the content of group norms is an important factor influencing the quality of group decision-making. In addition, the content of these norms is related to the proneness of the group to groupthink (Postmes et al., 2001).

2. *Group membership does not lead to hostility towards other groups (Level A).*

   A randomized controlled before-and-after study of third-party punishment found no evidence that group membership, by itself, leads to hostility towards other groups. This contradicts the longstanding thought in sociology and social psychology that mere membership in a group leads to hostility towards other groups (Goette et al., 2006).

3. *Threat to personal control seems to increase conformity to salient in-group norms (Level C).*

   In a 2017 experimental study, Stollberg et al. explored the effects of a threat to personal control on conformity to in-group norms. Findings indicated that reminding employees of their lack of personal control increased their commitment to organizational change when a pro-change norm was salient. The effect was specific for commitment to change and did not generalize across other commitment domains. According to the authors, this indicates that rather than 'mindlessly' supporting their in-group, control-deprived people seem to be highly sensitive to in-group rules and norms, which then guides their (collective) behaviour (Stollberg et al., 2017).

4. *A focus on process accountability seems to increase the risk for excessive conformity, whereas self-focused norms can mitigate this effect (Level C).*

   A 2017 experimental study by Patil et al. investigated the effects of process and outcome accountability on the susceptibility to conform to rules. The results indicated that a focus on process accountability can increase the risk for excessive conformity, whereas self-focused norms mitigate this effect. The authors explained these findings as follows: "Because they strive to be distinct, people in self-focused groups tend to be more concerned with self-enhancement goals: they look to maximize individual gains regardless of what the 'wisdom of the crowd' dictates. For these reasons, researchers have found that people in self-focused groups generally take deviant stances and challenge the status quo to express themselves." (p. 290).

5. *The productivity of men seems to be more strongly affected by peer pressure compared to women (Level C).*

   Results of a 2010 experimental study by Bellemare et al. found that the productivity of women was not so strongly affected by the level of peer pressure, when paid either a fixed wage or a piece rate. The productivity of men, however, was strongly affected by peer pressure, both with fixed wages and piece rates. High levels of peer pressure were found to have a significant negative effect on productivity. Moreover, conformism and self-motivation considerations appear to be muted when male workers were paid piece rates (Bellemare et al., 2010).

Conclusion

As stated previously, the claim that people have the desire or need to be part of a group is substantiated. Conformity is an important and well-researched concept in relation to this 'need to belong.' Our specific research shows the impact of norms of critical thinking versus consensus norms in decision-making, in-group-out-group dynamics, the role of personal threat and outcome accountability, and productivity and peer pressure including gender differences and the role of financial incentives in behavioural change. An excess of conformity that impedes critical thinking can negatively impact the overall quality of decision-making and might increase groupthink. Peer pressure, which can occur if a person wants to be or remain part of the group, can have negative effects on productivity of men (especially when they are paid fixed wages). Notwithstanding the potential negative effects of conformity, being part of a group does not have to be negative, as groups can fulfil socially intrinsic human needs.

Practical reflections

Conformity is instrumental in organizing and changing; it helps people 'march to the same drummer.' On the other hand, it may also lead to a lack of reflection, poor feedback, groupthink, and suboptimal decision-making. Groups can increase the quality of decision-making by having critical norms within a group. These norms are very important in the case of change that can be very impactful for organizations and their people. Change cannot be taken for granted; it is not a 'given.' People should think critically and evaluate to make the right decisions for their organization and all the people involved. In addition, there is a risk of groupthink when people conform to certain group norms, which can have negative consequences.

Notwithstanding the potential risk and dangers of too much conformity, some positive aspects of conformity, specifically for organizational change, must also be mentioned. The available research indicates that commitment to organizational change might be increased when shared pro-change norms are in effect. Organizational change often threatens employees' control and certainty and may thus cause personal resistance. However, that threat may improve employees' commitment to the change when they understand their efforts as being part of a collective endeavour shared by their colleagues (Stollberg et al., 2017, p. 381). The following section about a closely related bias, groupthink, describes several possible negative implications of too much conformity together with interventions to prevent or correct them. Examples of these interventions are assigning someone to play the devil's advocate, using a critical reviewer, planning open sessions to reconsider alternatives, and discussing group ideas with people outside the group.

Groupthink

What is groupthink?

Groupthink is a psychological phenomenon that occurs when a group of people make faulty decisions because of the desire to maintain harmony and conformity in the group. It thus illustrates the failure of groups to consider all available and relevant information in decision-making (Janis, 1972). In scientific literature, groupthink is defined as "group members' effort to collectively reduce the potential damage from threat and to ward off negative images of the group that produces . . . the genuine sharing of illusory beliefs" (Turner et al., 1992). Janis (1972), the founding father of groupthink, considered group cohesion the most important antecedent of groupthink. Festinger (1950) defined group cohesion as "the resultant of all the forces acting on the members to remain in the group." Festinger elaborated on this and stated: "these forces may depend on the attractiveness or unattractiveness of either the prestige of the group, members in the group or the activities in which the group engages." A more recent definition of groupthink is the unity or solidarity of a group, including the integration of the group for both social and task-related purposes. Group cohesion can thus involve both socially cohesive elements (e.g., trust, social support, and identification) and task-cohesive elements (e.g., task and goal interdependence) (Bernthal & Insko, 1993; Chang & Bordia, 2001). Since its introduction in 1971, the concept of groupthink has been researched extensively in a variety of disciplines, including psychology, business, politics, and communication. Most of the research dates back to the 1980s and 1990s, but more recent studies (Goncalo et al., 2010; Riccobono et al., 2015) also illustrate the popularity of groupthink as a research topic. One well-known example of groupthink was the bombing of Pearl Harbour in December 1941. Even though Japanese messages had been intercepted by Washington DC indicating a potential attack by Japan, the group of American senior officers at Pearl Harbour did not take warnings by Washington DC seriously, as they assumed that the Japanese wouldn't dare to attempt an assault against the United States. These shared illusions and group rationalizations presumably contributed to the lack of precaution taken by the United States (Janis, 1982). A second infamous example is the Bay of Pigs invasion in 1961. This invasion, approved by former American president Eisenhower in order to overthrow the new communist regime in Cuba, was rapidly approved by the Kennedy-administration, presumably without questioning whether the Central Intelligence Agency information made sense. The mission is now perceived as one of the greatest U.S. foreign policy failures, and its defeat only further solidified Castro's role as a national hero and widened the political division between the United States and Cuba. According to Arthur Schlesinger, Jr., one of the advisors present at the meetings, Kennedy's advisors never voiced their concerns even though they had good reason to think the mission would fail. "Senior officials . . . were unanimous for going ahead. . . . Had one senior advisor opposed the adventure, I believe that Kennedy would have cancelled it. No one spoke against it" (Sunstein, 2006).

A phenomenon relating to groupthink is the so-called 'bandwagon effect.' This effect is the tendency for people to support and adopt certain beliefs, attitudes, or behaviours as they become more popular. Simply put, as more people come to believe in something, adopt a certain style or behave in a certain way, others are prone to 'hop on the bandwagon' as well. An example of the bandwagon effect is fashion trends, wherein the increasing popularity of a certain style encourages more and more people to adopt it as well (Long et al., 2007). This tendency supposedly stems from our need to belong, as conforming to the norms or attitudes of the majority ensures some degree of inclusion and social acceptance.

Secondary biases related to groupthink

Bandwagon effect—the tendency to support and adopt certain beliefs, attitudes, or behaviours as they become more popular

Notwithstanding the available research and real-world examples of the phenomenon of groupthink, Fiske (2004) is critical and clear: "Although an appealing theory that deserves to be true, and although evidence from descriptive studies seemed supportive, nonetheless groupthink experiments failed to pin it down clearly. . . . General models of group problem-solving currently seem more useful."

What is the relevance of groupthink to organizations and change?

Despite of the clear and critical reflection of Fiske (2004), groupthink is a very popular concept in organizational contexts and part of the vocabulary of a lot of managers and consultants. The problem it aims to describe and address is related to subjects like change vision, change capacity, leadership, team development (group dynamics, group problem-solving and decision-making), communication, organizational culture, and communication. Popular belief is that groupthink can occur when certain preconditions are met, for example when the group is highly cohesive, has no access to contrary options, and is ruled by a directive leader. These conditions can lead to negative outcomes such as having only a few alternatives for a problem and the favoured solution never being critically examined. In other words, expert opinion is not sought, and the group only selects information that is positive for their 'well-founded solution.'

One example of groupthink comes from the management of the Coca Cola Company that asked its board to approve its proposed equity compensation plan for 2014. One of the board members was the now-famous American investor Warren Buffet, who owned almost 10 percent of the company. Buffet disapproved the proposed plan, criticizing stock options and comparing them with 'lottery tickets.' Interestingly, however, Buffet chose to abstain from voting either in favour or against the plan. His statement clearly illustrates the investors' desire to maintain the harmony of the group: "I love Coke. I love the management, I love the directors. So, I didn't want to vote no. It's kind of un-American to vote no at a Coke-meeting." Buffet also stated that this is often how it works, thereby addressing the persistent presence of groupthink within organizations: "I've never yet heard at any of the 19 boards I was on, anybody say in the meeting they were against a compensation plan" (Sibony, 2019).

Such examples, combined with the popularity of the concept and its links with relevant topics from the organizational context make it worth further analysing groupthink and its evidence.

Search strategy

Relevant databases were searched using the term 'groupthink' both separately and in combination with the terms 'organisation*,' 'work,' 'employ*,' 'leader*,' or 'chang*.' The search yielded almost 400 articles. After removing the duplicates and thorough examination, 0 meta-analyses, 0 systematic reviews, and 6 studies were included.

Main findings

1. *Social-emotional cohesive groups are more likely to fall victim to groupthink than task cohesive groups (Level B).*

   In a 1993 experimental study, Bernthal and Insko investigated the interaction between cohesion and groupthink in work groups and explored potential techniques in avoiding the occurrence of groupthink. The findings indicated that groupthink was strongest in groups where social-emotional cohesion was relatively strong, that is, when the focus of the group members was on maintaining the social aspects of the group. Conversely, groupthink appeared to be lower when task-oriented cohesion exceeded social-emotional cohesion, that is, when groups continued to focus on the requirements of the task regardless the level of social/relational conflict among the members.

2. *When task cohesion is high, social-emotional cohesion does not necessarily lead to groupthink (Level B).*

   In their article, Bernthal and Insko conclude that when both task cohesion and social cohesion within groups are high, groupthink will not necessarily increase if the reasons for forming the group are clear and the group follows procedures designed to counteract the possibility of groupthink (Bernthal & Insko, 1993; Mullen, 1994).

3. *Groups with dominant individuals produce higher quality decisions and are less likely to be affected by groupthink compared to groups without dominant individuals (Level B).*

   In a controlled before-and-after study that involved over a hundred participants, Callaway et al. (1985) found that groups with dominant individuals make more statements of agreement and disagreement and use more time to make a decision compared to groups with less dominant people. Being less affected by groupthink, high-dominance groups produced higher quality decisions compared to low-dominance groups. These findings resonate with an earlier statement by Janis in 1972 that suggests that some individuals and groups of individuals "are extraordinarily self-confident and may not need the support of a cohesive group" in dealing with the stresses of decision-making (Callaway et al., 1985).

4. *Groupthink reduces intragroup stress (Level B).*

   The aforementioned study by Callaway et al. also found evidence supporting the idea proposed by Janis (1972) that groupthink is essentially a stress-reduction process. By providing support to their members, cohesive groups reduce conflict and disagreement and, hence, stress. Results showed that high-dominance groups reported lower levels of state anxiety. This supports the proposition that some individuals are less likely to avoid disagreement to reduce stress (Callaway et al., 1985).

5. *High group confidence in the early stages of a group assignment leads to more groupthink, thereby negatively affecting group performance (Level B).*

   In two longitudinal studies of classroom project teams, Goncalo et al. (2010) investigated the effects of group confidence in different stages of a group assignment. The results indicated that in the early stages of a group project, (too much) group confidence can result in fewer conflicts. However, conflicts may be beneficial in the early phase of a group project, as this stimulates the consideration of alternatives. Adversely, fewer conflicts early on will likely encourage groupthink and suppress the consideration of alternatives (Goncalo et al., 2010).

6. *Groupthink in groups' decision-making processes negatively impacts project performance (Level B).*

   In a longitudinal controlled field experiment, which included 18 business process reengineering projects, Riccobono et al. (2015) explored the impact of 'groupthink concurrence-seeking behaviour' (GTB) on project performance. Concurrence-seeking is defined as the distinctive behaviour of the groupthink phenomenon and explains the meaning of groupthink itself, "thinking like the group." Findings showed that GTB negatively impacted group project performance (as rated by an independent project evaluator).

Conclusion

Fiske (2004) points to the groupthink experiments that failed and the possibly more useful general models of group problem-solving. Having said that, we see a set of studies in the organizational context that resulted in a collection of evidence and relevant insights. The evidence provides insights into the perception of groupthink and the relationship between task and social emotional cohesion. The evidence also provides insights into the kind of group members and the effect on the quality of decision-making. In addition, the research provides insights into conflicts, group confidence and performance, and the conceptualization of groupthink as a stress-reduction process.

Practical reflections

Assuming that groupthink can threaten the effectiveness of groups and has the potential to undermine their performance and change programmes, the following counteractive guidelines can be helpful. These guidelines are based on and inspired by the evidence presented. For example, the first part is based on the research of Bernthal and Insko (1993). They state: "As long as the reasons for forming the group are clear and the group follows procedures designed to counteract the possibility of groupthink, high levels of social-emotional cohesion should not present a problem." A possible solution is to assign someone to play the devil's advocate in a group (on a rotating basis) and use a critical reviewer when making important group decisions. Do not allow individuals to express their preferences in advance and plan open sessions to reconsider alternatives. Stimulate honest consideration of all alternatives before making a final decision. Form subgroups to allow a more detailed discussion and discuss group ideas with people outside the group. Invite experts to regularly and actively join group meetings. It must be noted that having high group cohesion does not necessarily mean that groupthink lurks around every corner. The research indicates that particularly when the task cohesion is low and the social cohesion is high, groupthink can become a dangerous force to be reckoned with.

Social desirability bias

What is the social desirability bias?

The social desirability bias (SDB) is a type of response bias where people under-report perceived undesirable behaviour and over-report perceived desirable behaviour in a manner that will be viewed favourably by others. This bias occurs for example in questionnaires and inventories in which respondents 'self-report' their views or behaviour, and it potentially influences people's answers to a degree that threatens the accuracy and practical relevance of the findings.

The term 'social desirability' was first introduced in the field of psychology by Allen L. Edwards in 1953. In an experimental study, participants had to rate 140 personality traits on a scale of social desirability, which were then tested on a second group of participants as a normal personality inventory. The results showed that the more the personality traits were perceived as socially desirable the more likely the participants were to endorse these traits as self-descriptions. This begged the question whether personality inventories were measuring the actual traits reflecting the personality of respondents or merely personality traits being perceived as socially desirable. Although Edwards' initial experiment on the social desirability bias focused on personality traits only, the bias can be extended to other areas such as ethical or political opinions, religious beliefs, or intellectual achievements. A typical example of the social desirability bias concerning environmental behaviour is participants reporting that they regularly sort and recycle household waste even if this is not true. This type of misreporting might account for the often-observed mismatch between self-reported and observed pro-environmental behaviour (Vesely & Klöckner, 2020).

The introduction of this bias had a profound impact on the field of psychology, as most of the methods for measuring personality traits, attitudes, and opinions are self-report questionnaires and inventories. However, as Edward's study illustrated, findings obtained from such methods may not reflect reality. Scientists in the field of psychology have been struggling with this problem for decades and have been trying to minimize the impact of the SDB on their respective fields of research.

One example of the social desirability bias is the 'Bradley effect' (Payne & Ratzan, 1986), which refers to the tendency of African American and other minority political candidates to perform better in opinion polls than in the actual election when facing a white opponent. The term was introduced after Tom Bradley, a Democratic African American who ran for Governor of California in 1982, ended up losing to his white Republican opponent George Deukmejan, while earlier in the opinion polls, the majority of voters responded that they were going to vote for Bradley. The central idea behind the Bradley effect is that people do not want to be perceived as prejudiced and thus claim they are going to vote for a minority candidate, even if they have no intentions of actually doing so. A response bias strongly related to the social desirability bias, is the 'courtesy bias' or the tendency of not fully stating unhappiness with a service or product because of the willingness be polite towards the questioner.

Secondary biases related to the social desirability bias

Courtesy bias—the tendency of not (fully) stating unhappiness with a service or product because of the willingness to be polite towards the questioner

What is the relevance of the social desirability bias to organizations and change?

The degree to which people show socially desirable behaviour has an impact on multiple facets of organizations, for example in governance and risk-management. In the case of internal audits or investigations, the bias can obscure serious problems, such as unethical, illegal, or unsafe behaviours by organizational members. This decreased ability to determine whether laws, regulations, or internal policies are being violated by organizational members poses a serious threat to organizations and prevents them from taking the subsequent corrective actions or installing measures to combat these problems.

Despite its negative consequences, the tendency to alter one's responses to appear in a favourable light has a function, namely, to enhance social interactions. By exhibiting socially desirable behaviour, organizational members are adhering to the social norms, which in turn, might help strengthen group cohesion and trust. From the perspective of organization and change, these social norms are strongly related to organizational culture and cultural change. Fiske (2004) relates social norms to the combination of the core social motives belonging and understanding. Fiske states: "People need shared norms, such as equity and exchange systems, communal norms or other relational models, to understand what rules apply to different relationships. In order to belong to groups, people want to understand the shared ground rules about different kinds of relationships" (2004, p. 309).

Concerning the relevance to organizational change, SDB is thought to obscure the true feelings or intentions people have while facing a change, which prevents them from expressing potential fear or worry. This is related to the courtesy bias. However, in organizational change, identifying true opinions and feelings is an integral part of taking away resistance. Bridges (1991) also emphasizes the importance of understanding resistance and its causes: "It's the process of letting go that people resist, not the change itself. Their resistance can take the form of foot-dragging or sabotage, and it is necessary to understand the pattern of loss to adequately deal with the resistance and keep it from getting out of hand" (Ten Have et al., 2019). Furthermore, communicating and listening to possible valuable remarks and additions from the organization can help the desired change to advance and succeed.

Search strategy

Relevant databases were searched using the term 'social desirability' both separately and in combination with the terms 'organisation*,' 'work,' 'employ*,' 'leader*,' or 'chang*.' The search yielded 93 results. After removing the duplicates and thorough examination, 9 meta-analyses, 2 systematic reviews, and 1 study were included.

Main findings

1. *People under-report perceived undesirable behaviour and over-report perceived desirable behaviour in a manner that will be viewed favourably by others (Level A).*

   Blair et al. (2020) conducted a meta-analysis of 264 experiments concerning political behaviours and attitudes. Findings indicated a systematic over-reporting of socially desirable behaviours and attitudes and under-reporting of undesirable behaviours and attitudes, although its influence differed per context. Other meta-analyses and systematic reviews have confirmed these results (Vesely & Klöckner, 2020; Vilar et al., 2020; Larson & Bradshaw, 2017; Sugarman & Hotaling, 1997; Perinelli & Gremigni, 2016).

2. *People under-report perceived undesirable behaviour and over-report perceived desirable behaviour through conscious and unconscious processes (Level A).*

   Blair et al. (2020) identified two dimensions of SDB in their meta-analysis: impression management and self-deceptive enhancement.

Impression management refers to the tendency to consciously over-report desirable behaviours and under-report undesirable behaviours and is proposed to be influenced by contextual factors. Self-deceptive enhancement represents unconscious response distortion and is the tendency to provide an honest but overly positive representation of oneself. Various high-quality studies (meta-analyses and systematic reviews) have also researched these two components of social desirability (Dwight & Feigelson, 2000; Viswesvaran et al., 2001; Perinelli & Gremigni, 2016; Moorman & Podsakoff, 1992).

3. *Social desirability is likely to be related to personality traits such as conscientiousness and emotional stability (Level B).*

   Ones et al. (1996) found that social desirability was positively related to individual differences in emotional stability and conscientiousness. This was confirmed 20 years later by Connelly and Chang (2016), who found that social desirability scales were most strongly related to the personality traits emotional stability, conscientiousness, and agreeableness. These findings suggest that SDB seems to be an extension of these personality traits and is less of a general response bias.

4. *Social desirability might be related to organizational constructs such as locus of control, organizational commitment, role ambiguity, and general job satisfaction (Level B).*

   A meta-analysis by Moorman and Podsakoff (1992) found that SDB and specifically impression management correlates to several organizational constructs (locus of control, organizational commitment, role ambiguity, and general job satisfaction). Although these effects were small to moderate in size, the authors conclude that researchers should be especially attentive if a study includes any combination of these variables, since they were shown in their research to be somewhat more susceptible to socially desirable responses than other commonly used measures.

Conclusion

Social desirability is a well-researched concept with clear relevance in the organizational context and change. High-level evidence confirms the existence of SDB, although its influence could differ from context to context. Factors such as social referents, environmental factors, personal cost, and anonymity need to be considered in minimizing people's susceptibility to this bias (Blair et al., 2020). Most of the included research indicates that the social desirability bias comprises two components: impression management (conscious) and self-deceptive enhancement (unconscious). Available evidence suggests that SDB is an extension of personality traits such as emotional stability and conscientiousness and is less of a general response bias.

Practical reflections

First and foremost, the evidence leaves no doubt that people are influenced by the social desirability bias. Although this adherence to social norms might provide them a sense of belonging, the social desirability bias runs the risk of overshadowing negative feelings or even resistance of employees facing an organizational change. This could be strengthened when employees feel that voicing dissent is frowned upon or leads to punishment. Leaders and management practitioners should be sensitive to this fact and stimulate voices of dissent. Focusing on resistance to change, Kriegel and Brandt (1996) point to the classic paper "How to Deal with Resistance to Change" (1954) by Harvard Business School professor Paul Lawrence. Lawrence describes "how failing to understand workers' resistance can sabotage the whole effort." Heifetz et al. (2009) pleads for the protection of the voices of dissent. He states:

> The voices of dissent are the naysayers, the sceptics, who not only question this initiative but question whatever is on the agenda of today. They are princes of darkness, often resting on the negative. But they are valuable for implementing adaptive change because they are canaries in the coal mine, early-warning systems, and because in addition to being unproductive and annoying much of the time, they have the uncanny capacity for asking the tough key question that you have been unwilling to face up to yourself or that others have been unwilling to raise. In many organisations, dissenters get marginalized, silenced, or even fired, which deprives the organisation of their valuable, if unpopular service.

The evidence on social desirability also provides some possible practical guidelines for leaders and (other) (change) management practitioners. Notwithstanding the absence of high-level scientific evidence supporting the fact that SDB impacts personality questionnaires, some caution is warranted, as organizational members' natural tendency to portray a socially desirable image of themselves might lead to skewed perceptions of actual feelings, attitudes, or opinions. When trying to minimize the risk of this bias, specific contextual factors need to be taken into account. Blair et al. (2020) suggested four criteria to keep into account when trying to decide whether or not to worry about the SDB. If the answer to these questions is 'no,' respondents are less likely to be influenced by this bias.

1. Is there a social referent respondents have in mind when answering?
2. Do respondents believe the social referent can infer their answers exactly or approximately?
3. Do respondents perceive that the social referent prefers a particular answer to the question?

4. Do respondents believe they (or others) will suffer costs if that preferred response is not provided?

   In short, when administering questionnaires or interviews, being alone at the time of responding, being able to back-track answers, knowing whether there is a socially desirable response (from an organizational point of view vs. employee/individual point of view), and whether a personal cost is attached to an individual's response all seem to influence the susceptibility to SDB (Blair et al., 2020). Additionally, practitioners should keep in mind that questionnaires, including those about organizational commitment, job satisfaction, or role ambiguity are relatively sensitive to a socially desirable response (Moorman & Podsakoff, 1992).

Status quo bias

What is the status quo bias?

The status quo bias describes the tendency to have a clear preference for the current state of affairs. The status quo is taken as a baseline or reference point, and the new situation is defined by anything that moves away from this baseline. Samuelson and Zeckhauser (1988) were the first to find empirical evidence for the status quo bias. In their paper "Status Quo Bias in Decision-Making," they investigated how making one option the default choice (i.e., status quo framing) affected decision-making. The researchers gave a questionnaire to participants, which asked them to make hypothetical decisions, offering either a default option (status quo option) or not. The results showed that participants chose a default or status quo option when it was offered. The status quo bias is seen in important real-life decisions and can have significant consequences on our choices concerning health, politics, and consumption. For example, rates of organ donation registrations are proposed to be powerfully influenced by the default policy in effect ('opt-in' vs. 'opt-out'). Since the default option is often opt-in (e.g., not being a donor) and changing this to being a donor requires action by individuals, this could result in fewer registered organ donors and, ultimately, fewer people being saved (Davidai et al., 2012). A bias strongly related to this is 'inertia,' or a tendency to prefer the default option unless motivated to reject this option. The two concepts are very similar. However, there is one important distinction: where inertia involves inaction regarding changing circumstances, the status quo bias concerns a strong commitment to the current situation, which may also result in taking action to maintain this situation. One recent example illustrative of the difference between the status quo bias and inertia was visible in 2021 when a dozen of the world's richest football clubs announced the formation of a breakaway European club competition, thereby splitting from the existing Champions League. Football fans exhibiting inertia would let this new situation unfold without protest because stopping it would require action. The status quo bias, on the other hand, would cause fans to actively protest because of their preference for the current situation over a new one.

The status quo bias is also related to the 'omission bias,' which is the preference for harm caused by omissions over equal harm caused by acts. This is illustrated in the COVID-19 pandemic, as many people are opposed to vaccinations against COVID-19. In 1990, Ritov and Baron explained such vaccination oppositions as follows: Many people consider the risk of harm from vaccination as more serious than the risk of omitting vaccination, even when the probability that the vaccination will cause death is less likely than death from the disease prevented. The status quo bias shares overlap with other biases too, such as the endowment effect (chapter 6, Self-enhancing), loss aversion (chapter 4, Controlling) and sunk-cost fallacy (chapter 6, Self-enhancing). The main findings concerning the status quo bias might thus also be applied to these biases.

Secondary biases related to the status quo bias

Omission bias—the tendency to prefer harm caused by omissions over equal or lesser harm caused by acts

Inertia—the tendency to prefer the default option unless motivated to reject this option.

What is the relevance of the status quo bias to organizations and change?

Numerous examples of status quo bias can be seen in the organizational context. Take, for example, the annual budget process. As a rule, in most organizations, headquarters review the budget of each organization unit separately instead of exercising reallocation involving all the units. Because of this approach, the 'default' choice is to modify resource allocation only marginally (Sibony, 2019). Within organizations and teams, the status quo bias usually takes the form of resistance. Because deviations from the status quo are psychologically threatening, they are unlikely to be supported, leading to resistance to change. Leaders and management practitioners implementing organizational change have to be aware that a new situation deviating from the status quo can sometimes be met with resistance. The status quo bias might impact an organization's competitive advantage since always sticking with the default option can cause it to miss out on opportunities that would be beneficial for business. This prohibits organizations from making progress and impedes learning processes.

Search strategy

Relevant databases were searched for the term 'status quo' and 'inertia' both separately and in combination with the terms 'organisation*,' 'work,' 'employ*,' 'leader*,' and 'chang*.' This yielded 56 results. After removing the duplicates and thorough examination, 3 meta-analyses, 2 systematic reviews, and 13 studies were included.

Main findings

1. *People tend to choose a default or status quo option when it is offered (Level A).*

   An experimental study on the effect of the status quo bias on economic decision-making by Samuelson and Zeckhauser (1988) found that when presented with a default option, people generally tend to choose this option. This finding was confirmed by a meta-analysis of 48 studies by Fillion et al. (2020). In a systematic review by Ackerson and Preston (2009), maintaining the status quo was found to be one of the main reasons why women with access to healthcare still chose not to adhere to regular breast cancer screening. Additionally experimental research by Gunaydin et al. (2018) found support for the status quo bias in mate choice and romantic relationships. Results of their randomized controlled study showed that people tend to prefer traits found in their current partners, even when more desirable traits were given as alternatives. According to the authors, these findings indicate that when it comes to matters of the heart, we tend to love what we currently have (i.e., the status quo).

2. *The further a new situation differs from the status quo, the more resistance is experienced (Level A).*

   The aforementioned study by Fillion et al. (2020) found that the further a situation differs from the routine (i.e., status quo) the more negative emotions and regret are experienced. Adding to this, Stamkou et al. (2016) found in their meta-analysis of more than 1,700 participants that people in higher places of power within organizations were less likely to grant power to norm violators (dissidents to the status quo) than people in lower places of power. These findings could be explained by the fact that for people in higher places of power, the status quo would change more in comparison to people lower in the hierarchy when granting power to people challenging the status quo.

3. *Framing the status quo differently may help overcome the status quo bias (Level A).*

   A systematic review on women's choices concerning breast cancer screening by Ackerson and Preston (2009) found that women who did adhere to regular breast cancer screening tests framed their status quo differently than women who did not adhere to regular care. While women who did not adhere framed their current situation as one where no medical procedures existed or where necessary, women who adhered framed regular medical care as 'normal.' According to the researchers, framing the current situation in a different light might encourage adherence to proper medical care and help people leverage the status quo bias. Additionally, Hu and Shealy (2020) found that sustainable framing by government officials affected the recommendations participants gave in favour of green sustainable infrastructure. In their study, participants who received information about a new green resolution in advance were more likely to recommend a green/sustainable solution over a default setting (status quo). Lastly, a randomized controlled study by Merriman et al. (2016) found that framing sustainable reforms as being financially beneficial was more effective in lowering resistance to change within financial organizations (as opposed to framing it in moral arguments). These findings show that different contexts can benefit from different kinds of framing to overcome the status quo bias.

4. *The status quo bias can be a barrier to implementing change and interventions and needs to be considered by managers and organizations (Level A).*

   In a systematic review in 2019, Dawkins et al. identified being locked in the status quo to be one of the top barriers when implementing interventions for sustainable consumption by governments. Further evidence that the status quo bias impacts change projects was found by Long et al. (2020), who found that having too few reviews during a project makes it less likely for subjects to abandon a project that should be abandoned. This is also partly explained by the status quo bias.

Conclusion

Ever since 1988, when Samuelson and Zeckhauser first identified the status quo bias, high-quality scientific research has been showing the effect of the status quo bias in our everyday lives on various aspects, such as our economic and health decisions, our attitudes towards the environment and our significant others, and even in the organizational or change context. Framing can influence the status quo bias. By framing a situation differently, and thereby changing a person's reference point in relation to the status quo, the bias can be leveraged.

Practical reflections

Scientific evidence shows that people have a need to maintain their current state of affairs, which incorporates their social norms, behavioural routines and daily habits. Anything that deviates from this state of affairs, or status quo, can be met with fear or resistance. This also applies to organizational members. Managers should be aware of the status quo bias and how it can affect people in their organizations. Leaders and practitioners are advised to consider the way employees perceive their current status quo and then frame organizational changes in a way that is more congruent with the situation, thereby lessening potential fear and resistance. The status quo bias potentially blocks organizations from questioning their choices, leading to suboptimal business decisions. Therefore, leaders and change practitioners are advised to challenge the status quo, or to 'create a routine to change the routine.'

System-justification bias

What is the system-justification bias?

The system-justification bias stems from the system-justification theory. Specifically, this bias states that people tend to maintain views of their social systems, and their attendant norms, rules, and social structures, and perceive these as relatively legitimate, even when confronted with information suggesting the opposite. At its core, people's system-justification motive presumably arises from the psychological threat or anxiety produced by acknowledging that a particular system one is embedded in may be flawed or illegitimate (Proudfoot & Kay, 2014). Researchers Jost and Banaji first introduced the system-justification theory in 1994 to further explain and understand why some people tend to legitimize the prevailing social systems, despite these being against their interests. The theory, expanding on other popular social psychological theories such as social identity theory and social dominance theory, soon sparked interest among social psychologists and scientists, and experimental research followed soon after the introduction of the system-justification theory. According to Kay and Friesen (2011), more than a decade of research from the perspective of system-justification theory has demonstrated that people engage in motivated psychological processes that bolster and support the status quo. Additionally, Kay and Friesen consider the motivated psychological processes that bolster and support the status quo to be highly contextual. Groups and individuals do not always justify their social systems but are more likely to do so under certain circumstances. They distinguish four categories of circumstances or contexts in which groups and individuals are prone to engage in system-justifying processes: system threat, system dependence, system inescapability, and low personal control.

Paradoxically, system-justification is sometimes strongest among those who are most harmed by the status quo (Jost et al., 2004). This paradox can be explained by the logic of 'cognitive dissonance,' which is a form of mental discomfort or psychological stress that is experienced by someone who simultaneously holds two or more contradictory beliefs, ideas, convictions, or values. The discomfort or stress that results from the internal inconsistency motivates people to reduce the cognitive dissonance, either by changing the belief, justify the belief by adding new beliefs, and ignore or deny information that conflicts with existing beliefs. According to system-justification theory, "people who are most disadvantaged by the status quo would have the greatest psychological need to reduce ideological dissonance and would therefore be most likely to support, defend and justify existing social systems, authorities and outcomes" (Jost et al., 2003).

In essence, the system-justification bias provides a perspective that helps understand social arrangements, hierarchies, and differences in status within and between groups, and their justification. Related to this is the social dominance orientation, one's degree of preference for inequality among social groups. Research into social dominance shows that high social dominance-orientated people seek hierarchy-enhancing professional roles and people with a low orientation seek hierarchy-attenuating roles. In addition, social dominance orientation is related to beliefs in a large number of social and political ideologies that support group-based hierarchy and policies that have implications for intergroup relations (Pratto et al., 1994). Related to social dominance orientation are legitimating myths or ideologies that intellectually and morally justify the superiority of high-status groups in the existing social structure (Sidanius et al., 2001). One common example of system justification affecting our judgements and beliefs concerns wage disparities among men and women. Research suggests that women generally believe they are paid lesser than men because they do not deserve equal pay (Hogue & Yoder, 2003). System-justification theorists have suggested this illustrates how people of low-status groups incorporate their inferiority to justify the status quo (Jost & Hunyady, 2003).

A closely related bias to the system-justification bias is the authority bias, which is the proposed tendency to attribute greater accuracy to the opinion of an authority figure and to be more influenced by that opinion. Despite the questionable research methods a well-known example of the authority bias is the social psychological Milgram experiment, which allegedly illustrated that people tend to comply when being requested by an authority figure. Presumably, the perceived legitimacy that comes with being an authority figure leads people to accept and obey requests by these figures (Ramos, 2018). This strongly relates to system-justification bias in its position that people tend to believe in the steadiness and justness of their current social system.

Secondary biases related to the system-justification bias

Authority bias—the tendency to attribute greater accuracy to the opinion of an authority figure and to be more influenced by that opinion

What is the relevance of the system-justification bias to organizations and change?

The system-justification bias provides a very insightful perspective that helps to understand organizational behaviour and change in organizations. It contributes to the understanding of certain motives and dynamics in and between groups. From the perspective of organization and change, it is particularly relevant to topics like resistance to change, commitment, cooperation, communication, organizational culture(s), and change vision. Organizations, teams, and subgroups within an organization can be seen as systems in line with this bias. As such, the bias posits that existing organizational structures and (unwritten) policies are likely to be reinforced, rather than questioned. This potentially prohibits the organization to learn from its mistakes and to engage in trial and error.

Considering organizational change, the social justification bias provides insight into the psychological processes that may hinder and promote interest in change. Contrary to popular belief that communicating a sense of organizational 'crisis' may provide an opportune context for instigating change, social justification bias suggests that generally, because deviations from the status quo are psychologically threatening, they are unlikely to be supported, especially in contexts where people's system-justification motive is heightened, such as when their system is faced with external threats to its legitimacy (Proudfoot & Kay, 2014). Adding to this, Jost and Hunyady (2003) propose that system-justifying ideologies, in particular in the case of conflicts with other interest and motives, "serve a palliative function in that they reduce anxiety, guilt, dissonance, discomfort and uncertainty for those who are advantaged and disadvantaged". The system justification helps to further understand the reasons for resistance to organizational change.

Search strategy

Relevant databases were searched using the terms 'justification theory' and 'justification' both separately and in combination with the terms organisation*,' 'work,' 'employ*,' 'leader*,' and 'chang*.' The search yielded more than 200 results. After removing the duplicates and thorough examination, 0 meta-analyses, 0 systematic reviews, and 3 studies were included.

Main Findings

1. *System-justification hinders organizational change when communicating a sense of organizational crisis (Level C).*

   In an extensive literature review on system-justification theory, Proudfoot and Kay (2014) investigate the implications of system justification for the field of organizations and organizational change. Drawing on theoretical and empirical work on system-justification theory, the authors propose that people's desire to view prevailing structural arrangements in a positive light may provide unique insight into the psychological processes that may hinder and promote interest in organizational change. "Stemming from the basic idea that people have a desire to defend and legitimize the current state of affairs, research emerging from social justification theory demonstrates that, generally, because deviations from the status quo are psychologically threatening, they are unlikely to be supported, especially in contexts where people's system-justification motive is heightened, such as when their system is faced with external threats to its legitimacy" (Proudfoot & Kay, 2014).

2. *System-justification motives can override ego and group justification motives (Level C).*

   In a 2004 extensive literature review, Jost et al. integrated 10 years of research on system-justification. The available empirical evidence shows that members of groups that are low in socioeconomic success usually score higher than members of groups that are high in socioeconomic success on measures of right-wing authoritarianism (Altemeyer, 1981), political conservatism (Stacey & Green, 1971), power distance (Hofstede, 1997), and the belief in a just world (Hunt, 2000). This evidence contradicts prevailing assumptions that social and political attitudes generally reflect self-interest and group membership. Based on these findings, the authors conclude that the motives for system justification can be so strong that they override the ego and group justification motives associated with the protection of both individual and collective interests and esteem (Jost et al., 2004).

3. *System justification is a significant barrier in achieving equal opportunities in an organizational context (Level C).*

   An experimental study by Phelan and Rudman in 2011 examined whether system justification results in resistance to companies that promote diversity and equal opportunity. Findings indicated that system justification is a significant barrier to achieving equal opportunities in the organizational context, as it fosters resistance to social policies that use affirmative action to promote equal opportunity for women and minorities (in terms of race, colour, religion, sexual orientation, etc.). According to the authors, as system justifiers are motivated to perceive society as fair and just, they resist social-change policies designed to reduce inequality and thereby improve society's fairness.

Conclusion

Based on the research regarding system justification and social change, it can be concluded that the system-justification bias is very relevant and useful for the field of management and change. The research shows that system-justification may hinder organizational change and helps to explain resistance to change and how motives on the system, group, and individual level interact with one another in social contexts. It is presupposed that system-justification can even be stronger than the inclination to act in one's self-interest and group membership. Desirable changes such as improved equality and diversity can also be hampered by the system-justification bias.

This makes it possibly harder to attain commitment for changes with conceivable negative side effects.

Practical reflections

In managing change, leaders and change agents have to be aware of the system-justification bias and its possible consequences. Richter and König (2017) specifically warn of the adverse effects of system-justification in the face of downsizing, as system-justifying tendencies might reduce feelings of guilt and moral outrage and may therefore inhibit support of those suffering from layoffs. Additionally, the legitimization of downsizing might worsen organizations' treatment and care of the employees who lose their jobs because of downsizing and, as a result, impede the development of a fair layoff culture. Justifying downsizing as inevitable, for instance, might provoke a lack of interpersonal sensitivity while implementing layoffs. On a more general note, understanding the concept of system justification may prompt leaders and change agents not to take reactions to change initiatives at face value, particularly when those reactions come from people lower in the hierarchy. The system-justification bias helps understand why and how, and by whom, the dynamics of change are sometimes thwarted by the stability in insights, hierarchy, and positions desired by individuals and groups involved.

Bibliography

Ackerson, K., & Preston, S. D. (2009). A decision theory perspective on why women do or do not decide to have cancer screening: Systematic review. *Journal of advanced nursing, 65*(6), 1130–1140. https://doi.org/10.1111/j.1365-2648.2009.04981.x

Allen, V. L. (1965). Situational factors in conformity. *Advances in Experimental Social Psychology, 2*, 133–175. https://doi.org/10.1016/S0065-2601(08)60105-7

Altemeyer, B. (1981). *Right-wing authoritarianism*. University of Manitoba Press.

Bellemare, C., Lepage, P., & Shearer, B. (2010). Peer pressure, incentives, and gender: An experimental analysis of motivation in the workplace. *Labour Economics, 17*(1), 276–283. https://doi.org/10.1016/j.labeco.2009.07.004

Bernthal, P. R., & Insko, C. A. (1993). Cohesiveness without groupthink: The interactive effects of social and task cohesion. *Group & Organization Studies, 18*(1), 66–87. https://doi.org/10.1177/1059601193181005

Blair, G., Coppock, A., & Moor, M. (2020). When to worry about sensitivity bias: A social reference theory and evidence from 30 years of list experiments. *American Political Science Review, 114*(4), 1297–1315. https://doi.org/10.1017/s0003055420000374

Bridges, W. (1991). *Managing transitions: Making the most of change*. Addison-Wesley.

Callaway, M. R., Marriott, R. G., & Esser, J. K. (1985). Effects of dominance on group decision making: Toward a stress-reduction explanation of groupthink. *Journal of Personality and Social Psychology, 49*(4), 949–952. https://doi.org/10.1037/0022-3514.49.4.949

Chang, A., & Bordia, P. (2001). A multidimensional approach to the group cohesion-group performance relationship. *Small Group Research, 32*(4), 379–405. https://doi.org/10.1177/104649640103200401

Connelly, B. S., & Chang, L. (2016). A meta-analytic multitrait multirater separation of substance and style in social desirability scales. *Journal of Personality, 84*(3), 319–334. https://doi.org/10.1111/jopy.12161

Davidai, S., Gilovich, T., & Ross, L. D. (2012). The meaning of default options for potential organ donors. *Proceedings of the National Academy of Sciences, 109*(38), 15201–15205. https://doi.org/10.1073/pnas.1211695109

Dawkins, E., André, K., Axelsson, K., Benoist, L., Swartling, S. G., & Persson, S. (2019). Advancing sustainable consumption at the local government level: A literature review. *Journal of Cleaner Production, 231*, 1450–1462. https://doi.org/10.1016/j.jclepro.2019.05.176

Dwight, S. A., & Feigelson, M. E. (2000). A quantitative review of the effect of computerized testing on the measurement of social desirability. *Educational and Psychological Measurement, 60*(3), 340–360. https://doi.org/10.1177/00131640021970583

Festinger, L. (1950). Informal social communication. *Psychological Review, 57*(5), 271–282. https://doi.org/10.1037/h0056932

Fillion, A., Kutscher, L., & Feldman, G. (2020). Impact of past behaviour normality: Meta-analysis of exceptionality effect. *Cognition and Emotion, 35*(1), 129–149. https://doi.org/10.1080/02699931.2020.1816910

Fiske, S. T. (2004). *Social beings: Core motives in social psychology*. John Wiley & Sons.

Goette, L. F., Huffman, D., & Meier, S. (2006). The impact of group membership on cooperation and norm enforcement: Evidence using random assignment to real social groups. *The American Economic Review, 96*(2), 212–216. https://doi.org/10.2139/ssrn.892343

Goncalo, J. A., Polman, E., & Maslach, C. (2010). Can confidence come too soon? Collective efficacy, conflict and group performance over time. *Organizational Behavior and Human Decision Processes, 113*(1), 13–24. https://doi.org/10.1016/j.obhdp.2010.05.001

Gunaydin, G., Selcuk, E., Yilmaz, C., & Hazan, C. (2018). I have, therefore I love: Status quo preference in mate choice. *Personality and Social Psychology Bulletin, 44*(4), 589–600. https://doi.org/10.1177/0146167217746339

Heifetz, R. A., Grashow, A., & Linsky, M. (2009). *The practice of adaptive leadership: Tools and tactics for changing your organization and the world*. Harvard Business Review Press.

Hofstede, G. (1997). *Cultures and organizations*. New York: McGraw-Hill.

Hogue, M., & Yoder, J. D. (2003). The role of status in producing depressed entitlement in women's and men's payallocations. *Psychology of Women Quarterly, 27*(4), 330–337. https://doi.org/10.1111/1471-6402.00113

Hu, M., & Shealy, T. (2020). Overcoming status quo bias for resilient stormwater infrastructure: Empirical evidence in neurocognition and decision-making. *Journal of Management in Engineering, 36*(4), 1–12. https://doi.org/10.1061/(asce)me.1943-5479.0000771

Hunt, M. O. (2000). Status, religion, and the "belief in a just world": Comparing African Americans, Latinos, and Whites. *Social Science Quarterly, 81*(1), 325–343. https://www.jstor.org/stable/42864385

Janis, I. L. (1972). *Victims of groupthink*. Houghton Mifflin Company.

Janis, I. L. (1982). *Groupthink*. Houghton Mifflin Company.

Jost, J. T., & Banaji, M. R. (1994). The role of stereotyping in system-justification and the production of false consciousness. *British Journal of Social Psychology, 33*(1), 1–27. https://doi.org/10.1111/j.2044-8309.1994.tb01008.x

Jost, J. T., Banaji, M. R., & Nosek, B. A. (2004). A decade of system justification theory: Accumulated evidence of conscious and unconscious bolstering of the status quo. *Political Psychology, 25*(6), 881–919. https://doi.org/10.1111/j.1467-9221.2004.00402.x

Jost, J. T., & Hunyady, O. (2003). The psychology of system justification and the palliative function of ideology. *European Review of Social Psychology, 13*(1), 111–153. https://doi.org/10.1080/10463280240000046

Jost, J. T., Pelham, B. W., Sheldon, O., & Ni Sullivan, B. (2003). Social inequality and the reduction of ideological dissonance on behalf of the system: Evidence of enhanced system justification among the disadvantaged. *European Journal of Social Psychology, 33*(1), 13–36. https://doi.org/10.1002/ejsp.127

Kay, A. C., & Friesen, J. (2011). On social stability and social change. *Current Directions in Psychological Science, 20*(6), 360–364. https://doi.org/10.1177/0963721411422059

Kelman, H. C. (1958). Compliance, identification, and internalization three processes of attitude change. *Journal of Conflict Resolution, 2*(1), 51–60. https://doi.org/10.1177/002200275800200106

Kriegel, R. J., & Brandt, D. (1996). *Sacred cows make the best burgers*. Warner Books, Inc.

Larson, K. E., & Bradshaw, C. P. (2017). Cultural competence and social desirability among practitioners: A systematic review of the literature. *Children and Youth Services Review, 76*, 100–111. https://doi.org/10.1016/j.childyouth.2017.02.034

Lawrence, P. R. (1954). How to deal with resistance to change. *Harvard Business Review, 32*(3), 49–57.

Long, D. S., Fox, N. R., & York, T. (2007). *Calculated futures: Theology, ethics, and economics*. Baylor University Press.

Long, X., Nasiry, J., & Wu, Y. (2020). A behavioral study on abandonment decisions in multistage projects. *Management Science, 66*(5), 1999–2016. https://doi.org/10.1287/mnsc.2018.3270

Maurer, R. (2010). *Beyond the wall of resistance: Why 70% of all changes still fail—and what you can do about it*. Bard Press.

Merriman, K. K., Sen, S., Felo, A. J., & Litzky, B. E. (2016). Employees and sustainability: The role of in centives. *Journal of Managerial Psychology, 31*(4), 820–836. https://doi.org/10.1108/jmp-09-2014-0285

Moorman, R. H., & Podsakoff, P. M. (1992). A meta-analytic review and empirical test of the potential confounding effects of social desirability response sets in organizational behaviour research. *Journal of Occupational and Organizational Psychology, 65*(2), 131–149. https://doi.org/10.1111/j.2044-8325.1992.tb00490.x

Mullen, B., Anthony, T., Salas, E., & Driskell, J. E. (1994). Group cohesiveness and quality of decision making. *Small Group Research, 25*(2), 189–204. https://doi.org/10.1177/1046496494252003

Li, J., Jin, X., Zhao, T., & Ma, T. (2021). Conformity consumer behavior and external threats: An empirical analysis in China during the COVID-19 pandemic. *Sage Open, 11*(3). https://doi.org/10.1177/21582440211032152

Ones, D. S., Viswesvaran, C., & Reiss, A. D. (1996). Role of social desirability in personality testing for personnel selection: The red herring. *Journal of Applied Psychology, 81*(6), 660–679. https://doi.org/10.1037/0021-9010.81.6.660

Packer, D. J., Ungson, N. D., & Marsh, J. K. (2021). Conformity and reactions to deviance in the time of COVID-19. *Group Processes & Intergroup Relations, 24*(2), 311–317. https://doi.org/10.1177/1368430220981419

Patil, S. V., Tetlock, P. E., & Mellers, B. A. (2017). Accountability systems and group norms: Balancing the risks of mindless conformity and reckless deviation. *Journal of Behavioral Decision Making, 30*(2), 282–303. https://doi.org/10.1002/bdm.1933

Payne, J. G., & Ratzan, S. C. (1986). *Tom Bradley, the impossible dream: A biography*. Roundtable Pub.

Perinelli, E., & Gremigni, P. (2016). Use of social desirability scales in clinical psychology: A systematic review. *Journal of Clinical Psychology, 72*(6), 534–551. https://doi.org/10.1002/jclp.22284

Phelan, J. E., & Rudman, L. A. (2011). System justification beliefs, affirmative action, and resistance to equal opportunity organizations. *Social Cognition, 29*(3), 376–390. https://doi.org/10.1521/soco.2011.29.3.376

Postmes, T., Spears, R., & Cihangir, S. (2001). Quality of decision making and group norms. *Journal of Personality and Social Psychology, 80*(6), 918–930. https://doi.org/10.1037/0022-3514.80.6.918

Pratto, F., Sidanius, J., Stallworth, L. M., & Malle, B. F. (1994). Social dominance orientation: A personality variable predicting social and political attitudes. *Journal of Personality and Social Psychology, 67*(4), 741–763. https://doi.org/10.1037/0022-3514.67.4.741

Proudfoot, D., & Kay, A. C. (2014). System justification in organizational contexts: How a motivated preference for the status quo can affect organizational attitudes and behaviors. *Research in Organizational Behavior, 34*, 173–187. https://doi.org/10.1016/j.riob.2014.03.001

Ramos, V. J. (2018). *Analyzing the role of cognitive biases in the decision-making process*. IGI Global.

Riccobono, F., Bruccoleri, M., & Größler, A. (2015). Groupthink and project performance: The influence of personal traits and interpersonalties. *Production and Operations Management, 25*(4), 609–629. https://doi.org/10.1111/poms.12431

Richter, M., & König, C. J. (2017). Explaining individuals' justification of lay offs. *Journal of Applied Social Psychology, 47*(6), 331–346. https://doi.org/10.1111/jasp.12442

Ritov, I., & Baron, J. (1990). Reluctance to vaccinate: Omission bias and ambiguity. *Journal of Behavioral Decision Making, 3*(4), 263–277. https://doi.org/10.1002/bdm.3960030404

Samuelson, W., & Zeckhauser, R. (1988). Status quo bias in decision making. *Journal of Risk and Uncertainty, 1*(1), 7–59. https://doi.org/10.1007/bf00055564

Sibony, O. (2019). *You're about to make a terrible mistake: How biases distort decision-making and what you can do to fight them*. Little, Brown Spark.

Sidanius, J., Levin, S., Federico, C. M., & Pratto, F. (2001). Legitimizing ideologies: The social dominance approach. In J. T. Jost & B. Major (Eds.), *The psychology of legitimacy: Emerging perspectives on ideology, justice, and intergroup relations* (pp. 307–331). Cambridge University Press.

Stacey, B. G., & Green, R. T. (1971). Working-class conservatism: A review and an empirical study. *British Journal of Social and Clinical Psychology, 10*(1), 10–26. https://doi.org/10.1111/j.2044-8260.1971.tb00708.x

Stamkou, E., van Kleef, G. A., Homan, A. C., & Galinsky, A. D. (2016). How norm violations shape social hierarchies: Those who stand on top block norm violators from rising up. *Group Processes & Intergroup Relations, 19*(5), 608–629. https://doi.org/10.1177/1368430216641305

Stollberg J., Fritsche I., & Jonas, E. (2017). The groupy shift: Conformity to liberal in-group norms as a group-based response to threatened personal control. *Social cognition, 35*(4), 374–394.

Sugarman, D. B., & Hotaling, G. T. (1997). Intimate violence and social desirability. *Journal of Interpersonal Violence, 12*(2), 275–290. https://doi.org/10.1177/088626097012002008
Sunstein, C. R. (2006). *Infotopia*. Oxford: Oxford University Press.
Ten Have, S., Rijsman, J., Ten Have, W., & Westhof, J. (2019). *The social psychology of change management: Theories and an evidence-based perspective on social and organizational beings*. Abingdon: Routledge.
Turner, M. E., Pratkanis, A. R., Probasco, P., & Leve, C. (1992). Threat, cohesion, and group effectiveness: Testing a social identity maintenance perspective on groupthink. *Journal of Personality and Social Psychology, 63*(5), 781–796. https://doi.org/10.1037/0022-3514.63.5.781
Vesely, S., & Klöckner, C. A. (2020). Social desirability in environmental psychology research: Three meta-analyses. *Frontiers in Psychology, 11*(1395), 1–9. https://doi.org/10.3389/fpsyg.2020.01395
Vilar, R., Milfont, T. L., & Sibley, C. G. (2020). The role of social desirability responding in the longitudinal relations between intention and behaviour. *Journal of Environmental Psychology, 70*, https://doi.org/10.1016/j.jenvp.2020.101457
Viswesvaran, C., Ones, D. S., & Hough, L. M. (2001). Do impression management scales in personality inventories predict managerial job performance ratings? *International Journal of Selection and Assessment, 9*(4), 277–289. https://doi.org/10.1111/1468-2389.00180

8 The impact of bias on organizational behaviour and change

Cornell Vernooij, Judith Stuijt, Steven ten Have, and Wouter ten Have

Introduction

Humans are social animals, and change is a social process. To understand this social process and explain the thoughts, feelings, and behaviours of individuals, knowledge of how people are influenced by the presence of others is crucial. Social psychology, being the scientific attempt to do so, is thus essential for effective (behavioural) change. In a continuous endeavour to make sense of the world and understand themselves and their surroundings, humans make predictions about what will happen next and create theories to explain events or behaviours about themselves and others. Their predictions and theories, however, are not as formalized as those of a professional scientist. Instead, people see the world through their own lenses, based on their uniquely organized systems of construction, which they use to anticipate events or behaviours. As humans are prone to making irrational mental shortcuts, they do not conform to the economists' theoretical model of rational decision-making. The systematic, nonrandom, and predictable deviations from economic reality are called biases. An organization is exclusively made up of and governed by humans that are all embodied with biased thinking, which makes organizations eminently prone to biased behaviour.

The preceding sentences were the leading notions in the first chapter. They may seem obvious and self-evident, but practice and science suggest otherwise. The reality of businesses and institutions leaves little to no room for recognizing and acknowledging these biases, as organizations are understood to perform objectively, resolutely, and effectively based on their purpose—their economic or social remit—and to change where required (Bower, 2000). Change management literature shows that subjects such as collaboration, decision-making, resistance to change, participation, and culture are crucial for this field of research and its organizational context. Almost without exception, cognitive and social biases, by influencing human thinking, feeling, and behaviour, provide the insights and knowledge that are helpful, if not essential, to understand, optimize, or reduce these subjects if necessary.

The essential basis of each profession and each science exists in its 'body of knowledge,' the systematic and validated formal knowledge (Greenwood,

DOI: 10.4324/9781003288237-8

1957; Barber, 1963; Freidson, 1973; Abbot, 1988). The process we started was focused on collecting, analysing, and presenting or making available knowledge relevant to organizational behaviour and change in an encyclopaedic, coherent, and evidence-based way. By doing so, we contribute to diminishing, the meta-bias that fosters all biases—the bias blind spot, which causes people to believe they are less biased in their judgements than others (see chapter 1 for an elaboration on the bias blind spot). Creating awareness of biased behaviour in a person helps reduce the possible negative effects of biases. This book helps create knowledge and awareness regarding biases, which can subsequently be used to create meaningful and effective interventions within organizations to reduce the possible negative effects of biases or leverage the positive effects of biases.

As stated in chapter 1, while we are writing this book, we felt supported by standing on the shoulders of giants. Kahneman and Tversky and other scientists have done considerable valuable research and have shown us the irrationality in human behaviour. While referring to organizational behaviour and change, we, stand on another group of giants with strong shoulders like Lewin, Schein, Weick, Argyris, and Oreg, who have built change management as a discipline primarily from the (social) psychological perspective. We once more want to express our gratitude to all scholars that added to the establishment of this base of knowledge. In writing this book, we have made use of and built upon the knowledge and understanding of major thinkers who have gone before us. In chapters 3–7, we presented the results of our systematic research process. This last chapter is dedicated to integration and reflection: What are the lessons and insights and their relationships from all the biases for the field of organizational behaviour and change management? What does a more evidence-based, systematic, and integrative approach bring to practice and research?

A story of social motives, biases, organizational behaviour, and change

Chapters 3–7 contain 29 primary cognitive and social biases. They were categorized into five core social motives—understanding, controlling, trusting, self-enhancing, and belonging—and comprised five short stories. Taken together, they make up the story of the social motives, biases, organizational behaviour, and change:

Understanding

Understanding is the need for shared meaning and prediction. People are naturally motivated to understand, predict, and give meaning to their environment, as this enables their functioning and survival in groups. This also accounts for people within the organizational and change context;

understanding relates to several important topics; for example, organizational mission culture, change vision, and resistance to change. In an urge to understand the world around them, people rely on mental shortcuts; tend to be selective about the information they attend to; and focus specifically on things that are emotional, arousing, and personally relevant to them (attentional bias). In forming judgements about probabilities or frequencies, people seem to rely on comparable instances that come to mind (availability bias). People also falsely assume that multiple specific conditions are more probable than a single generic one (conjunction fallacy). The way a message is framed influences people's perceptions, evaluations, and decisions, and people are specifically influenced when messages contain emotional information (framing effect). Priming is a valid phenomenon in social interactions. When people are primed with certain stereotypical information, they rapidly form a mental categorization of the other and make social judgements according to that social category (priming effect). Recent information is generally weighed more heavily than preceding information when forming judgements (recency effect). In social judgements specifically, physically attractive people are generally evaluated more positively those that are not (halo effect). Lastly, there are signs that people evaluate those they perceive to be similar to them in a more favourable light (similarity bias).

Controlling

Controlling is the need for perceived contingency between behaviour and outcomes. A certain sense of control urges people to improve or learn from past or present situations to increase their control even further. In times of organizational change, people may find their existing sense of control and competence challenged or threatened. The replacement or adjustment of routines, habits, cultural patterns, and cognitive schemes necessary for change could lead to serious stress and resistance to change. To foster their sense of control, people tend to overestimate the degree of control over events that are in essence uncontrollable (illusion of control). The heightened perception of control and competence spans over past, present, and future situations. For instance, people tend to overestimate their foresight knowledge of an event after the event has occurred, with the potential repercussions of overestimating the responsibility of others and limiting (organizational) learning (hindsight bias). The longing for control is also present in decision-making. People might sometimes tend to seek more and more information, even when it cannot affect the outcome of the decision (information bias). Furthermore, in most cases, people attach more weight to avoiding losses than to acquiring equivalent gains (prospect theory). Lastly, people tend to prefer smaller immediate rewards over larger later rewards, which is associated with impulsive, risk-taking, and procrastinating behaviour (delay discounting). Notwithstanding the popular belief that people are prone to display more risk-taking behaviour when safety measures are in place, scientific research has not found support for this claim (risk compensation).

Trusting

Trusting is the need to view others as basically benign and to see the world as a benevolent place. Trust in leadership as well as organizational trust have beneficial effects on commitment, job satisfaction, and performance. Conversely, a lack of trust in the organization's leaders may hinder change by causing or aggravating resistance to change. To be able to have confidence or faith in the people and the world around us, people rely on several mental shortcuts. People tend to prefer information because of repeated exposure to that information (mere exposure effect). Thus, to create trust, organizational leaders should increase their own visibility as leaders of the change and that of the change in the organization. People tend to judge the trustworthiness of information by relying on the - either positive or negative - valence of information. They put greater weight on negative events or stimuli compared to positive instances (negativity bias). As people perceive themselves to be more likely to experience positive events compared to others (optimism bias), they are likely to become overly optimistic about the time they need to complete a certain task. People make (inaccurate) decisions by assigning causes to their own behaviour and those of others (attributional bias). Better understanding of attributions can help design and develop well-thought-out and contextual, sensitive, and sensible 'paths to change' and to being more able to deal with resistance to change.

Self-enhancing

Self-enhancing is the need to view the self as basically worthy or improvable. In an organizational context, self-enhancement is related to change vision, change capacity, commitment and resistance to change, cooperation, leadership, and culture. People want to feel good about themselves and see themselves in a positive light. To be able to do so, they rely on several mental shortcuts. When making judgements, they tend to rely on their own perspectives versus those of others (egocentric bias). This can be lessened by providing feedback, treating people fairly, and training/remembering (e.g., by nudging or exemplary behaviour) to help perceive certain situations from other vantage points. People are overly confident in themselves and the social group they identify with (overconfidence effect). Forming diverse teams and organizing activities enhancing organizational identity (e.g., team-building exercises) or informational campaigns could help to reduce this tendency. Furthermore, people seem to tend to seek out, interpret, favour, and recall information consistent with their own expectations (confirmation bias). To minimize its influence, firms and leaders should communicate changes in a vivid, in-depth way regarding the purpose of the change. For group discussions, it could be wise to appoint someone a devil's advocate. While testing or analysing change initiatives, people influence the research outcomes through their own convictions and expectations (experimenter bias). Double-blind research techniques can help reduce this. People prefer retaining an object they possess rather than acquiring the same object if they do not own it (endowment effect). This leads to the tendency of attaching a higher value to objects when owned. Becoming aware of these dynamics and the role of both selling and buying parties is likely to minimize the effect. While making decisions, people tend to continue an already initiated endeavour because of the time, effort, or money they have invested (sunk-cost fallacy). Barriers can be implemented to overcome this, such as activating a decision-maker's need to externally justify the project-related decisions, distributing responsibility to various decision-makers, or stimulating to focus on alternatives and consider opportunity costs.

Belonging

Belonging—the need for strong stable relationships—is the central and most fundamental core social motive. It can be seen as the essence of human motivation. The formation and sustainability of social connections are the most powerful, universal, and influential human drives. The need to belong shapes human emotion, cognition, and behaviour. Belongingness is related to change and management topics such as mission, leadership, organizational culture, resistance to change, commitment, compliance, change capacity, and vision. As people have the urge to connect with and belong to a group, they tend to converge their thoughts, feelings, or behaviour towards a social or group norm (conformity). By having critical norms, groups can increase the quality of decision-making. People also want to maintain harmony and conformity in a group, which can lead to faulty decisions (groupthink). Clarity about the reasons for forming the group and setting clear group goals can minimize the tendency to engage in groupthink. Additionally, people tend to show socially desirable behaviour (social desirability bias), which may overshadow negative feelings when faced with an organizational change. This can be overcome by stimulating alternative opinions and voices of dissent. People tend to have a clear preference for the current state of affairs (status quo bias), and anything that deviates from this state of affairs can be met with fear or resistance. Actively challenging the status quo could help to reduce this bias. Lastly, people seek to maintain views of their social systems as relatively legitimate even when confronted with information suggesting the opposite (system-justification bias).

Overview of biases and their probability

The preceding story contains essential conclusions to be able to understand and explain how individuals' thoughts, feelings, and behaviours are influenced by the presence of others. Incorporating the conclusions from 29 primary biases into one story is a huge step. From thousands of scientific articles to conclusions in about 170 pages in chapters 3–7, to approximately a story 1,500 words. At the same time, it still is a whole lot to grasp, comprehend, and remember. For reasons of clarity and oversight, we therefore assembled the primary biases in one overview (see Table 8.1).

As we concluded in chapters 3–7, the quantity and quality (level of evidence) of scientific research per bias vary. Therefore, we provided each of the biases with a probability level (addressed in an additional column in Table 8.2). This probability level indicates the degree to which we reasonably assume that, based on all the evidence gathered, the bias is likely to occur in human thinking. We, as the authors and research team, analysed the level of evidence of the main findings and assigned a probability level (ranging from '−' to '+++') to each bias to provide this indication. We did so based on the appraisal criteria as developed by the Center for Evidence-Based Management (Barends & Rousseau, 2018); see Table 2.3 and for further explanation, see chapter 2.

In Table 8.1, approximately 20 primary biases are assigned the probability levels, '++' or '+++.' This means for each of these biases we assume based on scientific evidence that it is likely, or more than likely, to influence human thinking. For approximately 10 primary biases, with the indication '+/−' or '+' we have to be cautious about drawing definite conclusions ('it could be' or 'there are signs that'). One indication of '−' given to risk compensation catches the eye. Notwithstanding the popular belief that people would display more risk-taking behaviour when safety measures are in place, scientific evidence shows the opposite effect.

Table 8.1 Elaboration on Evidence Levels and Probability Levels

Evidence level	*Methodological appropriateness*	*Estimated trustworthiness*	*Interpretation*	*Probability level*
A	High	90%	It is shown that . . .	+++
B	Moderate	80%	It is likely that . . .	++
C	Limited	70%	It could be that . . .	+
D	Low	60%	There are signs that . . .	+/-
None	NA	NA	We cannot assume that . . .	-

Table 8.2 Overview of Biases and Their Probability Levels

Belonging

Bias	*What does this bias say?*	*Probability level*
Conformity	People tend to convergence their thoughts, feelings, or behaviour towards a social or group norm	+++
Groupthink	Groups tend to have the desire to maintain harmony and conformity in the group	+ +
Social desirability bias	People tend to report their behaviours in a manner that will be viewed favourably by others	+ +
Status quo bias	People are prone to have a clear preference for the current state of affairs	+
System-justification bias	People tend to maintain their social systems—their attendant norms, rules, and social structures—and see them as legitimate, even when confronted with information suggesting the opposite	+

Understanding

Bias	*What does this bias say?*	*Probability level*
Attentional bias	People tend to be selective in the information they attend to	+ + +
Availability bias	People judge the frequency or prevalence of events by the ease with which relevant instances come to mind	+/-
Conjunction fallacy	People tend to assume that multiple specific conditions are more probable than a simple generic one	+ +
Framing effect	The way a message is presented to people influences perceptions, evaluations, and decisions	+ +
Priming effect	The introduction of one stimulus influences how people perceive and respond to a subsequent stimulus	+ +
Recency bias	People are prone to give more weight to recently presented information over earlier presented information	+ +
Halo effect	Positive impressions of a stimulus in one area positively influence perceptions of that stimulus in other areas	+ +
Similarity bias	People evaluate others they perceive as similar to them in a more favourable light	+/-

Controlling

Bias	*What does this bias say?*	*Probability level*
Illusion of control	People tend to overestimate the degree of control over uncontrollable events	+ +
Hindsight bias	People tend to overestimate their foresight knowledge of an event after the event occurs	+ + +

Information bias	People tend to seek more information even when it cannot affect the outcome	+/-
Risk compensation	People are prone to display more risk-taking behaviour when safety measures are in place	-
Prospect theory	People tend to prefer avoiding losses to acquiring equivalent gains in decision-making	+ +
Delay discounting	People tend to prefer smaller immediate rewards over larger later rewards	+ + +

Trusting

Bias	*What does this bias say?*	*Probability level*
Mere exposure effect	People tend to develop preferences for things they are familiar with	+ + +
Negativity bias	People tend to give more weight to negative information compared to positive information	+ + +
Optimism bias	People tend to perceive they are more likely to experience positive events than others	+ + +
Attributional bias	People tend to make systematic errors when assigning causes to their own behaviours and those of others	+ +

Enhancing-self

Bias	*What does this bias say?*	*Probability level*
Egocentric bias	People tend to rely on their own perspective and have a higher opinion of themselves than reality reflects	+
Overconfidence effect	People tend to be overbearing regarding the accuracy of their judgements or their abilities	+
Confirmation bias	People tend to prefer information that is consistent with their own prior beliefs and expectations	+
Experimenter bias	Experimenters or observers tend to influence their participants, data, or outcomes	+ + +
Endowment effect	People tend to attach a higher value to objects when they own these objects	+
Sunk-cost fallacy	People tend to continue an endeavour once an investment in money, effort, or time has been made	+ + +

An evidence-based perspective on change management

In addition to the theoretical and conceptual or more deductive contribution of cognitive and social psychological biases to organizational behaviour and change, we gathered specific evidence. This was done to feed change management from the inductive or empirical perspective with evidence that resulted from the application of cognitive and social psychological biases in the organizational context correlated to change management topics and

Table 8.3 Change Management Topics

Mission, vision, strategy	*Performance management*	*Resistance*
Leadership	Change capacity	Commitment
Culture	Change vision	Cooperation
Structure	Teams/team development	Participation
Systems	Communication	

issues. Reflecting from the perspective of organizational behaviour and change, the question for each bias was what the specific relevance could be (section 2 of the REA format, see chapter 2). The perspective was operationalized by using a set of change management topics, resulting from earlier evidence-based research and a team analysis (Ten Have et al., 2016). The topics are displayed in Table 8.1. These topics were also used in describing the conclusion and/or practical reflections with regard to each bias and change management (sections 5 and 6 of the REA format). In this final chapter, we give five illustrations or examples, one per core social motive, by presenting an exemplary bias and a summary of the specific evidence.

Understanding—Framing effect

As a bias related to the core social motive of understanding, the framing effect provided a set of relevant insights based on evidence specific to the organizational context. It is relevant to topics such as mission, vision, and strategy, change vision, communication, culture, cooperation, and commitment. The basic notion is that how a message is presented influences people's perceptions, evaluations, and decisions. The evidence shows that during decision-making processes, people are influenced by frames, and frames are more persuasive when they induce stronger emotions. Also, loss framing is likely to be more effective for stimulating behavioural change than gain framing. In communicating the rationale for the change, focusing on what's at stake or what there will be missed if the organization fails to act (i.e., creating a sense of urgency) can help incite people to take action. However, some caution is warranted in the usage of negative frames to create a sense of urgency, especially on the long term. Negative frames can help create urgency and can help incite people to take action; however, in the long run, they can also create an atmosphere of negativity. Positive frames, on the other hand, mirroring positive emotions and feelings, create more self-efficacy and action control in dealing with changes and challenges, stimulating change, and improving performances for a longer period.

Controlling—Illusion of control

The illusion of control is related to the core social motive of controlling. The basic notion of the bias is that people tend to overestimate their degree of control over uncontrollable events. The bias is relevant to leadership, performance management, change vision, change capacity, and commitment. The illusion of control appears constantly in various situations, even when the different conceptualizations and methods are considered. For the organizational context, the evidence indicates that a strong perception of organizational control by top management could lead to an overestimation of the success of their organization in forecasts due to inadequate risk assessment, which can lead to unattainable organizational goals and all related consequences. A proper forecast ability, on the other hand, can be seen as a competitive advantage, which in turn could lead to above-average performances. A possible way to mitigate this bias could be a heightened level of awareness of the illusion of control through education, training, and discussion of potential situations in which an illusion of control may appear. This way leaders and employees can, in that case, focus more on the things they have control over instead of wasting time on uncontrollable variables.

Trusting—Optimism bias

The optimism bias is related to the core social motive of trusting. People tend to perceive that they are more likely than others to experience positive events. The optimism bias is related to change management topics such as mission, vision and strategy, leadership, performance management, teams/team development, and communication. Organizations falling prey to the optimism bias are inclined to engage in high-risk decision-making and venture into loss-making activities. Furthermore, the evidence shows that group discussions heighten the group members' tendency to be overly optimistic about the time they predict to need to complete a certain task. It would, therefore, be useful for organizational leaders to be aware of this bias and its possible impact on their business. In this way, this cognitive error can be prematurely recognized before exerting its influence on the organization. Forming concrete action plans that specify when, where, and how to act to reach goals seem particularly helpful in reducing the effects of this tendency on organizational planning.

Self-enhancing—Sunk-cost fallacy

The sunk-cost fallacy, related to the core social motive of self-enhancing, provides relevant insights for the organizational context, and specifically decision-making behaviour. The basic notion is that people tend to continue an endeavour once they have invested money, effort, or time into it. The sunk-cost fallacy relates to structure, systems, performance management, resistance, commitment, cooperation, and participation. The evidence shows that people are influenced in their decision-making by earlier investments made. Barriers can be implemented to overcome this, such as activating a decision-maker's need to externally justify the project-related decisions, distributing responsibility to various decision-makers, or stimulating to focus on alternatives and consider opportunity costs.

Belonging—Conformity

Conformity relates to the social core motive of belonging. People tend to converge their thoughts, feelings, or behaviour towards a social or group norm. It is relevant for change management topics such as teams/team development, culture, commitment, cooperation, and participation. Notwithstanding the potential negative effects of conformity, being part of a group does not have to be negative, as groups can fulfil socially intrinsic human needs. An excess of conformity that impedes critical thinking can have a negative impact on the overall quality of decision-making and might increase groupthink. Peer pressure, which can occur if a person wants to be or remain part of the group, can have specific negative effects on the productivity of men (especially when they are paid fixed wages). The evidence shows that groups can increase their quality of decision-making by having critical norms within the group. This can, for instance, be created by appointing someone to play the devil's advocate (on a rotating basis). Additionally, having norms that focus on the self and self-enhancement can decrease conformity, but this can have other negative effects such as egocentric behaviour.

Developing the change management framework from the perspective of biases

The categorization based on Fiske's core social motives provides an initial framework that helps structure, relate, and integrate the numerous findings from the 29 biases with the purpose of (further) developing the knowledge on the biases and their application in change management. From the perspective of education, science, and practice, there are at least three reasons for continuing to conceptualize biases in a model regarding the core social motives and the change-competence model. The first was already introduced in chapter 2. Research (Gage & Berliner, 1992) shows that students who study models before a lecture may recall as much as 57 percent more on questions concerning conceptual information compared with students who receive instruction without the advantage of seeing and discussing the models. The second is inspired by Bower (2000), who states: "It is one thing to recognize that a corporation is a complex non-linear system interacting with a very rich and changing environment. It is another to provide a map of that system that permits managers to act in an intentionally rational fashion." From the change management perspective, we had already developed an initial version of such a map (Ten Have et al., 2015). The map or model of change competence and the purposive change ("what it should be and how it should be accomplished" and the combination of 'change vision' and 'change capacity') of Bower (2000) has already been introduced in chapter 2. Chapters 1 and

2 also have the perspective of social psychology with the five core social models visualized in the same way as the change-competence model, with the two lemniscates (Ten Have et al., 2019). In this book, we have provided a new layer on top of both models and have deepened the body of knowledge of change management by enriching it with cognitive and social biases.

The third reason for a model is related to the first two reasons, and in particular the second, and has to do with the interrelatedness between the social psychological motives, biases, and factors of organizational behaviour and change. The motives can be seen as interrelated in positive or negative ways, in terms of synergies or trade-offs, and as protagonists and antagonists. To illustrate this, one can imagine a synergy between understanding and controlling, that a lack of trust can hamper a feeling of belongingness, and that there could be a trade-off between controlling and trusting. The same can be said about biases. For instance, people who are strongly influenced by the negativity bias are most likely to also be prone to loss aversion (prospect theory). Another interplay between biases is that the behaviour of people affected by the status quo bias can be altered by framing the status quo differently. Based on the interrelatedness and combinations of the biases and the core social motives, the right use of the model can result in a model that is larger than the sum of its parts.

The change-competence model and the core social motives can be assembled on top of each other, as has been shown in chapter 2. Figure 8.1 gives an example of five change management topics that are each specifically related to one or more of the five factors of the model. Mission, for example, is positioned in the field of the rationale and understanding, because a mission is the grand story of why an organization exists and what its goals are. Performance management is related to effect in combination with focus. It is directed at managing and controlling the organizational goals, which can be extracted from the organizational strategy. Structure is placed in the focus and trusting factor because an adequate structure creates psychological safety in the organization due to clear roles, rules, and guidelines. Resistance can be caused by a variety of reasons, spread over the five factors of the model, but generally comes to the surface in the factor energy. As said earlier, an organization is made up of (irrational) people and without the contribution of these people there would be no organization or change possible. The final topic is, teams, which is placed under connection in combination with focus. Teams are essential building blocks in organizations and belongingness to solid teams is therefore paramount. In this chapter, we illustrate how the aforementioned changemanagement topics can be better understood by using social psychological biases and providing a limited but illustrative set of examples.

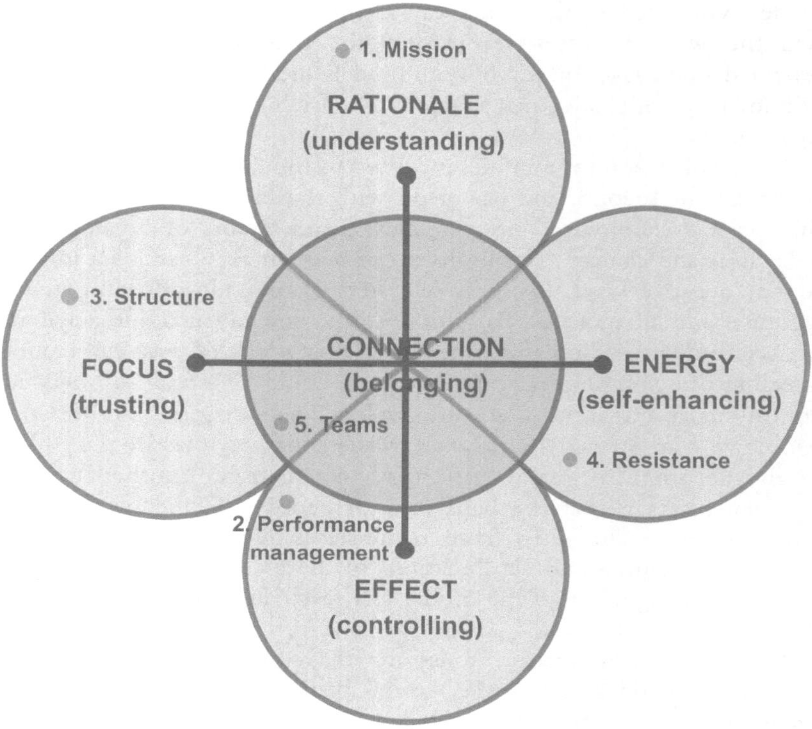

Figure 8.1 The Change-Competence Model Enriched with the Core Social Motives and One Related Change Management Topic Per Factor

Table 8.4 Change Management Topics, Social Motives, and Social Psychological Biases Illustrated

Change Management Topic/Factor	*Core Social Motives(s)*	*Social Psychological Bias (illustration, Examples)*
1. Mission (strategy)	Understanding	Attentional bias
2. Performance management (management)	Controlling	Prospect theory
3. Structure	Trusting	Optimism bias
4. Resistance (leadership)	Self-enhancing	Confirmation bias
5. Teams (culture)	Belonging	Groupthink

Example 1: Mission, vision and strategy, and attentional bias

In starting a change process, a clear rationale as part of the "what should it be" question of Bower (2000) and his 'purposive change' is helpful and important, if not necessary. The mission of the organization provides a relevant point of reference for Bower's purposive change, which by definition has to contribute to the mission and must fit the purpose. Having a mission in itself is not sufficient to satisfy the core social motive of understanding, the need for shared meaning and orientation. One of the often-heard critiques in practice that does not resonate is that the mission (or a strategic or change vision) is well formulated and coherent but does not move people. An energising, inspiring vision (the picture that drives all the action) could be key to mobilizing support (Belasco, 1990). In change processes, attentional bias helps understand why having a sense of mission that resonates with people is crucial for getting people 'on board' with the change. As the specific evidence on attentional bias shows, people tend to focus more on messages that are arousing and highly relevant to them. To capture organizational members' attention and, consequently, mobilize support for the change, leaders and managers should use positive, powerful language and make sure that their word usage aligns with the perception, interests, and emotions of their employees. In this way, they capture their employees' attention and can, in turn, positively influence employees' attitude towards change. Storytelling, which is the technique of incorporating inspiring stories and story structures in communicating organizational change, is a powerful tool to do this.

Example 2: Resistance to change and confirmation bias

Resistance to change has many causes and can take different forms. It can be related to all five change-competence factors as well as all five core social needs. For example, a weak rationale for change will not help the development of shared understanding, and, if a change process does not satisfy the need for self-enhancement, energy will leak away. Avoiding resistance is difficult, if not impossible to accomplish. As Maurer (2010) states: "Progress without resistance is impossible. People will always have doubts and questions. Even when you are the champion of change, you will still have doubts. Will this really work? Have I given the idea sufficient thought? Resistance is a natural part of any change." Even so, resistance to change cannot be avoided, it is worthwhile to understand how to minimize its influence. A bias that is essential to understand resistance to change is confirmation bias. According to the conformation bias, people are more prone to seek out, interpret, favour, and recall information that is consistent with their own expectations. Changing initial beliefs takes a considerable amount of time and effort, and thus people tend to disregard new, alternative ideas, or perspectives. People in organizations confronted with change initiatives that are not in line with their own existing mental framework are likely to resist change and could be difficult to persuade. It is helpful to understand this bias and its underlying mechanisms to be better able to deal with factual or possible resistance. As scientific evidence indicates, presentations prompting a deeper, more analytical, and critical processing of the information could reduce the confirmation bias. As such, in communicating about a change, it is advisable to make presentations and methods to ensure analytical and critical processing, such as organizing subgroup discussions, in which in-depth explanations can be given and questions can be answered. In addition, leaders and managers are advised to take note of certain situations in which the confirmation bias is most likely to exert its influence; for example, situations in which individuals tend to be highly motivated to voice their own point of view or defend their arguments. In these situations, it is advisable to appoint someone to play the devil's advocate.

Example 3: Structure and optimism bias

Structure—not only meaning organizational schemes or organograms but also systems, procedures, responsibilities, and roles—is strongly related to the core social motive of trusting. The optimism bias gives valuable insights into why structure and systems, as part of the factor focus, are important. The optimism bias posits that people tend to perceive they are more likely than others to experience positive events. This bias can have detrimental effects on the planning and execution of projects by causing an overestimation of benefits or financial gains, and underestimation of costs or completion time. This is where clear and aligned systems, procedures, responsibilities, and roles play an important role. They provide organizational structure and specific guidelines, which aim at countering the unwanted consequences of unbridled optimism, such as engaging in high-risk decision-making and investments in loss-making activities and executing poor project planning. For example, while planning for a certain (change-) project, managers, or project leaders should be aware of the effects of the optimism bias on time judgements, since employees tend to be overly optimistic regarding their estimates of the time it will take to complete the project (-phase). To combat this, it is advisable to provide structure; for example, forming concrete action plans that specify when, where, and how to act to reach particular goals.

Example 4: Performance management and prospect theory

Performance management is related to both the running and changing of organizations. From a social psychological perspective, performance management is strongly related to the social motive of controlling. People need perceived contingency between behaviour and outcomes (Fiske, 2004). Prospect theory helps understand how effect, through controlling, works in organizational and change contexts. It deepens the insights into change and behaviour by shedding light on an important cognitive mechanism. The prospect theory states that people tend to prefer avoiding losses over acquiring equivalent gains, which is illustrated by the well-known phrase "losses loom larger than gains." This can be translated to performance management.

For example, framing certain job tasks as being preventative of organizational failure (loss framing), can be effective in enhancing employee productivity.

Example 5: Teams and groupthink

Teams and team development become essential when we understand that it is deeply related to the most fundamental core social motive—belonging. The need for strong, stable relationships is a, if not the, defining characteristic of humans as social or organizational animals. For the organizational context, from a social psychological perspective, groupthink is important for the need to belong as such, and for teams and team development in particular, as it influences the behaviour of the individual and the team. Groupthink is the social psychological phenomenon that occurs when the desire of members to maintain harmony and conformity in a group results in faulty decisions. Several guidelines can help reduce groupthink; for example, making use of a critical reviewer, not allowing individuals to express their preferences in advance, planning open sessions to reconsider alternatives, stimulating honest consideration of all alternatives, and forming subgroups to allow a more detailed discussions.

Notions and thoughts about our journey so far

The purpose of our research and book is to provide scientists and practitioners with the best available evidence linking biases to organizational behaviour and change. This research and book do not stand by themselves. We regard this book and our earlier projects as a journey in the development of change management in an evidence-based way of working. Our book *Reconsidering Change Management* (Ten Have et al., 2016) was a 'stopping place' and 'starting point' for the next stages of the journey towards effective change management to make better organizations that work and contribute. We accomplished this by collecting, analysing, and presenting the scientific research and insights available, focusing on more, better, relevant, and useful or helpful evidence for practice (and science).

The subsequent book *The Social Psychology of Change Management* (Ten Have et al., 2019) had the same focus and can be seen as the next stage of the journey. In this book, we presented 40 social psychological theories relevant to change management in an encyclopaedic, coherent, and evidence-based way. It can be seen as the driving force of our current destination: *Organizational Behaviour and Change Management—The Impact of Social and Cognitive Biases*. With this book, we have reached the next 'inn' where we tell our story and share our experiences, the insights, and the evidence we gathered with other travellers, so they are possibly better prepared for the next stages of their scientific or practical journey.

About the next stages, the question from a research and methodological perspective could be "What's next?" The short answer is: making more, better, relevant, and useful evidence available for the science and practice related to change management; that is, providing additional evidence in terms of quantity, level (of evidence), specificity, and fitness for the purpose.

Notions and thoughts for future research

Reflecting on the results of our research, we formulate thoughts and notions that may be helpful in the way forward. To begin with, related to the field of change management, we have the conceptual and empirical insights of 29 biases. This base of evidence can be further exploited and developed in future research. Thus, the evidence regarding the biases in themselves (i.e., not specifically related to organizational behaviour and change) will develop further. This will provide additional insights also relevant to organizational behaviour and change. This book shows that there is a large potential regarding the specific relationship between social psychological biases and the context of organization behaviour and change. Of course, we hope that this will motivate researchers to 'dive deeper' into biases and the specific context of organizational behaviour and change. In addition, we look at the experience of practitioners as an important source of evidence, which needs further exploration from the perspectives of a researcher and a practitioner. Through reflection by practitioners and with the help of scientists, the evidence can be made available and provided to other practitioners.

Lastly, we have a more practical suggestion for future research. In our research, we used the rapid evidence assessment (REA) method. A REA, by applying a systematic review method to search and critically appraise studies, provides a balanced assessment of what is known in the scientific literature. For REAs used in this book, concessions have been made in terms of the breadth and depth of the search process, to be able to make it rapid. This includes the exclusion of articles not written in English. This results in a predominantly Western orientation of this book and its main findings. We have not focused on the manifestation of social psychological biases in, for example, Eastern or Asian cultures. Therefore, it is valid to question whether the main findings yielded can be universally applied to other cultures, or if cultural differences could play a significant role. For example, one of the proposed ways in which Asian cultures differ from Western cultures is that group identity is placed over individual identity. This importance of group identity could manifest itself, for example, in more groupthink or conformity in Asian cultures compared to Western cultures. However, future research is needed to further explore such assumptions.

Final remarks

With this book, we provide an overview of the current state of scientific knowledge regarding biases, relevant to organizational behaviour and change. We have structured them into a coherent model, analysed the available knowledge, and put this knowledge in an organizational context. We believe it to be essential to approach biases in an appreciative and balanced manner and not follow the negative frame surrounding biases. We believe that biases must be viewed with both a practical and holistic outlook so that organizational frameworks and behaviour can be changed effectively and adequately. Knowledge about certain built-in cognitive pathways can help make organizational behaviour more predictable and recognizable. Understanding the tendencies that all humans bear helps understand and subsequently reshape certain unwanted behaviours in oneself, others, teams, and organizations.

Changes usually concern issues with a great organizational, emotional, economic, and social impact. Therefore, this book goes beyond the domain of organizational sciences. We hope that our journey, and this book as an integral part, will provide you with the knowledge and the wisdom to use biases with purpose and to help the world make a better place.

Bibliography

Abbot, A. (1988). *System of professions: Essay on the division of expert labour.* The University of Chicago Press.

Barber, B. (1963). Some problems in the sociology of professions. *Daedalus, 92*(4), 669–688. https://www.jstor.org/stable/20026806

Barends, E., & Rousseau, D. M. (2018). *Evidence-based management: How to use evidence to make better organizational decisions*. Kogan Page Publishers.

Belasco, J. A. (1990). *Teaching the elephant to dance: Empowering change in your organization.* New York, NY: Crown Publishers.

Bower, J. L. (2000). The purpose of change, a commentary on Jensen and Senge. In M. Beer & N. Nohria (Eds.), *Breaking the code of change*. Harvard Business School Press.

Fiske, S. T. (2004). *Social beings: Core motives in social psychology*. John Wiley & Sons.

Freidson, E. (1973). *The professions and their prospects*. Sage Publications, Inc.

Gage, N. L., & Berliner, D. C. (1992). *Educational psychology* (5th ed.). Houghton Mifflin Company.

Greenwood, E. (1957). Attributes of a profession. *Social Work, 2*(3), 44–55. https://www.jstor.org/stable/23707630

Maurer, R. (2010). *Beyond the wall of resistance: Why 70% of all changes still fail—and what you can do about it.* Bard Press.

Ten Have, S., Rijsman, J., Ten Have, W., & Westhof, J. (2019). *The social psychology of change management: Theories and an evidence-based perspective on social and organizational beings*. Routledge.

Ten Have, S., Ten Have, W. D., Huijsmans, A. B., & Otto, M. (2016). *Reconsidering change management: Applying evidence-based insights in change management practice*. Routledge.

Ten Have, S., Ten Have, W., Huijsmans, A. B., & Van der Eng, N. (2015). *Change competence: Implementing effective change*. Routledge.

Appendix A

Overview of primary and secondary biases

Understanding: **Need for shared meaning and prediction—first cognitive motive**

1. **Attentional bias**—the tendency to be selective in the information people attend to.
   1. ***Frequency illusion***—the tendency to notice something more often after having noticed it once, leading to the belief that it has a high frequency
   2. ***Focusing effect***—the proneness to magnify the importance of something because of heightened attention to it
   3. ***Distinction bias***—the tendency to over-value the distinctions between two options when evaluating them simultaneously
2. **Availability bias**—the tendency to judge the frequency of prevalence of events by the ease with which relevant instances come to mind
   1. ***Availability cascade***—the self-reinforcing process where a certain perception or stance gains increasing plausibility in public discourse through its rising its availability
   2. ***Illusory correlation***—the proneness to perceive a relationship between variables (events, people, or actions) even when no such relationship actually exists
   3. ***Apophenia***—the tendency to perceive a meaningful connection or pattern between unrelated objects or ideas based on the recognition of a few components or stimuli
   4. ***Pareidolia***—a certain type of apophenia concerning the perceived connection between (usually) visual stimuli (e.g., the perception of a face within an inanimate object)
   5. ***Well-travelled-road effect***—the tendency of 'travellers' to appraise the time taken to cross routes differently depending on their familiarity with those routes

3. **Conjunction fallacy**—the tendency to assume that multiple specific conditions are more probable than a simple generic one
   1. ***Representativeness heuristic***—a mental shortcut used to come to judgements by comparing novel situations and information to familiar mental concepts or 'internal stereotypes'
   2. ***Base-rate fallacy***—the tendency to rely on specific information rather than statistics
4. **Framing effect**—the tendency to let the presentation of the message influence choices, perceptions, evaluations, and decisions
   1. ***Affect heuristic/Projection bias***—type of mental shortcut in which people make decisions influenced by their current emotions
   2. ***Unit bias***—the tendency to want to complete a unit of a given item or task
5. **Priming effect**—the tendency to let the introduction of one stimulus influence the perception and response to a subsequent stimuli
   1. ***Anchoring***—the tendency to compare stimuli to a particular reference point ('anchor')
   2. ***Conservatism bias***—the tendency to revise one's belief insufficiently when presented with new evidence
   3. ***Semmelweis effect***—the tendency to reject new evidence or new knowledge because it contradicts established knowledge, norms, or standards
   4. ***Law of the instrument***—the tendency to over-rely on familiar tools
6. **Recency effect**—the tendency to give more weight to recently presented information over earlier presented information
7. **Halo effect**—the tendency to let the positive impressions of a stimulus in one area positively influence perceptions of that stimulus in other areas
   1. ***The law of small numbers***—the tendency to generalize about all members of a certain group based on information about just one or very few people
8. **Similarity bias**—the tendency to evaluate those perceived as similar to oneself in a more favourable light

Controlling—: **Need for perceived contingency between behaviour and outcomes—second cognitive motive**

9. **Illusion of control**—the tendency to overestimate the degree of control over events that are in fact uncontrollable
   1. ***Illusory superiority***—the tendency to overestimates one's own qualities and abilities compared to those of others

2. ***Self-serving bias***—the tendency to hold a distorted perception of reality to maintain and enhance self-esteem or any other favourable perception of oneself

3. ***Planning fallacy***—the tendency to make overconfident estimations about the duration of a future task and underestimation of the time needed

10. **Hindsight bias**—the tendency to overestimate our foresight knowledge of an event after the event occurs

    1. ***Outcome bias***—the tendency to focus primarily on the outcome rather than on other available information at the time, in deciding if a past decision was correctly made

11. **Information bias**—the tendency to seek information even when it cannot affect the outcome

    1. ***Zero-risk bias***—the tendency to prefer the complete elimination of risks (and benefits) of certain element, even when alternative options produce a greater overall risk reduction
    2. ***Ambiguity effect***—the tendency to prefer an option for which the odds of a favourable outcome are known over one for which they are unknown
    3. ***Parkinson's law***—the tendency to increase the complexity or expand the duration of a task to fill the time available for its completion

12. **Risk compensation**—the tendency towards a more risk-taking behaviour when safety measures are in place

    1. ***Reactance***—the tendency to respond when a person feels that someone or something is taking away their choices or limiting the range of alternatives

13. **Prospect theory**—the tendency to prefer avoiding losses to acquiring equivalent gains in decision-making

    1. ***Disposition effect***—the tendency of investors to sell assets that have increased in value, while holding assets that have lost value
    2. ***Dread aversion***—the tendency to attach more weight to possible negative future events as opposed to positive future events
    3. ***Pseudo-certainty effect***—the tendency to prefer an apparent certain option even though it is factually uncertain
    4. ***The neglect of probability***—the tendency to disregard probability when making a decision under uncertainty
    5. ***Sunk-cost fallacy***—the tendency to follow through on an endeavour if time, effort, or money are already invested into it

14. **Delay (hyperbolic) discounting**—the tendency to prefer smaller immediate rewards over larger later rewards

    1. ***Money illusion***—the tendency to mistakenly value money at face value (nominal value) instead of its purchasing power (real value)

***Trusting*: Need for seeing others as basically benign—first affective motive**

15. **Mere exposure effect—**the tendency to develop preferences for familiar things

    1. ***Illusory truth effect***—the tendency to judge information as more valid after being exposed to it numerous times
    2. ***Rhyme-as-reason effect***—the tendency to judge a saying or aphorism as more accurate or valid when written in rhyme
    3. ***Automation bias***—the proneness to prefer suggestions from automated systems and to falsely ignore contradictory information made without automation (i.e., by humans)

16. **Negativity bias**—the tendency to give more weight to negative information compared to positive information

    1. ***Truthiness*—**the tendency to judge a claim or statement as valid because of a personal feeling or desire for it to be true regardless of the absence of supporting facts or evidence
    2. ***Subjective validation***—the tendency to judge a statement or another piece of information to be correct if it has any personal meaning or significance
    3. ***Declinism*—**the belief that a society is tending towards decline
    4. ***Pessimism bias*** -—the tendency to overestimate the likelihood of negative events while underestimating positive events

17. **Optimism bias**—the tendency to perceive that is more likely to experience positive events compared to others

    1. ***Normalcy bias***—the tendency to respond to threat warnings with disbelief or minimization and to underestimate a disasters' potential adverse effects
    2. ***Pro-innovation bias***—the belief that all members of a social system should adopt and diffuse an innovation rapidly, without considering or allowing for an alteration to that innovation

18. **(Hostile) attribution bias**—the tendency to make systematic errors when assigning causes to behaviour of themselves and others

    1. ***Fundamental attribution error***—the tendency to overvalue dispositional explanations of others' behaviours (i.e., make internal attributions) while undervaluing dispositional explanations

2. ***Actor–observer bias***—the tendency to assign causes of behaviour differently depending on whether one is an actor or an observer
3. ***Third-person bias***—the proneness to overestimate the effects of mass media communication on others compared to oneself
4. ***Empathy gap***—the tendency to underestimate the influence of varying mental states on self behaviour and make decisions that only satisfy one's current emotion, feeling, or state of being
5. ***Hostile attribution bias***—the tendency to interpret others' ambiguous behaviours as hostile rather than benign

***Self-enhancing*: Need for viewing self as basically worthy or improvable—second affective motive**

19. **Egocentric bias**—the tendency to rely on their own perspective and to have a higher opinion of themselves than reality reflects

    1. ***Self-serving bias***—the tendency to take undue credit for positive events or outcomes, while blaming external factors for negative events
    2. ***Spotlight effect***—the proneness to overestimate the amount of attention others pay to oneself
    3. ***Forer effect***—the tendency to believe that generic personality descriptions apply specifically to oneself
    4. ***Zero-sum bias***—the tendency to intuitively judge that one person's gain would be another's loss (e.g., a zero-sum situation) even when this is not the case
    5. ***Reactive devaluation***—the proneness to disparage proposals made by another (antagonistic) party
    6. ***Not-invented-here syndrome***—the tendency to avoid using knowledge or buying products from an external party
    7. ***Curse of knowledge***—the susceptibility to assume others share the same background knowledge on a certain topic that one has expertise in

20. **Overconfidence effect**—the tendency to be overbearing regarding the accuracy of one's judgements or abilities

    1. ***Restraint bias***—the tendency to overestimate one's ability to control impulsive behaviour
    2. ***Moral credential effect***—when a status or reputation of being egalitarian establishes an unconscious license in someone that increases the likelihood of them showing less egalitarian behaviour later on
    3. ***Ostrich effect***—the tendency to avoid negative information that threatens to confirm negative self-beliefs

4. ***Choice-supportive bias***—the tendency to retroactively exaggerate the positive attributes of an option one has chosen and to downgrade the renounced alternatives
5. ***Bias blind spot***—the tendency of people to believe they are less biased in their judgements than others
6. ***Dunning-Kruger effect***—people with limited knowledge or competence in a given domain greatly overestimate their own knowledge or competence in that domain for people with high knowledge or competence the opposite is true

21. **Confirmation bias**—the tendency to prefer information that is consistent with one's prior beliefs and expectations

    1. ***Continued influence effect***—the tendency to continue to rely on misinformation and false claims in reasoning, even long after this information has been proven false
    2. ***Congruence bias***—the tendency to over-rely on testing one's initial hypothesis
    3. ***Illusion of validity***—the tendency to overrate one's ability to make accurate predictions and interpret data subjectively to strengthen one's assumptions and predictions
    4. ***Backfire bias***—the tendency to strengthen one's initial beliefs when encountering evidence that supports the opposite
    5. ***Selection bias***—the tendency to select individuals, groups, or data for analysis in such a way that proper randomization is not achieved, thereby failing to ensure that the sample obtained is representative of the population intended to be analysed

22. **Experimenter bias**—Experimenters or observers tend to influence their participants, data or outcomes

    1. ***Funding bias***—the tendency of a scientific study to support the (business) interests of the study's financial sponsor

23. **Endowment effect**—the tendency to attach a higher value to objects when owned
24. **Sunk-cost fallacy**—the tendency to continue an endeavour once an investment in money, effort, or time has been made

***Belonging*: Need for strong, stable relationships—fundamental core social motive**

25. **Conformity**—the tendency to converge thoughts, feelings, or behaviour towards a social or group norm
26. **Groupthink**—the tendency to want to maintain harmony and conformity in the group

    1. ***Bandwagon effect***—the tendency to support and adopt certain beliefs, attitudes or behaviours as they become more popular

27. **Social desirability bias**—the tendency to report their behaviours in a manner that will be viewed favourably by others

    1. ***Courtesy bias***—The tendency of not fully stating unhappiness with a service or product because of the willingness to be polite towards the questioner

28. **Status quo bias**—the tendency to have a clear preference for the current state of affairs

    1. ***Omission bias***—the tendency to prefer harm caused by omissions over equal or lesser harm caused by acts
    2. ***Inertia***—the tendency to prefer the default option unless motivated to reject this option

29. **System-justification bias**—the tendency to maintain social systems and attendant norms, rules, and social structures and see them as legitimate even when confronted with information suggesting the opposite

    1. ***Authority bias***—the tendency to attribute greater accuracy to the opinion of an authority figure and to be more influenced by that opinion

Appendix B

Examples of Matrix for Each Core Social Motive

1. Understanding

Attentional Bias

Author and Year	*Design*	*Sector/ Population*	*Moderator/ Mediator*	*Main Finding*	*Limitations*	*Level*
Pool et al. (2016)	Meta-analysis of 150 articles (k = 243, n = 9.120), controlled studies using a within-subject design	Healthy adults	Attentional bias subcomponents Attentional paradigm Measure Cue-target onset asynchrony Valence Arousal Relevance to specific concerns Types of positive stimuli Stimulus format Positive value	Despite an initial focus on negative threatening stimuli, researchers have more recently expanded the investigation of attentional biases towards positive rewarding stimuli. The present meta-analysis compared attentional bias for positive compared with neutral visual stimuli. Overall, results showed a significant, albeit modest (Hedges' $g = .258$ (=small)), attentional bias for positive as compared with neutral stimuli. Moderator analyses revealed that the magnitude of this attentional bias varied as a function of arousal ($p = .099$) and that this bias was significantly larger when the emotional stimulus was relevant to specific concerns (e.g., being presented food-related stimuli when hungry) of the participants compared with other positive stimuli that were less relevant to the participants' concerns ($p <.001$).	The methodlogical quality of each study was not assessed or it was not described clearly.	A-

(Continued)

(Continued)

Author and Year	*Design*	*Sector/ Population*	*Moderator/ Mediator*	*Main Finding*	*Limitations*	*Level*
Shin et al. (2011)	Randomized controlled before and after study. Sample size: 147	Students	NA	A fear-induced shift in attention to threatening cues was associated with increased levels of later anxiety ($p = .04$, $R^2 = .14$ (medium)). A happiness-induced shift in attention to emotional cues (both threatening and pleasant) was associated with increased levels of later life satisfaction (pleasant: $p = .006$, $R^2 = .17$) (medium), threatening $p = .01$, $R^2 = .15$ (medium)). Our finding that shifts in attention to potentially salient (threatening and pleasant) cues after the induction of happy mood were associated with higher levels of well-being over a follow-up period of 3 weeks is consistent with Fredrickson's broaden-and-build theory of positive emotion (Fredrickson, 1998, 2001). This theory suggests that in contrast to negative emotions, which are associated with specific thought-action repertoires, positive emotions generally broaden cognition. This allows for creative exploration and the building of resources required for well-being and resilience. Interpreted in light of this theory, broadening one's attention to both threatening and pleasant stimuli in one's environment may allow for the detection of resources and information that may be important for well-being.	NA	A
Cai et al. (2018)	Randomized controlled before- and after study. Sample size: 77	NA	NA	The aim of this study is to examine whether attentional bias modification (ABM) can be used to modify high test-anxiety (nonclinical) individuals' attention to emotional information. The ABM consisted of a dot probe test, a computerized attention task in which participants are trained to avoid the threat. The behavioural findings suggested that attentional bias towards threat information significantly decreased after the 5-day training away from the threat ($p = 0.047$, Cohen' $d = 0.392$ (small to medium)). They started to pay more attention to the positive words than the threat words after the 5-day training. In contrast, the participants in the placebo and waiting list groups tended to allocate their attention towards threatening stimuli with the approaching exam.	NA	A-

Author and Year	*Design*	*Sector/ Population*	*Moderator/ Mediator*	*Main Finding*	*Limitations*	*Level*
Crum et al. (2017)	Randomized controlled study. Sample size: 113	Students	NA	The aim of the current study was to explore whether stress responses can be altered by changing individuals' mindsets about the nature of stress in general. Results: only when the stress was evaluated as a challenge (= when given positive feedback), a stress-is enhancing mindset produced heightened attentional bias towards positive stimuli ($p = .037$, $\eta^2 = .047$ (small to medium)). In contrast, those with a stress-is-debilitating mindset experienced worse cognitive flexibility and less bias to happy faces despite being given positive feedback. So, whenever possible, people should attempt to evaluate stressors as challenging (as opposed to threatening).	NA	
Jamieson (2012)	Randomized controlled study. Sample size: 55	Not specified	NA	We examined whether reappraising stress-induced arousal could improve cardiovascular outcomes and decrease attentional bias for emotionally negative information. Relative to controls, participants instructed to reappraise their arousal showed decreased attentional bias compared to the ignore condition ($p = .013$, $d = .77$ (large)), and the no-intervention controls ($p = 0.55$, $d = .58$ (medium-large))	Relatively small sample size.	
Morrison and O'Conner (2008)	Randomized controlled study. Sample size: 81	Students	NA	This experimental study examines the relationship between rumination and attentional bias. In combination with negative mood, inducing rumination decreased positive attentional bias ($M = 84.20$, $SD = 175.14$), whilst inducing distraction increased positive attentional bias ($M = -147.47$, $SD = 407.51$).	Relatively small sample size.	

(*Continued*)

(Continued)

Author and Year	*Design*	*Sector/ Population*	*Moderator/Mediator*	*Main Finding*	*Limitations*	*Level*
Tian et al. (2011)	Nonrandomized controlled before and after study. Sample size: 34	NA	NA	During moderate-intensity exercise, participants exhibited significantly greater attentional bias scores to pleasant compared with unpleasant faces ($p = .005$, $n^2 = .219$ (large)), whereas attentional bias scores to emotional faces did not differ at rest or during high-intensity exercise ($p > .05$). In addition, attentional bias to unpleasant faces was significantly reduced during moderate-intensity exercise compared with that during rest ($p = .025$). The results suggest that moderate-intensity exercise may prime the appetitive motivational system linked to visual attention. The results also suggest that defensive motivational circuits linked to visual attention to faces may be inhibited during moderate intensity exercise but not high-intensity exercise. Our hypothesis is that moderate-intensity exercise, when compared with rest, may promote a shift in attentional bias that may help promote improved mood.	Very small sample size.	B-
Jiang et al. (2017)	Randomized controlled study. Sample size: 62	Chinese male under-graduates	NA	The present study investigated the influence of acute psychosocial stress on attentional bias to threatening stimuli using behavioural and electrophysiological measures. Results: attention was equally allocated to angry and neutral faces in stressed participants, indicating a stress-induced suppression of attentional bias. This finding could be further evidence supporting the idea that attention orientation to threat is suppressed under stress. In summary, our results suggest that acute psychosocial stress impairs attentional bias. Acute stress may lead to indiscriminate selective response to threat and reduced efficiency of cortical processing.	Relatively small sample size.	C

2. Controlling

Illusion of Control

Author and Year	*Design*	*Sector/ Population*	*Moderator/ Mediator*	*Main Finding*	*Limitations*	*Level*
Presson and Benassi (1996)	Meta-analysis (53 studies from 29 articles)	Not specified	4 moderators (Note: the authors apprehend that this are identified as possible moderators): Participants' awareness of the possibility that task outcomes were random Type of illusion measured Type of situational variable Type of control assessment	An analysis on illusory control following Langer's (1975) study that first coined the term 'illusory control'. Some studies before Langer's one were used on the basis of reference lists by other studies and Langer's. Definition of illusion of control: "an expectancy of a personal success probability inappropriately higher than the objective probability would warrant (Langer, 1975, p. 313) ◊ i.e. a judgement is illusory when it is higher than some accepted standard, "The present meta-analysis showed a positive, consistent, and moderately strong illusion of control effect—not a single effect size estimate was negative" (p. 506). The overall weighted mean effect size was d=0.68. The effect sizes per situational variables were (p. 501:0 Outcome Frequency: d=.87 Choice: d= 0.95 Involvement (Actor vs. Observer): d=.51 Outcome Sequence: d=.93 Competition: d=.51 Foreknowledge: d=.74 Familiarity (With Task): d=.62 Familiarity (With Stimulus): d=1.27 Extrinsic Reward: d=.95 Involvement (not actor vs. observer): d=.52 Instructional set: d=1.14 Conclusions:	Most studies did not (or is unclear) use a control group and random assignment. It is unclear whether most studies included a control group or a before and after measurement. The method-logical quality of each study was not assessed or it was not described clearly.	B-

(Continued)

(Continued)

Author and Year	*Design*	*Sector/ Population*	*Moderator/ Mediator*	*Main Finding*	*Limitations*	*Level*
				"The present meta-analysis showed a positive, consistent, and moderately strong illusion of control effect—not a single effect size estimate was negative" (p. 506). The overall meta-analysis showed no moderating effect of illusion type, but when further meta-analyses are conducted on experiments that measured control and prediction judgement◊ control measures produced a smaller effect size than measures of prediction. The authors concede that illusory control (i.e., illusion of control) is not the adequate term for the meta-analysis. Rather, they suggest that 'illusory judgement' the correct term, due to the fact that not all the review studies necessarily had to do with the concept of control: "there is some question as to whether illusion of control researchers have examined a single underlying construct" (p. 502). For the authors, if Langer (1975) herself did not actually measure illusion of control, as she did not include a direct measure of control. "We suggest that had a more direct measure of perceived control been included in Langer's experiment, the effect might have been smaller than what was obtained using the willingness to exchange measure." The general line of the findings is thus while the effects have been found, they cannot necessarily all be attributed to the 'illusion of control' but rather 'illusory judgement' because this would be more in line with the findings.		

Author and Year	Design	Sector/ Population	Moderator/ Mediator	Main Finding	Limitations	Level
Stefan and David (2013)	Meta-analysis (34 studies, from 20 articles	Not specified	No moderators specified	"The purpose of this meta-analytic review involves offering effect-size estimates for the factors manipulated to induce the illusion of control and for the different conceptualizations of the phenomenon since 1996" (p. 378) in this year the meta-analysis by Preston & Bernassi was published. Overall weighted mean effect size (D) at a 95% confidence interval about the mean .49 to .75 D=.62 "The value indicates a medium effect size and shows that the manipulation of different factors in order to promote illusion of control has always been effective, even if alternative con-conceptualizations of the phenomenon were used." (p. 383) Main findings: Larger effect sizes seem to be associated with judgements related to the skill involved in solving the experimental task and direct estimates of personal control. More indirect measures such as behavioural responses (e.g., the amount he/she is willing to bet) or decisions to become an active agent in the experimental situation tend to be associated with moderate effect sizes. This finding does not seem to confirm the conclusion of the earlier meta-analysis, as Presson and Benassi (1996) found that direct measures produced smaller effect sizes than did indirect measures "To summarize, experiments designed to induce the illusion of control tend to obtain medium effect sizes using different independent variables and different conceptualizations of the phenomenon. The illusion of control seems to be a reliable phenomenon that appears constantly, to variable degrees, in association with numerous situational and psychological factors." (p. 384).	Most studies did not (or is unclear) use a control group and random assignment. It is unclear whether most studies included a control group or a before and after measurement. The method-logical quality of each study was not assessed or it was not described clearly.	B-

(Continued)

(Continued)

Author and Year	*Design*	*Sector/ Population*	*Moderator/ Mediator*	*Main Finding*	*Limitations*	*Level*
				The study echoes the sentiment of Preston and Bernassi (1996) in observing that there is no scholarly consensus on the exact meaning of 'illusion of control' or 'illusory control', as Stefan and David (2013, p. 384) state: "there seems to be a lack of agreement in terms of the concept's definition and measurement, as many studies approach this concept either as a judgement or subjective feeling, or as a specific behaviour, and these different facets of the concept could be of a different underlying nature." Connecting the different concepts seems to be large bone of contention that the authors seem to raise. Exploring the connections and relations between the different concepts could clarify the concept of illusory control in future research.		
Durand (2003)	Cross-sectional study survey on 785 CEO's of different firms	French industries in 1997	Not specified	Recent research shows that forecasting ability is an organizational distinctive competence. We propose and test a model accounting for interfirm differences in forecasting ability. After controlling for reciprocal effects, we find that two principal firm-level factors (i.e., organizational illusion of control and organizational attention) influence both bias and magnitude of errors in estimates. High organizational illusion of control increases positive forecast bias. A firm's illusion of control, manifested by higher relative investments in dynamic resources and high self-perception, increases positive forecast biases. It also tends to increase absolute value of errors as the positive and significant coefficients of Self-Perception and Relative R&D (even if less so) demonstrate. Moreover, organizational attention to external information, manifested by higher relative investments in marketing information, reduces positive forecast biases and the magnitude of errors. It also significantly moderates forecast biases associated with illusion of control, resulting in improved accuracy. Finally, organizational attention to internal information, manifested by higher relative investments in employee education, increases negative forecast bias and reduces average absolute error only for the highest observed values of illusion of control.	Sample was not randomly selected	D-

Author and Year	*Design*	*Sector/ Population*	*Moderator/ Mediator*	*Main Finding*	*Limitations*	*Level*
Keil et al. (2007)	Cross-sectional study Sample sizes: 178 subjects	All subjects were under-graduate students at an urban university in the south-eastern United States and enrolled in either an upper-level CIS course (82) or a marketing course (96)	NA	Our role-playing experiment was conducted in an unstructured problem context and the results suggest that, in such a setting, both problem recognition and cognitive biases affect escalation. Furthermore, cognitive Biases can affect the decision process either at the beginning (i.e., problem recognition stage) or at the end (i.e., actual decision stage). In particular, this study demonstrates the effects of two cognitive biases that have not been previously explored in relation to escalation of commitment: (1) selective perception and (2) illusion of control. As expected, we saw a significant positive relationship between marketing illusion of control and proclivity to launch as planned. One explanation for this finding is that individuals who believe they can control the odds associated with introducing a new product to the market will feel little or no pressure to depart from the planned launch schedule. In addition to the direct effect, we also observed a mediated effect through software quality problem recognition. Specifically, those subjects who exhibited a greater marketing illusion of control were less likely to recognize the software quality problem embedded in the scenario. This reduced problem recognition, in turn, led to a greater proclivity to launch as planned. In summary, the software quality assurance subjects were more apt to recognize problems associated with software quality, and this caused them to exercise greater restraint in launching the product as planned. Moreover, because of their functional affiliation as software quality assurance professionals, these subjects exhibited greater reluctance	It is unclear whether sample was randomly selected	D-

(Continued)

(Continued)

Author and Year	*Design*	*Sector/ Population*	*Moderator/ Mediator*	*Main Finding*	*Limitations*	*Level*
				to commercialize a buggy software product. In other words, when faced with a problem that they were tuned to selectively perceive, they were less likely to exhibit escalation behaviour. In contrast, the marketing subjects were less apt to recognize the software quality problem. At the same time, they were more apt to exhibit an illusion of control regarding their ability to successfully commercialize a buggy software product. This combination made them more willing to engage in escalation behaviour. Finally, illusion of control may be a bias that is both subtle and difficult to counter. An organization is likely to desire an individual familiar with the nature of the work to be performed, but familiarity can induce an illusion of control. One approach to this situation may be to elevate the level of awareness of the issue through education, training, and discussion of potential situations in which illusion of control may act.		
Fenton-O'Creevy et al. (2003)	Noncontrolled post-test study only: Study 107	Traders in four City of London investment banks	Not specified	p. 65: This study offers evidence that illusion of control is an important form of cognitive bias affecting traders and that traders with higher levels of illusion of control perform less well than those with lower levels. p. 65: These results make a contribution to two relates theoretical debates. The first debate concerns whether positive illusions are beneficial or harmful. This study illustrates one set of conditions in which positive illusion may be harmful to performance. The second concerns whether perceptions of high control are always adaptive. These results add to a body of evidence suggesting that high control beliefs are maladaptive in some circumstances where control is unlikely or impossible.	It is unclear whether the intervention was independent of other changes over time	D-

Mere Exposure Effect

Author and Year	*Design*	*Sector/ Population*	*Moderator/ Mediator*	*Main Finding*	*Limitations*	*Level*
Yariitu et al. (2015)	Noncontrolled post-test study only: two experiments	Not specified	NA	The results of the two experiments presented here provide little support for the motivational approach. From this approach it is argued that people must be personally involved in trying to obtain the outcome, and their self- esteem at risk, for the illusion to occur (Alloy et al., 1985; Thompson, 1999; Thompson et al., 1998). This claim lies on the idea that the illusion of control is a self-serving bias that activates when the relationship judged is relevant to self-esteem (e.g., Alloy & Abramson, 1979; Dudley, 1999; Koenig et al., 1992). However, we did not find an effect of personal involvement when it was tested independently of p(C). Participants of the Yoked Group showed the illusion of control even though their judgements were not relevant to protect their self-esteem. Moreover, we found a strong effect of p(C). As we have noted earlier, this p(C) effect could explain the results that had been often attributed to personal involvement in previous research, given that participants who are more involved tend to perform more actions to obtain the outcome. The main contribution of the present experiments is that the effects of personal involvement and probability of the cause are tested independently of each other. Even though the predictions of the motivational and the cognitive approaches can often be identical (because increased motivation produces more active behaviour), when these two variables are tested separately, the predictions of the two approaches become clearly different. The motivational approach predicts, for these cases, that only those who act to obtain the outcome should develop the illusion. The cognitive approach predicts that only p(C) should influence the illusion. In our experiments,	It is unclear whether data was gathered at two points in time after the intervention.	D-

(*Continued*)

(Continued)

Author and Year	*Design*	*Sector/ Population*	*Moderator/ Mediator*	*Main Finding*	*Limitations*	*Level*
				the judgements of participants who were involved in obtaining the outcome can be directly contrasted to the judgements of those who simply observed the identical events. Under these conditions, the results showed that the probability of the potential cause was the only variable that clearly influenced the participants' judgements. Although our results suggest that personal involvement has no influence on the illusion of control, we must acknowledge that our conclusions are based on the absence of significant differences with respect to this variable		

3. Trusting

Optimistic Bias

Author and Year	*Design*	*Sector/ Population*	*Moderator/ Mediator*	*Main Finding and effect sizes*	*Limitations*	*Level*
Klein and Helweg-larsen (2002)	Meta-analysis of 22 articles (total N = 5,142 with 27 effect sizes	Students	Nationality Student status Risk status Type of optimistic bias measure used	Greater perceived control was significantly related to greater optimistic bias with an average r of 0.31 (medium). Moderators played a significant role in this relationship. Nationality: only us participants: r=0.53 (large). Non-us participants: r=0.18 (small) Student status: Students: r=0.43 (medium). Nonstudents: r=0.24 (small) Risk status: no risk sample: r=0.43 (medium). At risk sample: r=0.04 (too small) Type of optimistic bias: direct optimistic bias: r=0.43 (medium). Indirect optimistic bias: r=0.18 (small)	The method-logical quality of each study was not assessed or it was not described clearly.	B-

Author and Year	*Design*	*Sector/ Population*	*Moderator/ Mediator*	*Main Finding and effect sizes*	*Limitations*	*Level*
Buehler et al. (2005)	Randomized controlled before-after study. 3 studies (S1 N = 64, S2 N= 216, S3 N = 267).	Students	Mediator: Informational focus at the time of prediction	Group discussion heightened participants' tendency to focus primarily on factors promoting successful task completion, and this selective focus on "planning for success" enhanced their optimistic outlook. Study 1: F (1, 14) D 15.90, $p < .001$ (strong effect) indicating that participants generated more optimistic predictions through group discussion than they did individually. Study 2: predictions were shorter in the group discussion conditions (M D 12.26, SD D 2.02) than in the individual condition (M D 13.08, SD D 1.37), t (64) D 2.07, $p < .05$. This is a small effect. Study 3: participants expected the assignment would take less time in the discussion conditions than in the individual conditions t (80) =2.57, p=.01. This is a strong effect. The mediator was tested and had the following effects: z=2.36, $p < .02$. This is a significant effect therefore informational focus is a mediator on the relationship between group discussion and optimistic bias.	The method for randomly assigned participants is not (clearly) described. The sample size was not big enough for every study.	B
Koole and Van 't Spijker (2000)	Randomized controlled before-after study. (N = 120)	Undergraduate students	NA	Implementation intentions/planning is correlated with increasing optimism bias. r=0.55 (large effect size). It is also important to note that implementation intentions were also correlated with an increase in actual goal completion, which is described as a positive thing. Keeping these two effects in mind, the overall effect was positive in the sense that in the end there was a significant reduction in optimistic bias in completion predictions.	It is unclear how the random assignment of participants took place.	B

(Continued)

4. Self-Enhancing

Experimenter Bias

Author and Year	*Design & sample size*	*Sector/ Population*	*Moderator/ Mediator*	*Main Finding*	*Effect level*	*Limitations*	*Level*
Hróbiartsson et al. (2013)	Systematic review (N = 24)	Patients & assessors	Blinded and nonblinded trials on significant results	Nonblinded experimental trials significantly report higher p-values and significant effects than blinded trials	Large	The method-logical quality of each study was not assessed or it was not described clearly.	A-
Strickland and Suben (2012)	Experimental randomized control trial (N = 19)	Students	Effects of experimenter bias on randomized experimental trials	Experimenters significantly obtained their own hypothesized results	Large ($p<0.01$) & not significant	NA	A

Author and Year	*Design & sample size*	*Sector/ Population*	*Moderator/ Mediator*	*Main Finding*	*Effect level*	*Limitations*	*Level*
Hróbiartsson et al. (2012)	Systematic review (N= 21)	Patients & assessors	Observer bias in blinded/ nonblinded assessors in trials with binary outcomes	Non blinded assessors generated more optimistic patient assessments by a ratio of 36%	Large	The method-logical quality of each study was not assessed or it was not described clearly.	A
Stubbs et al. (2014)	Cross-sectional research	Populations from 156 (3 worldwide property rights indexes were used)	Knowledge about economic growth influencing property rights decisions	A clear observer bias was detected across 2 indexes. Property rights subjective coding was consistently more positive when a country experienced economic growth.	$P<0.032$ Moderate	It is possible some studies were missed. The process of selecting studies was not clearly defined. The method-logical quality of each study was not assessed or it was not described clearly.	NA

(Continued)

(Continued)

Author and Year	*Design & sample size*	*Sector/ Population*	*Moderator/ Mediator*	*Main Finding*	*Effect level*	*Limitations*	*Level*
Holman et al. (2015)	Meta-analysis & literature review (systematic review using text mining) N = 93 papers & N = 7644 papers	Not specified	Observer bias blinded and nonblinded trials in the field of life sciences	Blinded trials showed significantly lower effect sizes compared to nonblinded trials	$P < 0.032$ Moderate	It is possible some studies were missed. The process of selecting studies was not clearly defined. The methodological quality of each study was not assessed or it was not described clearly.	C-

5. Belonging

Social Desirability

Author and Year	*Design*	*Sector/ Population*	*Moderator/ Mediator*	*Main Finding*	*Effect level*	*Limitations*	*Level*
Blair et al. (2020)	Meta-analysis of 264 list experiments in 92 papers	Not specified	Direct Indirect questioning	Depending on the context social desirability can differ. Voter turnout turned out to be systematically over-reported. The authors accrue this to sensitivity bias and not to memory or recall bias. But there was no indication (against expectations) of socially desirable answers concerning prejudice. In fact, people over-reported on their own prejudices instead of under-reported (which was hypothesized). In contrast there were significant effects found in support for authoritarian regimes. The authors argue that there is higher order of consequences than impression management such as fear of imprisonment that cause socially desirable answers.	Medium—Nonsignificant	They state that it is possible experiments were missed. They do not mention methodological quality of each study. The method-logical quality of each study was not assessed or it was not described clearly.	A-
Moorman and Podsakoff (1992)	Meta-analysis 33 studies	Students/ employees	Social desirability on work related constructs	Student samples appear to be more likely to be affected by socially desirable response bias than employee samples, neither the true V value for the student sample (r = .15), nor the r value for the organizational sample {r = .04) were significantly different from zero as noted by the confidence interval. Locus of control (—.22), general job	Small-medium	NA	B-

(Continued)

(Continued)

Author and Year	*Design*	*Sector/ Population*	*Moderator/ Mediator*	*Main Finding*	*Effect level*	*Limitations*	*Level*
				satisfaction (.22), role conflict (—.18), role ambiguity (—.24) and organizational commitment (.18) were all found to correlate with s.d. While these correlations may not be excessively high, they were all outside the .05 confidence interval. The remaining variables, self-esteem, satisfaction with supervisor, initiating structure and performance, were not similarly related to s.d.			
Ones & Viswesvaran (1996)	Meta-analysis >700 studies	Work force (>18<65) N=409,496	Social desirability on big 5 personality traits and job-related performance	Found that social desirability (a) is not a predictor in its own right, (b) does not function as a worthwhile suppressor variable, and (c) does not mediate the relationship between personality and job performance are all new to the field of applied psychology	Nonsignificant	The method-logical quality of each study was not assessed or it was not described clearly.	B-
Dwight and Feigelson (2000)	Meta-analysis 30 studies	Studies with children were excluded	Impression management and self-deceptive enhancement on computer	A small but statistically significant effect (d = -0.08) was found for impression management, with impression management being lower when assessed by computer. Correlational analysis revealed, however, that the strength of the effect of computer	Small-non-significant	They state it is possible that articles were missed. The method-logical quality	B-

Author and Year	*Design*	*Sector/ Population*	*Moderator/ Mediator*	*Main Finding*	*Effect level*	*Limitations*	*Level*
			person ability test vs. paper & pencil test.	administration on impression management appeared to diminish over time such that more recent studies have found small or no effects. No effect was found for S.D.E. As people become more familiar with computers this effect will probably decline to zero. This is in line with Ones & Viswesvaran (1996) that S.D. is not a useful predictor of job performance or enhances criterion-validity personality constructs.		of each study was not assessed or it was not described clearly.	
Ones and Viswesvaran (1998)	Literature review	NA	NA	Social desirability predicts a number of important work variables such as job satisfaction, organizational commitment, and supervisor ratings of training success, social desirability does not seem to be a predictor of overall job performance and is only very weakly related to specific dimensions of job performance such as technical proficiency and personal discipline. Social desirability does not moderate the criterion-related validities of personality variables or integrity tests. Controlling for social desirability in integrity or personality test scores leaves the operational validities intact, thereby suggesting that social desirability functions neither as a mediator nor as a suppressor variable in personality-performance and integrity-performance relations.	NA	NA	NA

(Continued)

(Continued)

Author and Year	*Design*	*Sector/ Population*	*Moderator/ Mediator*	*Main Finding*	*Effect level*	*Limitations*	*Level*
Viswesvaran & Ones (2001)	Meta-analysis 17 articles	Managers (N) = 20,069	Impression management on managerial performance	This research examined the correlation between impression management scale scores and overall job performance as well as its component dimensions for managerial jobs (one type of job requiring considerable interpersonal interaction). There appears to be little evidence that impression management scales predict job performance in at least one job category where interpersonal interactions are important (management).	Non-significant—small	The method-logical quality of each study was not assessed or it was not described clearly.	B-
Perinelli and Gremigni (2016)	Systematic review (35 studies from 2010–2015)	Adults	The effect of social desirability scales clinical psychology constructs	Perinelli and Gremigni (2016) found some evidence that SD is associated with several self-report variables in clinical psychology, such as attitude, knowledge and health behaviours, physical and mental symptoms, quality of life and well-being, and treatment variables and outcomes, suggesting that SD should be considered when addressing self-reports in clinical psychology, they attested to the suppressor role of personality variables on SD. Indeed, after controlling for personality variables such as neuroticism, impulsivity, self-esteem, dispositional optimism, or the Big Five dimensions, the association or influence of SD on clinical variables such as excessive eating, alexithymia, subjective well-being or intentions to cooperate, disappeared. Therefore, controlling for personality variables seems to be relevant to clarify the role of SD in self-reports, which might otherwise be overestimated.	Small-moderate	It is possible that older articles were missed. The method-logical quality of each study was not assessed or it was not described clearly.	B-

Author and Year	*Design*	*Sector/ Population*	*Moderator/ Mediator*	*Main Finding*	*Effect level*	*Limitations*	*Level*
Ray et al. (2013)	Meta-analysis (45 studies)	Adult population: Institutional: Prisoners, forensic, clinical Community: community undergraduate, mixed	Relations of psychopathy scales on distorted response styles	A concern among researchers is that self-report measures may not be valid indicators of psychopathic traits due to the core features of psychopathy (e.g., lying, deception/ manipulation). Despite several limitations (e.g., inclusion of only published studies, limited moderators, exclusion of other measures), the general findings temper concerns of positive response bias and underscore the validity of self-report psychopathy scales. The violence role hypothesis predicted that social desirability would be more strongly associated with the expression of intimate violence than with the sustaining of intimate violence. The meta-analytic results support this contention. Reports of the expression of violence against a partner were more highly correlated with social desirability than were reports of the suffering of intimate violence. This does not imply that victim reports are free of any social desirability effect. Rather, victim reports are just less correlated with social desirability. In contrast to the victim's role, one could argue that the perpetrator's role is more socially unacceptable, thus more related to a desire to protect one's social acceptability. A conclusion	Moderate	The method-logical quality of each study was not assessed or it was not described clearly.	B-

(Continued)

(Continued)

Author and Year	*Design*	*Sector/ Population*	*Moderator/ Mediator*	*Main Finding*	*Effect level*	*Limitations*	*Level*
Sugarman and Hotaling (2017)	Meta-analysis (7 studies)	Adult population (marital & courts hip violence	Role of social desirability in intimate violence	offered by others (Riggs, Murphy, & O'Leary, 1989). The findings clearly did not support the corollary to the violence role hypothesis that posited an expected positive relationship between reports of sustaining violence and social desirability responding. So, increasing one's association with the victim role does not serve as a strategy of self-enhancement. The sex hypothesis posited that men would exhibit a stronger relationship between reporting the use of intimate violence and a desire to be socially acceptable than would women. This hypothesis, however, was not supported: a conclusion also supported by others. Male and female college students were equally likely to indicate that they would admit engaging in violent acts against a partner if they had done so (Riggs et al., 1989). Thus, the sex of the perpetrator had little moderating effect on the violence reporting-social acceptability relationship.	Small-moderate	The method-logical quality of each study was not assessed or it was not described clearly.	B-
Larson and Bradshaw (2017)	Systematic review (15 studies)	Adults from the United States	Effect of social desirability on measuring cultural competence	The review and analysis of these studies suggested that cultural competence is positively correlated with social desirability bias, but the strength of this association varies as a function of the cultural competence scale used. Furthermore, race, gender, sexual orientation, years of experience, and training experiences were also significantly associated with cultural competence and/or social desirability. Implications for future research and professional development related to cultural competence are discussed.	Small-moderate	The method-logical quality of each study was not assessed or it was not described clearly.	B-

Author and Year	*Design*	*Sector/ Population*	*Moderator/ Mediator*	*Main Finding*	*Effect level*	*Limitations*	*Level*
Vesley and Kockler (2020)	Meta-analysis (29 studies)	Not specified	Social desirability on environmental factors	That social desirability might be a confounder of people's survey responses regarding environmental actions has been discussed for a long time. To produce evidence for or against this assumption, we conducted meta-analyses of correlations between social desirability scales and self-reports of environmentally relevant behaviours, intentions, and (broadly defined) attitudes, based on data from 29 previously published papers. The pooled correlations with social desirability are generally small, ranging from 0.06 to 0.11 (0.08–0.13 when correcting for measurement error attenuation). However, our results do not lead to the conclusion that social desirability can be completely disregarded by environmental psychologists as a potential confounder. For example, we found evidence of substantial heterogeneity across studies, so the effect of social desirability may be more pronounced in specific cases. Continued attention to social desirability bias is needed to fully understand its possible subtle effects.	Small	The methodological quality of each study was not assessed or it was not described clearly.	B–

(*Continued*)

(Continued)

Author and Year	*Design*	*Sector/ Population*	*Moderator/ Mediator*	*Main Finding*	*Effect level*	*Limitations*	*Level*
Conelly and Chang (2016)	Meta-analysis (8 studies)	Not specified	Effect of social desirability on performance and personality traits	The meta-analysis found that self-report method variance (a) was negatively related to performance, (b) would suppress personality-performance relationships for self-report measures, and (c) was (partially) assessed by SD scales. However, relative to the effects of self-report method variance, SD scales are even more strongly influenced by Conscientiousness, Emotional Stability, and Agreeableness. It is not the case that SD scales are insensitive to inflated responding but that their susceptibility to personality trait variance likely outweighs their benefits. We discuss the implications of these results for using SD scales in research and practice.	Moderate	Quite likely a few articles were missed. The method-logical quality of each study was not assessed or it was not described clearly.	C

Index

Note: Page numbers in *italics* indicate figures and in **bold** indicate tables on the corresponding pages.

ABI/INFORM Global 23
actor- observer bias **18**, 112, 132–133
Adams, J. 138
ambiguity effect **18**, 82, 91–92, 98, 230
anchoring **17**, 32, 55, 229
apophenia **17**, 32, 40, 228
Asch, S. E. 183–184
attachment theory 118
attentional bias **17**, 30–33, 228; conclusions on 38–39; defined 33–36; main findings on 36–38; practical reflections on 39; relevance for organization and change 36; search strategy on 36
attribution bias **18**, *111*–113, 231; conclusions on 136; defined 131–133; main findings on 134–136; practical reflections on 136–138; relevance for organization and change 134; search strategy on 134
attribution theory 131–132, 134–136
authority bias **19**, 183, 202, 234
automation bias **18**, 112, 114–115, 231
availability bias **17**, 30–*31*, 33, 228; conclusions on 42–43; defined 39–41; main findings on 42; practical reflections on 43; relevance for organization and change 41; search strategy on 41–42
availability cascade **17**, 32, 40, 228

backfire bias **19**, 145, 160, 233
Banaji, M. R. 160, 201
Bandura, A. 34, 133
bandwagon effect **19**, 183, 188, 233
base rate fallacy 17, 32, 45, 229
Baumeister, R. F. 120, 127, 155
Belasco, J. A. 223
belonging 8, **14**, **19**, 233; conformity and 183–187; groupthink and 187–192; social desirability bias and 192–197; status quo bias and 197–201; system justification bias and 201–205
bias blind spot 3, 145, 152–153, 211, 233
Biased: 50 Powerful Cognitive Biases That Impair Our Judgment 17
Biased: Uncovering the Hidden Prejudice That Shapes What We See, Think, and Do 17
biases: the evolutionary origin of 4–6; a selection of leading cognitive and social psychological 16–21; social motives underlying 7–9; using to our advantage 6–7
Biases and Heuristics The Complete Collection of Cognitive Biases and Heuristics That Impair Decisions in Banking, Finance and Everything Else 17
body of thought 3
Bower, J. L. 3, 15, 210, 220, 222–223
Bowlby, J. 118
Brandt, D. 111, 196
Bridges, W. 137, 164, 172
broaden-and-build theory 37
Business Source Premier 23

Campbell, A. 25
causal attributions in decision making 134–135
change: attentional bias and 222–223; attributional bias and 134; availability bias and 41; belonging and 214; biases, organizational behaviour and 2–3; competence model 15–16; confirmation bias and 161; conformity and 184–185; conjunction fallacy and

45–46; controlling and 212–213; delay discounting and 102–103; egocentric bias and 148–149; endowment effect and 169; enhancing self and 214–215; experimenter bias and 161; framing effect and 52; groupthink and 189; halo effect and 64–65; hindsight bias and 87–88; illusion of control and 83–84; the impact of bias on organisational behaviour and 210–227; information bias and 92; mere-exposure effect and 115; negativity bias and 121–122; optimism bias and 127–128; overconfidence bias and 155; priming effect and 56–57; prospect theory and 99; recency effect and 60–61; risk compensation and 95; social desirability bias and 193–194; similarity bias and 71; status quo bias and 198; a story of social motives, biases, organisational behaviour and 211–214; sunk cost fallacy and 173–174; system justification bias and 202–203; trusting and 213; understanding and 211–212
change capacity 15
change commitment 110–111, 218–220
change management: developing the framework from the perspective of biases 220–222; an evidence-based perspective on 217–220; topics 218
change vision 15
choice-supportive bias **19**, 233
cognitive dissonance 201
Cohen's rule of thumb 26
cohesion: social 190, 192; task 190, 192
Colquitt, J. A. 111
confirmation bias **19**, 143–145, 233; conclusions on 163; defined 157–160; main findings on 161–163; practical reflections on 163–164; relevance for organization and change 161; search strategy on 161
conformity **19**, 181–182, 233; conclusions on 186; defined 183–184; main findings on 185–186; practical reflections on 187; relevance for organization and change 184–185; search strategy on 185
congruence bias **19**, 145, 158, 160, 233
conjunction fallacy **17**, 30–*31*, 33, 229; conclusions on 48–49; defined 44–45; main findings on 46–48; practical reflections on 49; relevance for organization and change 45–46; search strategy on 46
conservatism bias **17**, 32, 55, 229
continued influence effect **19**, 145, 160, 233
controlling 8–9, **14**, **18**, 229; delay discounting and 102–106; hindsight bias and 86–91; illusion of control and 82–86; information bias and 91–93; prospect theory and 97–102; risk compensation and 93–97
courtesy bias **19**, 183, 193–194, 234
critical norms 180, 187
curse of knowledge **18**, 145, 147–149, 232

Darley, J. M. 159
data extraction 22, 24, 27
decision-making, group 41–43, 135–136, 138, 190–191
Decline of the West, The 121
delay discounting **18**, 80–82, 231; conclusions on 105; defined 102; main findings on 103–105; practical reflections on 105–106; relevance for organization and change 102–103; search strategy on 103
Deutsch, M. 70
Diclinism **18**
Dirks, K. T. 111
disposition effect 18, 82, 98, 99, 230
distinction bias **17**, 32, 35–36, 228
distributive justice 138
downsizing: system justification in the face of 205
dread aversion 18, 82, 98–99, 230

Eagly, A. H. 66
EBSCO 23
effect sizes 24, 26
egocentric bias **18**, 143–145, 232; conclusions on 150; defined 145–148; main findings on 149–150; practical reflections on 150–151; relevance for organization and change 148–149; search strategy on 149
empathy gap **18**, 112, 132–133, 232
endowment effect **19**, 143–145, 233; conclusions on 171; defined 168–169; main findings on 170–171; practical reflections on 171–172; relevance for organization and change 169; search strategy on 169
ERIC 23
evaluation apprehension 147
evidence-based methodology: the importance of 21–22

expectancy theory 83
experimenter bias **19**, 143–145, 233; conclusions on 167; defined 164–165; main findings on 166–167; practical reflections on 168; relevance for organization and change 165; search strategy on 166

Ferrin, D. L. 111
Festinger, L. 188
Fiske, S. T. 8, 11–14, 15, 16–17, 19, 220; on compliance 13; on core social motives 8–9, 12; on groupthink 189; on self-enhancing 144; on social norms 194; on trust 110
focusing effect **17**, 32, 35, 228
Folkman, S. 151
forer effect **18**, 145–147, 232
framing effect **17**, 30–*31*, 229; conclusions on 54; defined 49–52; main findings on 52–53; practical reflections on 54; relevance for organization and change 52; search strategy on 52
Fredrickson, B. 37
frequency illusion **17**, 32, 35, 228
Friesen, J. 201
Fugate, M. 111
fundamental attribution error **18**, 132, 231
funding bias 19, 165, 233

Goncalo, J. A. 135, 137
Gonzalez-Morales, M. 138
Google Scholar 23
Greenberg, J. 150
group cohesion 187–188, 192–193
groupthink **19**, 181–183, 185–187, 233; conclusions on 191; defined 187–189; main findings on 190–191; practical reflections on 191–192; relevance for organization and change 189; search strategy on 189–190

halo effect **17**, 30–32, 229; conclusions on 68; defined 63–64; main findings on 65–68; practical reflections on 68–70; relevance for organization and change 64–65; search strategy on 65
Harris, S. G. 5
Heider, F. 132
Heifetz, R. A. 137, 196
Heller, J. 130
hindsight bias **18**, 80–82, 230; conclusions on 90; defined 86–87; main findings on 88–90; practical reflections on 90–91; relevance for organization and change 87–88; search strategy on 88
hostile attribution bias **18**, 133–134, 137, 231
Hovland, C. I. 55
How to Deal with Resistance to Change 196
Hunyady, O. 202–203

illusion of control **18**, 80–82, 229; conclusions on 85–86; defined 82–83; main findings on 84–85; practical reflections on 86; relevance for organization and change 83–84; search strategy on 84
illusion of validity **19**, 145, 160, 233
illusory correlation **17**, 41, 228
illusory superiority **18**, 83, 229
illusory truth effect **18**, 112, 114, 231
inertia **19**, 197–198, 234
information bias **18**, 80–82, 230; conclusions on 93; defined 91–92; main findings on 93; practical reflections on 93; relevance for organization and change 92; search strategy on 92
Insko, C. A. 188, 190, 191–192
interactional justice 138, 150

Janis, I. L. 187–188, 190
job performance: priming and 58–59
Jost, J. T. 160, 201–204
Judgement Under Uncertainty: Heuristics and Biases 17
justice theory 138

Kay, A. C. 201
Kelman, H. C. 183
Kotter, J. P. 124
Kouznes, J. M. 125
Kriegel, R. J. X; on resistance to change 111

law of small numbers, the **17**, 64, 68, 229
law of the instrument **17**, 32, 55, 229
Lawrence, P. 196
Lazarus, R. S. 151
Lewin, K. 11, 211
loss aversion 53–54, 98–102

Manz, C. C. 166
Marx, K. 154
Maurer, R. 184, 223
mere exposure effect **18**, 110–112, 231; conclusions on 118; defined 113–115;

main findings on 116–118; practical reflections on 118–119; relevance for organization and change 115; search strategy on 115–116
method of loci 12
Michel, A. 138
Milgram, S. 202
mission and attentional bias 222–223
mnemonics 12–13
monetary incentives 59
money illusion **18**, 82, 102, 231
moral credential effect **19**, 145, 152–153, 232
moral disengagement 133
Morgan, G. 119
Moscovici, S. 55

negative bias about bias 4
negativity bias **18**, 110–112, 231; conclusions on 124; defined 119–121; main findings on 122–124; practical reflections on 124–125; relevance for organization and change 121–122; search strategy on 122
neglect of probability, the **18**, 98, 99, 230
normalcy bias **18**, 112, 126, 231
not invented here syndrome **18**, 145, 147–148, 232

omission bias **19**, 183, 198, 234
Ones, D. S. 195
optimism bias **18**, 112–113, 231; conclusions on 130; defined 125–127; main findings on 128–130; practical reflections on 130–131; relevance for organization and change 127–128; search strategy on 128
Oreg, S. 211
organisational identity 143, 157, 213
ostrich effect **19**, 145, 153, 232
outcome bias **18**, 82, 87, 230
overconfidence bias **19**, 143–145, 232–233; conclusions on 156–157; defined 151–155; main findings on 155–156; practical reflections on 157; relevance for organization and change 155; search strategy on 155
Ovid 23

Pareidolia **17**, 40, 228
Parkinson's law **18**, 91, 92, 230
performance management and prospect theory 224
pessimism bias **18**, 120, 121, 231
Petticrew, M. 22, 25
planning fallacy **18**, 126–130, 230
Power of Bad: how the negativity effect rules us and how we can rule, The 120
Pratto, F. 202
priming effect **17**, 30–32, 229; conclusions on 58–59; defined 54–55; main findings on 57–58; practical reflections on 59; relevance for organization and change 56–57; search strategy on 57
pro-innovation bias **18**, 126, 231
projection bias **17**, 50, 52, 229
ProQuest 23
prospect theory **18**, 80–82, 230; conclusions on 101; defined 97; main findings on 100–101; practical reflections on 101–102; relevance for organization and change 99; search strategy on 99–100
pseudo certainty effect **18**, 82, 98–99, 230
PsychINFO 23
PubMed 23

rapid evidence assessment (REA) 22; added value of bias 26; basic assumption in 23; in change management 23; data extraction in 24; inclusion criteria for studies in 23; limitations 26; main findings 26; practical reflections 26; report and format per bias 27; search strategy in 23; study selection in 23; trustworthiness of evidence appraised in 25
reactance **18**, 94, 230
reactive devaluation **18**, 147–148, 232
recency effect **17**, 30–32, 229; conclusions on 62; defined 59–60; main findings on 61–62; practical reflections on 62–63; relevance for organization and change 60–61; search strategy on 61
Reconsidering Change Management 28
representativeness heuristic **17**, 45, 229
resistance to change: confirmation bias and 223
restraint bias **19**, 152–153, 232
rhyme as reason effect **18**, 114, 231
Rijsman, J. 7
risk compensation **18**, 80–82, 230; conclusions on 96; defined 93–94; main findings on 95–96; practical reflections on 97; relevance for organization and change 95; search strategy on 95

selection bias **19**, 160, 223
self-enhancing 9, **14**, **18–19**, 143–144; confirmation bias and 157–164; egocentric bias and 145–151; endowment effect and 168–172; experimenter bias and 164–168; overconfidence effect and 151–157; sunk-cost fallacy and 172–176
self-serving bias **18**, 146–147, 230, 232
semmelweis effect **17**, 55, 229
shared meaning 30
Sherif, M. 55
similarity bias **17**, 30–32, 229; conclusions on 73; defined 70; main findings on 72; practical reflections on 73–74; relevance for organization and change 71; search strategy on 71
social desirability bias **19**, 181–182, 234; conclusions on 195; defined 192; main findings on 194–195; practical reflections on 196; relevance for organization and change 193–194; search strategy on 194
social identity theory 44
social impact theory 70
social judgement theory 55
social learning theory 166
social motives: a dynamic and integrative model of 12; primary biases categorized by the five core 20; relationships among core **14**
Social Psychology of Change Management, The 2, 20, 225
spotlight effect **18**, 146–147, 150, 232
status quo bias **19**, 181–182, 234; conclusions on 200; defined X 197; main findings on 199–200; practical reflections on 200–201; relevance for organization and change 198; search strategy on 198–199
strategy and attentional bias 222–223
structure and optimism bias 224
subjective validation **18**, 120–121, 231
sunk-cost fallacy **18**, 80–82, 230; conclusions on 175; defined 172; main findings on 174–175; practical reflections on 175; relevance for organization and change 173; search strategy on 174
Swann, W. B., Jr. 143
system justification bias **19**, 181–182, 234; conclusions on 204–205; defined 201; main findings on 203–204; practical reflections on 205; relevance for organization and change 202–203; search strategy on 203

teams and groupthink 225
Thinking, Fast and Slow 1, 10, 17
third person bias **18**, 132–133
trusting 9, **14**, **19**, 110–111; attribution bias and 131–138; mere exposure effect and 113–119; negativity bias and 119–125; optimism bias and 125–131
truthiness **18**, 112, 120, 231

understanding 8, **14**, **17**, 30–31; attentional bias and 33–39; availability bias and 39–43; conjunction fallacy and 44–49; framing effect and 49–54; halo effect and 63–70; priming effect and 54–59; recency effect and 59–64; similarity bias and 70–74
unit bias **17**, 50, 52, 229

vision and attentional bias 222, 223
Viswesvaran, C. 195

Watkins, M. D. 164
Weibel, A. 59
Weick, K. E. 3, 211
well-travelled road effect **17**, 40, 41, 228
Wilson, J. Q. 11, 100

Zajonc, R. B. 113, 116, 147
zero-risk bias **18**, 91, 92, 94, 230
zero-sum bias **18**, 147, 148, 232

Taylor & Francis Group
an informa business

Taylor & Francis eBooks

www.taylorfrancis.com

A single destination for eBooks from Taylor & Francis with increased functionality and an improved user experience to meet the needs of our customers.

90,000+ eBooks of award-winning academic content in Humanities, Social Science, Science, Technology, Engineering, and Medical written by a global network of editors and authors.

TAYLOR & FRANCIS EBOOKS OFFERS:

A streamlined experience for our library customers

A single point of discovery for all of our eBook content

Improved search and discovery of content at both book and chapter level

REQUEST A FREE TRIAL

support@taylorfrancis.com

Routledge
Taylor & Francis Group

CRC Press
Taylor & Francis Group